A FEW FEET SHORT

A
FEW
FEET
SHORT

AN UNCOMMON JOURNEY
TO EVEREST

JAMEY GLASNOVIC

RMB

RMB | Rocky Mountain Books Ltd.
rmbooks.com
@rmbooks
facebook.com/rmbooks

Cataloguing data available from Library and Archives Canada
ISBN 9781771602914 (paperback)
ISBN 9781771602921 (electronic)

All photographs are by Jamey Glasnovic unless otherwise noted.
Maps by Jocey Asnong

Printed and bound in Canada by Friesens

Distributed in Canada by Heritage Group Distribution and in the U.S. by Publishers Group West

For information on purchasing bulk quantities of this book, or to obtain media excerpts or invite the author to speak at an event, please visit rmbooks.com and select the "Contact Us" tab.

We acknowledge the financial support of the Government of Canada through the Canada Book Fund and the Canada Council for the Arts, and of the province of British Columbia through the British Columbia Arts Council and the Book Publishing Tax Credit.

To my partner, Jocey –
who introduced me to the wonder that is Nepal.

CONTENTS

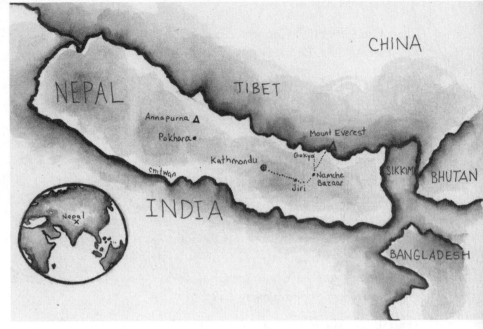

ASIA

NEPAL TRAVEL ROUTE

PART ONE

THE HIGH COUNTRY

1.

FREE AGAIN AT LAST

It's official: I'm scared shitless.

Even with the best efforts to get my act together, it's impossible to deny this feeling any longer. I am frightened right down to my core and I don't like it. What's most notable about this fairly common emotion, in this particular case, is the fear is coming to me in a way I've never experienced before in my life. I'm not startled or anxious; or even alarmed. That would be too superficial, too simple and too tame. No, the dread that is dominating this evening is more extreme and somehow more primal than that. I am, without doubt, terrified to the base of my being. The worst part is I have no idea what to do.

My partner, Jocey, and I have arrived in the Himalayan village of Machhermo, Nepal, just south of Gokyo and one valley over from Mount Everest, and I have a headache. That I have a headache is not notable in itself – I've been living with low-grade pain lurking behind my eyes since climbing up to Namche Bazaar four days ago, but this rattling inside my skull is a new sensation altogether and is way beyond anything I've ever felt.

"The Beast," as I have come to call it in the hours spent staring at the ceiling, wondering if I'm going to die, has the distinct characteristics of a bad migraine with all the attendant pain, nausea, and hypersensitivity to light and sound, but, just for good measure, the sensation is also peppered with an impending and overwhelming sense of doom. The thing is, "the Beast" also behaves like a mean tension headache, radiating up from my shoulders and pulling down at the back of my skull in a spectacularly irritating fashion. The whole experience is akin to a cranial tug-of-war, with my grey matter used as rope. Somehow even my hair hurts. I feel like a pair of giant dogs have me firmly locked in their jaws but haven't decided who gets the privilege of finishing me off.

Even in this vulnerable and addled state, however, I am struck by the idea that pure fear is a rare taste indeed. Frustration and aggravation and anxiety are easy to come by, and they all contain elements we can manipulate and control. To an extent, we ourselves even feed these lesser demons, giving them life. Real fear, on the other hand, exists wholly beyond our ability to cope, living unchecked and unmanaged, which makes it at once terrifying and exhilarating.

The fact that I don't know much about altitude sickness, or Acute Mountain Sickness as it's officially called, only compounds my sense of dread. Am I going to get up to go to the washroom only to pass out and never wake up? Am I going to start bleeding out the ears? Is the top of my head simply going to pop right off? I just don't know, and that helps feed the terror. But the worst part of the whole illness (once I ascertain this is probably an exercise in discomfort, not death) is that everyone in the guest house we're staying at has heard the Canadian is sick, and has a helpful thought or ten on treatment options. The truth is I'm beginning to feel like a sideshow attraction down at the county fair; I'm drawing attention to myself when all I want to do is curl up in a little ball and die already.

So, after ten straight hours of unrelenting agony and

uncertainty, I figure it is time to give in. I tap out. I surrender to my fate. Lesson learned and experience rendered. I am frightened and helpless and hopeless and small, and still, things could be worse. Things could be much, much worse. If the mother of all headaches does develop secondary symptoms like vomiting or diarrhea, then I will face the unenviable task of descending a narrow yak trail at 4400 metres in the dead of night. The trouble with that plan is that yak trail navigation at altitude is a skill I'm only beginning to master in broad daylight, thank you very much. As much pain as I may be in, the last thing I want to do is go stumbling around outside in the dark, even if it does bring some relief.

Of course, trekking in Nepal is a tremendous life experience for the adventure enthusiast even with these challenges. If not a vacation exactly, it does qualify as an endeavour worthy of pursuit for the adventurous type, and altitude sickness is just one of the inevitable complications associated with the attempt, along with washed-out trails, temperamental yaks, questionable water quality, dodgy toilets, rickety and/or sway-prone footbridges, guest houses of a wildly varying standard, thigh- and lung-searing climbs in which you take ten ridiculously small steps before stopping to wonder where all the air has gone, and, naturally, erratic mountain weather patterns.

This is a small price to pay, in my book, for deep, steep, tree-filled valleys; rivers that look like roaring molten steel; sweeping high mountain meadows; awe-inspiring, snow-covered peaks; and a unique glimpse into a culture and lifestyle still somewhat removed, both practically and geographically, from the consumption, commercialism, and greed that dominates everyday life in the "developed world." So I down some Diamox, generously provided by a group of Israelis staying down the hall, quit crying for my mommy already, and try to ride out the storm tearing around inside my head, because we've still got ten days left to go on our trek.

•••

Nine years later, I have returned to this little village high in the Himalaya, and I don't have a headache this time. Thank God. My recollections are a bit hazy, but Machhermo hasn't changed much from what I can remember. Outside the window of the dining room of Namgyal Lodge, prayer flags are being whipped about by a gathering wind, and a small cow is contentedly grazing in the inner courtyard. Here in the dining room, a colour bomb has gone off and distributed the full palette into every corner.

The set-up is fairly typical of modern guest houses: roughly ten tables placed on the periphery of a rectangular room, with a small wood stove at the centre. On the outside edge are benches covered with cushions and hand-crafted carpet with intricate designs in brown and orange and green and blue, the seats representing one consistent design, and the seat backs sporting another one entirely. The tablecloths are purple, and the metal folding chairs toward the centre of the room have red faux-leather seat cushions. The Tibetan-style trim on the windows is bright yellow, and the vaulted ceiling is painted with a collection of three- and four-foot-wide murals whose colour schemes encompass the rainbow. It should be an interior designer's nightmare, but somehow it all works. I would even go so far as to say it's beautiful in here.

Later today I will probably go out and explore. Machhermo is nestled by a small creek between two steep hillside spurs, and toward the head of the valley a jagged rocky peak dominates the skyline. Originally a summertime grazing area for yaks, the settlement now boasts a handful of lodges and a rescue post. The views from up on either of the hillside spurs are sublime, and the meticulously crafted stone walls enclosing each small pasture complete a scene that is at once pastoral and untamed. It is lovely here, and for the moment I am toasty warm and content. It's just too bad I was so ill the first time around that I barely remember the quiet and rugged charm of this place.

Obviously, I survived that original ordeal, or you wouldn't be reading an account of my return. After an uncomfortable day lounging around hoping the symptoms of my cerebral edema would simply pass, we were eventually forced down to Phortse, located at a more reasonable 3800 metres. My headache did clear up remarkably quickly after descending, and in time Jocey and I made it to one of our goals for that trip, which was Everest Base Camp.

Not that that part of our mountain adventure passed entirely without incident, mind you. Getting from the Gokyo Valley to the Khumbu Valley can be done in one of two ways. You can take the direct route, up and over the Cho La, which tops out at 5420 metres – a proposition that was completely out of the question after the experience in Machhermo – or you can take a few days and go around the formidable barrier created by Arakamtse, Cholatse and Tabuche Peak. At the time, that seemed like a much better idea, even if it took longer to get to our destination.

While we were in Phortse it began to rain overnight, and by morning the world was a damp and dreary place, but we had just taken a headache-inspired day off, so the only option appeared to be to push through it. Except for the rain, the day started out simply enough. The track was slick but straightforward, but unbeknownst to us the route we were about to attempt was more challenging than anything we'd come across to date. The tourist trail was over the river on the far side of the valley, lost somewhere in the heavy cloud cover and cut off from us by a bridge that had recently been washed out by heavy monsoon rains.

Rounding a bend on the now-treacherous trail in a persistent and drenching downpour was unpleasant enough, but before long we caught up to a group of porters and yaks struggling up a series of slick and crumbling stone steps cut right into the mountainside, creating what amounted to a traffic jam, pedestrian-style, on the path ahead. Unpleasant became unsettling, and it was obvious we were on a local's route, or a goat track, depending on how you choose to define these things.

During that first visit to Nepal, I was struck not only by the height and sheer mass of the mountains we were travelling through, although they are nothing short of spectacular, but also by how deep the valleys were. Back home in the Canadian Rockies where I live, you tend to get one of two perspectives: impressive craggy peaks high above when you travel through the valleys, or long views into those valleys as you ascend into the alpine. In the Khumbu region, many of the trails travel up away from the rivers to avoid impassable canyons, so the peaks can appear almost mundane in their muted splendour, until you look down and realize just how far away from the river you are. It can be 600 or 900 metres to the bottom of the valley, and it is not uncommon to climb beyond the sound of all that water rushing by below. And still the mountains continue to tower above. It is only then that you appreciate how mighty the Himalaya really are.

On the high route to the village of Dingboche, the cloud continued to fill the valley and distort perception, and in that circumstance the valley felt not just deep but bottomless, and I experienced a sudden bout of vertigo. For the rest of the morning I felt compelled to walk extremely close to the inside half of the narrow trail and never shook the sense of unease. At one point we passed a yak train coming in the opposite direction – an experience that rated somewhere close to terrifying. It wasn't until years later that I read a trail guide account by Jamie McGuinness of the ground we covered that morning that said, "If you're scared of heights and not happy walking along trails with steep drops beside them avoid this route."

Okay, good to know. Thanks for the heads up. One of these days I am going to have to do a little reading *before* setting out on a trip. But now that I'm back, with these challenges to relaxed travel staring me straight in the face once again, the question that comes to mind isn't "Why bother?" (although there are moments) but "What took me so long?"

Sure, I was in this region again in 2009, with Jocey and my parents, but we didn't venture up the Gokyo Valley, choosing to do a day trip up the Imja Khola Valley instead. The thing is, I haven't been anywhere interesting or had anything like an adventure since. It used to be that if I didn't go on a big trip every year or two I would start to go stir-crazy. Without realizing it, I would gradually become short-tempered and easily aggravated in my everyday interactions and would have no clear idea why.

And when, exactly, did I turn into such a slothful complainer? I hardly recognize the semi-inert being staring back at me from my mirror. He has an opinion on everything but no thoughts on how to defuse his wrath: he just likes to bitch and moan. I would love to know when that transformation happened.

I have been living my life in a perpetual state of unease but dismiss the sensation as normal, as part of "growing up," as part of being an adult. Now, seven years on from that last trip to the Khumbu, I see I am every single thing my younger self would loathe, and I simply can't live like that anymore. There is no doubt I have grown lazy and uninspired, and I have to take responsibility for that. But I have also become a zombie to the system, doing what needs to be done but never really getting anywhere, and the question that begs to be asked is: Why has there been this disconnect? What has been so consuming of my time and attention? What could possibly be more important than living an adventurous and fulfilling life?

The answer, of course, is work. A dirty, four-letter word if ever there was one. Work, that great disruptor, that energy sink, that deep black hole into which so much of our enthusiasm, time and good intentions disappear, often without a trace. If you grow up middle class in the Western world, certain expectations become a part of your everyday life, whether you like it or not. A home, children and a career are all but required of us as we drift toward middle age. It is what our grandparents did. It is what our parents did. Once we reach a certain age, it is what most of our friends do. It is how, right or wrong, our culture measures success.

The irony of this approach is that our relatives did what they did so we could have a better life – or at least that's how I have heard it justified. But what we learned was not to live better but to do more of the same. Our more personal aspirations and dreams, born in the blissfully ig-norant cocoon of adolescence, where we still believe any-thing is possible, are eventually diluted down to hobbies and interests. While still noteworthy, precious and per-haps even noble, most eventually wear away into foot-notes in the story of what might have been, annotations on who we might have become had we had the courage to try.

Forget that mine is the first generation since the in-dustrial revolution that will *not*, as a group, do better fi-nancially than our parents did. Forget that the modern economic system is inherently flawed, based as it is on rampant consumption, disposable everything and debt. It is a set-up dangerously susceptible to both corruption and greed, which collectively we appear incapable of re-sisting. We still call it good business. And let's not forget that many of my fellow Gen-Xers, endlessly bombarded by these images of wealth and success, often don't have the work ethic, discipline or opportunity to support those pricey wants. (Don't even get me started on the millen-nials). This is what we do in the Western world: we value our stuff to the extreme, whether we like it or not, and ul-timately find ourselves pursuing dreams that are not ours.

Or, with an air of privilege that has become all too common, we walk around feeling entitled to these bau-bles as part of our birthright.

Admittedly, money and the illusion of security that comes with it are compelling and attractive, in a demented kind of a way, as you look at them through the showroom window. In the end, they remain constructs. Artificial needs created to distract us from living in the present in favour of worrying about any number of possible futures that may never materialize. We are forever encouraged to live in a muted kind of fear, a fear of failure, a fear of poverty, a fear of our true selves. But success is the attempt we are supposed to make. So I tried. Lord knows, I tried.

More about that foolishness in good time; for now, it's all behind me. I have come back to the high Himalaya for a third time because I needed somewhere to go that would help feed a more personal demand, one that had nothing to do with finding a way to best survive the grind. One filled with adventure and discovery. If I'm lucky, I might even find a higher purpose for these actions, a deeper meaning to this wandering. For too long now I have day-dreamed about going somewhere and doing something that has some resonance on a more profound level. Even in my worn-out and jaded state, I still believe in inspiration and artistry and imagination as viable life choices. A counterpoint to our system of empty trophies that are more easily measured.

What I have been yearning for is a simple, old-fashioned stroll. A pilgrimage. An adventure. A quest. A trip from somewhere to somewhere that is all about the space in between. It is the simplicity of that process that has grown irresistible, and, as it turns out, Nepal is an incredibly interesting place to walk – or trek, as they call it in this small corner of the world.

Wedged between China to the north and India to the south, Nepal is a small and developing country that has only been open to the outside world since 1951. A former collection of mountain kingdoms with isolationist leanings, the landscape still makes travel difficult in many regions, but tourism has grown into a major player in the economy over the last few decades. Eight hundred kilometres long by 200 kilometres wide, about the size of Florida, it is dominated by the Himalaya, a robust line of mountains that rises along the northern edge of the country and slowly recedes to the south across Nepal's meagre width through the Middle Hills, before levelling out on the Terai, a flat, largely featureless geological formation that makes up the lowland plains of India.

Occupying that space are diverse cultures still separated into relatively small areas by the challenges of the landscape. Deep valleys, high ridges, a weak and disorganized central leadership and a comparatively poor infrastructure continue to make Nepal a land of districts that struggles to find a unified whole. In the end, modern Nepal remains a crazy enigma when seen through Western eyes. And at the moment I've got some money left in my pocket, no pressing commitments to hurry back to and a vast and rugged landscape to explore. After too many years of focused and determined, if at times largely uninspired, toil, I am free again at last.

PART TWO

THE MIDDLE HILLS

2.

KATHMANDU

Perspective is everything. Seven years after the second trip in 2009, I have come back to Kathmandu and am hardly culture-shocked at all. This disappoints me a little bit. Part of the wonder of travel is stunned awe, but having been here before, I knew what to expect, and that has taken the edge off. In the back of a minivan taxi with the window open, the warm evening breeze feels good on my skin; I've been cooped up too long in the carefully controlled environments of airplanes and airports. Clearing immigration was surprisingly fast and efficient, all my baggage arrived on the same flight I did and finding a taxi was no hassle at all. No trouble and no drama. Muted awe.

Up ahead, a dump truck dropping gravel at a building site at the edge of the tourist district of Thamel is completely blocking the road in both directions. This does not surprise me one bit, even though it's 11 o'clock on a Sunday night. That the driver now appears to be wedged between the building across the street and the gravel he's just left partway on the road is also no big deal. That's the thing about this town: crazy shit often happens, and when it does it's best to just roll with it. My driver seems to be taking the same laissez-faire approach. He hasn't said a word since leaving the airport, and simply kills the engine and sits back and waits for the bottleneck to be resolved.

There's maybe a dozen or so vehicles ahead of us, and

some of them are helpfully leaning on their horns in a show of support, while pedestrians, motorbikes and the occasional bicycle navigate the gridlock created by the truck. Nepali couples and groups of friends are out walking to or from one or another of the bars I've seen in the last couple of blocks, and are largely oblivious to the growing commotion. At the choke point there is much shouting and gesticulating in an attempt to help the driver unstick the truck, and the stray dogs just saunter past in their magnificent indifference.

Out the window to my left, a pair of young Nepali men in cycle rickshaws at the side of the road offer a friendly greeting to the newest tourist in town. They're just killing time, and based on their body language – reclining in the back with their feet up on the bike seats – don't seem especially intent on hustling a fare anytime soon. They also don't seem too concerned about the mess up ahead. I give them a tired smile and my first *namaste* of the trip. (This is the universal Hindu greeting that roughly translates as "I bow to the god within you.") Sitting back to wait, I reflect on this peace amid chaos: it is the Nepali way. I am alone and 11,000 kilometres from home, it's dark, I don't speak the language and I'm exhausted. Instead of being anxious and uncertain, as I was in the couple of weeks prior to departure, I feel peaceful and happy to be travelling again. Whatever comes, comes.

When you think of Nepal, you think of wintery mountain landscapes – at least, I did at first. Hard, sharp peaks and high valleys filled with ambitious climbers; Sherpas and Buddhism – that's what I envisioned. This is probably because so many of the stories about this place that make it out to the West are stories about Mount Everest. Mountaineering is both big business and a compelling narrative, and the rest of Nepal is often a footnote to those high-intensity exploits. In truth, in the Middle Hills and the lowlands, the influence is much more Indian than Tibetan, and the dominant religion is Hindu. The country is roughly 80 per cent Hindu, 10 per cent Buddhist and 4 per cent Muslim, with a mix of various other religions making up the difference.

Another minor surprise upon arrival is the climate. Tonight, after making it through the late-night traffic jam and checking in, it is pleasant to sit in shorts and a T-shirt on the open-air patio three storeys above the street at my guest house, even at midnight in mid-September. In fact, I'm sweating. Nepal is at the same latitude as Egypt, and although this is by no means a desert landscape, it can be remarkably warm, especially in the buildup to the monsoon in April and May, but autumn can also be more agreeable than you might expect.

Down below, just the odd car or motorcycle passes by on the street. Earlier there was music coming from somewhere out in the night, and the occasional sound of Nepali voices passing by, but it is mostly quiet now. Thamel has shut down for the night. As I pop the top of my second Everest Beer, Kathmandu begins to take on that mystic and mythic appeal that I remember so well – and there it is, right out in the dark beyond the edge of the building. I don't have a view, there are hotels and apartment buildings in every direction, but I know it's there. A city of exotic and confusing attraction, a city of contradictions, a place of poverty and of wonder, of deep history and strong religion mixed with the modern challenges of day-to-day survival.

I never dreamed of Nepal as a kid or longed to visit as an adult. But sometimes life surprises you, and what was simply a destination becomes much more. Sometimes a place finds a way to move your soul. This is one of those places. Accustomed to the obvious commonalities of modern cities, I didn't have high expectations before I found myself here that first time – this was just another city between where I was and where I wanted to go. It caught me completely off guard.

Not that I loved it right off the bat, mind you. The first time around I was completely shell-shocked. I knew intuitively that coming here for seven weeks of trekking and exploring in 2007 would be an unusual experience, and the three machine-gun-toting security guards patrolling the empty Singapore airport at four a.m. during one of three layovers certainly confirmed my suspicions. But even if you're prepared, arriving in Kathmandu in the daytime is an eye-widening jolt to the system.

The assault on the senses begins as soon as you step off the plane and onto the 1970s-style portable stairway that leads to the tarmac. It can be shockingly hot and muggy, and after standing around sweating in a dimly lit, poorly organized arrivals area to obtain a tourist visa, you clear customs and collect your luggage and are immediately attacked by representatives of various taxi companies, guest houses and tour companies. Everybody shouts and gesticulates madly. There are incessant offers of "good price" with no actual monetary value quoted, and it's impossible to carry your own bag three feet without someone offering to "carry your bag, sir?" with a generous tip implied. It's paparazzi rock-star treatment, with hundreds of locals clamouring for your dollar, and after four planes and 44 hours of bored transit (flight connections were decidedly more challenging back then), it feels like an instantaneous zero-to-60.

Kathmandu is a low-slung city of four- to six-storey buildings tucked into a valley just south of the mighty Himalaya. It is home to roughly two million souls if the extensive urban sprawl surrounding the city proper is included. Once you leave the airport, all that humanity is thrust upon you. Nepalis drive on the left side of the road, but it takes a few kilometres of riding in the back of one of the sub-compact cabs to know for sure. Any space on the exceedingly narrow streets is instantly filled with vehicles searching for an advantage. Cars, minibuses, motorcycles, bicycles and the occasional mini–flatbed delivery truck all jockey relentlessly in a barely contained chaos. Roundabouts are a congested mess. There are few stop signs, fewer traffic lights and the inconsistent road markings are virtually ignored. Sidewalks are practically nonexistent, away from the main arteries, and all over Nepal the horn is a mode of personal expression as much as a useful tool for averting collision.

After settling into the idea that you might die on your first day in the country – and possibly before you even reach the hotel – you start to notice some of the other eccentricities of Kathmandu. Particulate in the air that qualifies as something greater than smog stings the eyes and lungs, rundown shops press right to the road's edge, and rickshaws and pedestrians wander and weave, seemingly unaware they are basically playing in traffic. On the quieter side streets, unhealthy-looking cattle (yes, cattle in the city centre) and stray dogs pick through trash heaped in random piles by the side of the road and in vacant lots.

But Kathmandu is not just about these sights and sounds: smell also makes its presence known as exhaust fumes, urine, incense, ripe garbage and spices waft on every passing breeze. It is nothing short of a full-blown, no-holds-barred mindfuck to a jet-lagged and sleep-de-prived mind.

And that's what I have to look forward to tomorrow: a brand-new dose of relentless chaos.

I can't wait.

● ● ●

I've woken up this morning at six a.m. with exactly what I deserve: a three-beer, 27-hour-travel-day hangover. Super. The thing is, the beers here are served in quart bottles that are 650 millilitres each. A standard bottle of beer is 341 millilitres, so what I'm dealing with is more like a six-beer-and-all-the-rest-of-it hangover. Super duper. Unable to sleep, I've been fussing around my room for 20 minutes and have tried to unpack, but all I'm doing is walking in random circles, unable to focus on any one thing for more than 20 seconds. I'm up already but am largely useless, so I might as well go out and get breakfast before I come to my senses and go back to bed, where I likely won't sleep.

Out on the street, Thamel is just beginning to wake up. My guest house, Karma Travellers Home, is on Thamel Bhagwati Marg, a relatively quiet side street in the heart of the tourist district. The street is only six strides across, with five- and six-storey buildings pressing in on all sides. It feels more like a canyon than a roadway, and this early in the day the sun won't hit the street directly for another couple of hours. Most of the shops are still shuttered, but the convenience store next door is already open for busi-ness. It's more a kiosk than a store, six feet wide by ten feet deep, and filled with takeaway items. The proprietor and I exchange *namastes* as I pass.

On Chaksibari Marg, one of the main arteries through the district, things are a touch livelier, and at the corner I engage in the first instalment of what will be an ongoing exchange carried on throughout the city. In retrospect, it is unfortunate I have not been practising my "no, thank you," with any form of conviction, because a handful of taxi drivers are standing around their cabs, smoking and shooting the shit, and when they see me coming they shift into gear in an instant. Two or three of them start walking in my direction, clearly trying to get a jump on their cohorts. This is not like in big North American cities, where you step to the corner, wave and shout for a ride. Here they wave and shout at you.

"Taxi, sir? I take you to the airport, good price."

Never mind I have basically just come from there. I'm not even going to try and explain that.

"No, thank you," I say – a bit hesitantly, I guess, because he jumps on the opportunity to keep the conversation going.

"Where are you from?"

"Canada."

"Canada. A beautiful country."

"Yes, it is, and so is Nepal."

"Yes. First time in Nepal, sir?"

The trick here is to never stop walking and try not to engage in too much conversation beyond the expected pleasantries; otherwise you'll be standing around debating taxi fares all day. I have succeeded in the first and failed in the second, and now half a dozen guys are trailing along, trying to convince me theirs is the nicest cab of the bunch. In fact, the cabs are all exactly the same. I mumble something about having been here before and about needing breakfast and scurry off down the street.

In print, I have seen Thamel described many times as a tourist ghetto, but I think that is perhaps a bit harsh.

Technically, it fits the definition, as the majority of foreign tourists end up in this area, but the designation insinuates a level of privation that doesn't quite fit. Sure, Thamel is frayed at the edges, but it is not dirt cheap anymore. There are still bargains to be had, but the overall economic outcome of gathering the tourists in one place is a higher price point for many items, especially in restaurants and bars. It is crowded and loud once the day gets going, as you would expect, but there are other parts of the city that are not nearly as well-maintained.

As I walk along, there are people cleaning up the gutters and taking out the garbage on three-wheel bicycles with baskets strapped on the back, and the vendors who have opened up are taking care of their little piece of roadway. They're sweeping up yesterday's dust from front steps and splashing water on the street in a vain attempt to keep today's dust down, and it must be noted here that the term *roadway* might be a bit generous. It's not much more than an alley in places, and borders on the diabolical in terms of quality. It looks like big portions have been dug up for one reason or another, then hastily refilled with dirt and gravel but never resurfaced. In places where it is particularly uneven, pieces of stone and broken brick are used to level the grade. Stepping gingerly so as to not turn an ankle, I notice a few more people wandering around now, and there are even a few tourists out and about already.

One of the pleasing attractions of this part of town is the courtyards. Attached to guest houses or restaurants, these courtyards are a welcome escape from the hustle and bustle of the surrounding city, an oasis from the madness, if you will, and even though things have yet to kick off this morning, I duck into one that happens to be a favourite.

As a creature of habit, I always stop at Hotel Mandap for

a small pot of Nepali masala tea with lots of sugar and the "simple breakfast": two hard-boiled eggs, toast and fried potatoes with onions and green peppers. It's overcast and warm this morning and doesn't look like it's going to rain, thank goodness. At the back of the courtyard there are 11 tables, and a small evergreen grows near the centre. Closer to the street are four more tables, with potted plants and small ficus trees along the edges. The two outdoor seating areas are separated by a main indoor dining room and a small bakery shop that sits kitty-corner. When I want some peace and quiet, I sit in the back. When I want to be closer to the action, I sit in the front. Today it's the back. I settle in to take some notes, read, have my breakfast and maybe make a rough plan for the rest of the day.

After about an hour, I am refreshed and ready to take on the city – or, at least, in a perfect world I would be refreshed and ready. In reality, I'm not sure I'm up for it yet. Don't get me wrong, I am eager to wander the streets and explore the alleyways and investigate all the nooks and crannies of this place again. The bookshops, the restaurants, the bars and what the tour companies have to offer are compelling. I could easily spend a week checking everything out, but it will probably have to wait. The sun has come out and the day is heating up quickly, accentuating my hangover. It seems my meagre reserves of energy are draining away with every uptick on the thermometer, but at least I force myself to loop around the longer way back to the hotel.

When I turn onto Paryatan Marg, a sketchy-looking dude with a gold cap on one of his front teeth begins following me for a full block, offering all manner of services: trekking, flights, local guiding, rafting, jungle tours, spa, massage, whatever my heart desires. I shudder to think what would happen if I said all I wanted was a nap. No amount of "no, thank you" can shake him, and the rest of the sharks can smell blood in the water.

All of a sudden, inquiries on my need for "taxi," "Tiger Balm," "rickshaw ride" or "mini-violin" coming from all directions begin to erode the brand-new-arrival charm. I'm starting to get annoyed, and anyone who knows me realizes it doesn't take much. Instead of subjecting Thamel to a grumpy, jet-lagged me, I figure I better make my way back to Karma Travellers Home right quick, before I do something to wreck my karma.

3.

DURBAR SQUARE

Kathmandu has always been at the centre of things in the region that is now Nepal, and for 250 years Nepal has existed as a unified state in the modern sense. Historians use the date 1768 and the beginning of the reign of King Prithvi Narayan Shah for that transition, but the Kathmandu Valley was occupied for at least 2,000 years before that. For centuries it was a significant outpost on the trade route that linked Assam in the east to Kashmir in the west. It wasn't until the borders opened that it began to become known to a wider world. After a second day of absorbing the various charms of Thamel, I am keen on seeing the old town, where the modern history of this country began.

Overnight I worked out my strategy for dealing with forward vendors while keeping my annoyed-o-meter in check, and have settled on a "no, thank you" that's respectful but firmer than what I've managed so far, along with a vague and casual waist-high wave, executed mostly from the wrist. This is by no means effective in all circumstances, however.

Before escaping the southern edge of the Thamel district, I make my acquaintance with one of the hustler veterans. An older gentleman with obvious game, he penetrates my defences with ease, and within 30 seconds it's like we're lifelong friends. His smile is infectious, and even though I know he's trouble, I already like him. With his pot belly, round face and shaved head, if you put a maroon robe on him he'd be a dead ringer for a Buddhist monk. I finally agree to take his business card merely as an escape strategy, and now in addition to trekking and rafting, I know where to go for hash, opium, marijuana or a nice girl, with "happy ending no problem."

Last night's rain persists only in the form of a thin coating of sloppy, light-brown mud covering the streets, and I wish I'd worn my hiking boots instead of my shoes, but it's too late to go back now. I'm already dirty. The narrow streets are packed with pedestrians and the usual vehicle chaos, and it takes a little while to settle into the rhythm of it. It's an adventure in deft shoulder checks and funky sidesteps. The roadside shops gradually shift from tourist-oriented ventures – restaurants, T-shirt and pashmina shops and tour companies – to jewelry and clothing stores geared to a Nepali clientele.

What becomes apparent after a few blocks is that all the streets in this neighbourhood are virtually identical. There are millions of signs advertising everything under the sun, set against a backdrop of old buildings pressed right up to the edge of the street. What there aren't many of are street signs, but if I stop to consult my map to try and get my bearings, I am a target for another loveable scoundrel, so I let myself be swept up in the wave of humanity moving in my direction and hope I don't take a wrong turn. Amazingly, I don't, and it doesn't take long to reach my intended destination, Durbar Square.

Located at the heart of old Kathmandu, Durbar Square is a UNESCO World Heritage Site and a popular tourist attraction. Its name is actually a generic term used for all the royal palace squares from the three ancient kingdoms found in the Kathmandu Valley. Patan has a Durbar Square a few kilometres to the southeast, and Bhaktapur has one as well. At all three, the architecture – a testament to the skill of Newar craftsmen – is something of a mishmash of styles. Largely Hindu in influence, many of the buildings are of the pagoda design and were originally constructed between the 12th and 18th centuries by a succession of ruling monarchs. What is uniform almost without exception is the detail and intricacy of the woodcarving incorporated in much of the square. The Hanuman Dhoka Durbar Square Monument Zone leaflet describes the whole complex as a "living open museum of Nepal."

Entering Durbar Square from the northeast corner, I buy a ticket (1,000 Nepali rupees, or about $12 Canadian) and proceed directly to the site office at the far end to register. A passport photo and a little information, and I am issued a pass so I can come back to visit as many times as I like. With formalities out of the way, it's time to have a good look around, and what is obvious right away is the damage done by what has become known as the Gorkha earthquake and its major aftershocks in April and May of 2015. Nearly 9,000 people lost their lives, and over 20,000 were injured. Thousands upon thousands were made homeless across the central part of the country. To add insult to injury, many of the important cultural and religious sites across the region were among the most heavily damaged by the quake.

An indication of how important this square was to the early kingdom is Kasthmandap, a temple built in the pagoda style in the 12th century and dedicated to Gorakhnath, a founder of the Nath Hindu monastic movement in India. According to legend, the structure was built using wood from a single tree, and no nails were used in the construction. The name *Kathmandu* is said to originate from this particular temple. Tragically, it was completely destroyed in 2015. Standing in front of what is now just a few scattered piles of rubble is a chilling reminder of nature's power. Kasthmandap was not the only casualty of the quake in this historic square, unfortunately. Maju Dega, Narayan Vishnu and Trailokya Mohan were among the other buildings lost in a concentrated area at the southwest corner of the square.

You would think such extensive damage would diminish this place, but somehow it does not. Heavy wooden beams prop up temples and other buildings, and the site is splashed throughout with the tarps and scaffolding necessary in the reconstruction efforts, but surprisingly none of the significance or charm has been lost. It has only been bruised. The carefully salvaged brick piled in the corners of lots is a testament to the spirit of rebuilding.

Making my way out of the southeast corner of the square, past the rows of vendors hawking figurines, masks and *khukuri* knives in a large, brick-cobbled park, I make a quick visit to Freak Street, but I've clearly missed the party here. This was the heart of the happening scene in the '60s and '70s, when it was a stop on the hippy trail, but now it just reminds me of a mini-Thamel, so I don't stay long.

Coming back into the main square, I am still dazed and confused by it. You would need to be a serious nerd or a determined scholar of Nepali culture to understand the finer details and how it all fits together, but even to the layman it is remarkable and worth lingering in. Around lunchtime, I endeavour to find a high point from which to shoot a couple of pictures of Taleju Temple, which escaped major damage, and I end up on the rooftop patio of Jyona Belee Café and Restaurant, where I spend 30 contented minutes listening to the tapping and hammering of tools on wood and brick as labourers go about the slow process of restoring history.

• • •

I make my way back to Durbar Square late the next afternoon, convinced that although I have seen it, I have not yet experienced it – partly because, after three days, I don't feel like I've made any real connection with the people here. Paul Theroux, in the introduction to *The Tao of Travel*, lists as one of his early motivations to venture out in the world an interest in seeing how other people live. He writes, with obvious excitement, "They're just like us. They're not like us at all." Similarities between cultures remind us that despite our differences we are essentially the same, but those differences also celebrate our unique spirit as individual human beings. I will probably have more opportunity to engage in this once I leave the valley and start my trek, but I would like to find it here as well. Durbar Square seems as good a place to look as any.

Sure of the route this time, I easily find my way from the guest house to Durbar Square, and with no specific landmark to seek out, I just wander the square from north to south and back again, making sure to explore a few of the ancient alleyways to the south of the square. While I wait for the light on Jagannath Temple to change, in hopes of a better photo, a Nepali man sidles up to me. I have not seen him coming.

"You need guide?"

"No, thank you."

"If you know Durbar Square, you know Nepal. I can show you."

I have heard many times that this place is an important

part not only of the history of the country but of the local culture as well. That's why I chose it as my first destination on this trip. But again, too much chit-chat in this situation can lead to having a paid companion for a day. Not exactly what I'm looking for.

"No, thank you. I'm good."

"I know you are good." My new friend steps in half a pace and places his hands in the vicinity of my shoulders. He stands about five-foot-five. I'm close to six-two. "You are strong, yes."

It's an odd question.

"Yes, I guess so," I reply hesitantly.

"This is good, but I can help you know."

An interesting tactic, the implication being I could use help to understand the subtler nuances of this place – but I am not swayed.

"No, thank you."

"Are you sure? I am the best guide."

Realizing we are just going to go around and around in a circle if I stay engaged, I decide to try a different approach.

"I'll tell you what, if I change my mind I'll come and find you."

"When will you change your mind? Next life?" He says, with what I detect is a hint of sarcasm. My snappy comeback is right at the tip of my tongue for a change, not descending on me in a rush three hours later, so I let fly.

"Yes, maybe – you never know, my friend."

We both have a laugh and part ways.

The encounter makes me think there has to be another way to interact. I'm travelling solo, so I can't expect intense socializing when I have chosen to go it alone. I am also an introvert, so it's not like I need a ton of together time to begin with, but I wonder if every conversation for the next two months is going to revolve around the possibility of a transaction. Is there something here beyond the interactions facilitated by the business of tourism? There has to be. Mulling it over, I eventually find a perch on the steps of Kotilingeshwor Mahadev Temple and wait for night to fall.

As I sit here, no one bothers me for anything, which I don't actually notice for quite some time, and as the light fades, I begin to see a whole other aspect of the square. It is a historic and religious site, full of important monuments, but it is also a thoroughfare from one part of the old town to another. Tourists continue to mill about, but with the odd exception, they gradually disappear from the scene. Both yesterday and today, locals have been sitting on steps in groups of twos and threes, taking a break from the workday or enjoying a day off with friends. I'm sure I saw a couple of first dates. Increasingly as the sun sets, it's families – groups of men chatting about cricket or soccer, I'm betting, and groups of women enjoying themselves while keeping a vague eye on boisterous children running every which way.

Three young men, probably 20 years old at a guess, approach the area where I'm sitting, and I wonder what they're up to. Kids that age are always up to something, aren't they? But it turns out they're just looking for a quiet place to take a rest and maybe watch the girls go by. After a few minutes, Sabin, the most inquisitive of the group, leans over to ask where it is I'm from, and what *I'm* up to. I've had my notebook out and have been scribbling away, a habit that has a way of drawing attention. We spend a pleasant few minutes chatting while I try and figure out what the catch is. It turns out there isn't one.

Before long, two more young men, Sunil and Ujjsrul, come up the steps and take the space to my right. Also university-aged, they have many of the same questions. Where am I from? What have I seen in Nepal? Where am I going next? After awhile, Sabin leaves with his friends, but the other two appear intent on keeping the conversation going. As I loosen up, I find these young men delightful. They are educated and passionate about their country and their culture. In the space of 45 minutes, we talk travel, politics, religion and the differences in attitude between the East and the West. What we may lack in citation or hard fact, we more than make up for with intuition and belief. This is not rhetoric or argument, this is instinct and feeling, and at the root of it I get a sense that young Nepalis feel like they are being taken advantage of by a government that doesn't seem to care about the average citizen.

For a moment I'm desperate to record it all somehow. Bust out the notebook again, or maybe the voice recorder. Then I remember that sometimes a chat is just a chat, and settle into the moment of it. This is what I was looking for, and the boys deliver, with style and substance, and I am grateful. After we exchange Facebook handles so we can keep in touch, they wander off into the night to do whatever it is young men in Kathmandu do these days.

Making my way back into the fray, I do one more tour down to Freak Street, and upon my return notice there has been another subtle shift in the tempo of the square. Along the main walkway through the centre, street vendors have descended en masse, selling shoes, clothing and unmentionables to a local clientele. In an environment full of ambient energy, it is still an impressive display. One vendor in particular draws a big crowd with a show on par with that of a Southern U.S. auctioneer. Perhaps what I've failed to realize over the last few days is that culture, religion, commerce and the occasional flash of showmanship will forever be intertwined in this place. It is in the nature of the city.

• • •

After a couple of more days of wandering the streets and lounging around the guest house, it's time to address the elephant in the room. More specifically the oversized black bag tucked behind the door, which I have been ignoring with all my might. Inside the fancy reinforced heavy nylon is my bicycle, and there's no good reason for it to be here. You don't come to Nepal to ride a bike. You come to sightsee and shop and trek. Maybe you add in a jungle tour or some whitewater rafting at the end of your trip, if you have time. Yet there it is, sitting like an accusation, waiting for me muster up the nerve to do something with it.

The last time I was here, I rented a mountain bike and toured around town a couple of times. I am older now, and not as brave, and that is probably why I haven't even unzipped the bag. There's a bigger plan for the bike, of course – I didn't pack it away in the bottom of a plane on an intercontinental flight just to explore Kathmandu. For reasons that appear hazy now, I thought it would be cool to skip the usual methods of getting to a trailhead. People fly, take a bus or hire a four-by-four and driver. You can even start the Helambu trek by simply walking out of Kathmandu. But I just *had* to be different. Ride to Jiri before starting to walk? Sure. Great idea. In theory.

Breaking out the bike for the first warm-up ride turns out to be not so bad; it's just a bike, not some kind of torture device, and after spending a good hour unpacking and reassembling, I think I'm ready. I've been working on a personal psych-up job the entire time.

"I can do this. I've done it before," I say as I put on the wheels, adjust the seat height and reattach the handlebars.

"I need to ride, I need the exercise, I can't just walk everywhere," I keep telling myself as I pump up the tires, a tedious process with the shitty little bike pump I've packed.

"I want to feel the breeze on my face and get out past where a day trip on foot can reasonably take me."

It *is* time for a larger adventure. This is the argument, and I'm winning it.

"Come on man, you can do this!"

Ha, ha, ha, breeze on my face, that's a good one. More like dust and diesel fuel exhaust on my face, and in my eyes, and in my throat. Taking this on at midday may be a lapse in judgment on my part, and probably not the last one I'll make either, but here goes.

Traffic in the greater Kathmandu area, away from the tight alleyways near Thamel, is predictably chaotic, but not quite as dangerous as you might think. The key is speed – or, more precisely, the lack thereof. The city streets are either so congested or so poorly maintained that nobody can get up a full head of steam. Sure, the intensity of the honking and jostling and manoeuvring for position is decidedly unnerving, but without the element of speed, chaos rules more than danger – but only just – and you do have to get used to it. Riding on the left side of the road means shoulder checks and merges that are all ass-backwards, and I had forgotten about that. The destinations today are Boudhanath Stupa and Pashupatinath Temple, two important religious sites in Kathmandu, and already I'm going the wrong way.

Slipping out of Thamel, I'm swept up in the traffic on

Kanti Path and am too terrified to make a right turn across four lanes without getting my bearings first, so I end up travelling north on Lazimpat Road instead of moving east as I had planned. Compounding the early troubles, there's an annoying and persistent clicking sound coming from my back wheel, and the chain slips whenever I shift down to the easiest three gears on the rear chain ring. But the adrenalin is pumping now, so I just power forward and try to avoid the pedestrians, vehicles, motorbikes and three-wheel tuk-tuks coming at me from every which way. I don't even take a breath until the National Police Academy, a couple of kilometres away, where I finally stop to regain my composure.

A right turn in the proper direction is still out of the question, but the clicking sound is easily remedied. It was simply the end of the rear gear cable poking into the spokes. The actual gear problem will have to wait, and as I pass the American embassy, I begin to get a little more comfortable with how the rules of the road work. Locals on bicycles are easily overtaken, either because their bikes are so old and worn out that they can't maintain a head of steam, or because they're hauling some outrageous load. Fruits and vegetables, cooking gas canisters and neighbourhood garbage are common freight. Most of the bikes are also simple one-gear set-ups and not exactly built for speed.

The tuk-tuks are safe to draft behind for awhile and are also easily overtaken, because a tuk-tuk carrying five or six people doesn't go very fast. Motorcycles generally overtake a little too close for comfort – and on the right, which is weird – but also provide a honk or two to let you know they're coming. Dealing with cars and trucks and buses – well, that's just like urban riding everywhere. The competence of the vehicle operators you have to take on faith.

Approaching the Ring Road at the northern end of its circling of the city, I finally screw up the courage to venture out past the far left of my lane and attempt a right turn across the intersection. At the junction there's a roundabout with an island in the middle, where two energetic cops are giving directions and managing the flow of traffic. There are no lights – it's whistles and hand gestures only – and for all the commotion, it seems to work. My turning lane is brought to a standstill as other vehicles are given right of way. When it's our turn, we don't travel around the island as I'd expected but shortcut in front of it on the way to the far-left lane of the road to the right.

This being Nepal, however, there is always more than one thing going on at a time, so vehicles coming from the north and turning left onto the same section of Ring Road are also still moving. Making the turn means merging with them on my left while being passed by faster vehicles from my own lane on my right, with hundreds of horns bleating all around. If that doesn't get the heart racing, nothing will. Drivers don't give way so much as negotiate a non-verbal agreement based on positioning. You have to be assertive but not aggressive. Too timid and you'll never get across a major intersection. Too forceful and they'll be scraping you off the pavement and sending your stuff to the appropriate consulate.

But I think I've got it. At the first takeaway shop I come to, I take another breath, stop to check my map, and celebrate getting this far with a much-needed bottle of water. Enormous ducks come to pick through the litter in the park next to my bench, and some local kids come over and just stare. At first it's unnerving, and I try to make casual conversation to lighten the mood. They simply move to the far end of the bench without reply and continue to stare.

When I'm back on the bike and finally moving east, the Ring Road is downhill, and I move at pace with all the traffic. The cars, trucks and motorcycles are fellow vehicles and pass and are passed as momentum dictates. The challenge is the dogs and cows. It's early afternoon, which means it's hot and muggy, so most of them are taking a rest, right on the road. The road is wide and they stay close to the edge, but only kind of close. You still need to pay attention for fear of tumbling ass-over-teakettle on one that strays. Can you imagine trying to explain that to everyone back home?

"What on earth happened?"

"Hit a cow."

"Okaaay."

Nearing the junction with Boudhanath Sadak, the road steepens for a short stretch, and, despite the slipping low gears, I make it up without much trouble. This is where a cyclist excels in this city, on congested uphills surrounded by overloaded or underpowered vehicles. It makes you feel like a super-athlete. At the intersection it's a left turn from the left lane to a left lane. Simple, and I'm getting cocky. I'm beginning to feel like I was born to do this, which pretty much guarantees I'm about to get lost.

In my mind, Boudhanath Stupa sits on a hill and can be seen from everywhere, and I know I'm on the right road, so I don't even think about it. Boudhanath Sadak does turn into Boudha Road on my map after all – at some random point, it seems – but never mind that. I'll just ride until I see it. As it turns out, Boudhanath Sadak is very busy and is in unbelievably rough shape, and the stupa – traditionally a white or cream-coloured dome with a spire on top – is not visible from the roadside as I expect but tucked up into an old neighbourhood just away from the street. Naturally, I blow right past – but in my defence, that's easy to do when you're still concentrating on not getting killed.

The mud on the road is slick and thin and persistent, and the potholes – well, the potholes are enough to bring every vehicle nearly to a dead stop as the driver devises a plan of attack that will keep his axels intact. At one point, I tuck in behind a large flatbed truck for a couple of blocks before realizing his grossly overstacked load – large burlap sacks filled with god knows what – leans precariously every time he hits an uneven bit of road. It's piled so high that if the truck leans a degree or two more, it might go over. If the ropes holding everything in place give way, I won't stand a chance. So I slip by and get between a motorcycle and a scooter, each of us taking our own third of the space normally occupied by a car.

No surprise: I miss the sign for the stupa in among the barrage of signage, most of it advertisements, and eventually it dawns on me I must have gone too far, so I stop and ask for directions. Apparently, the stupa is back the way I came and to the right. Sounds dubious, but I'll give it another try. My map also indicates that's where it should be.

Backtracking but still distracted by the commotion in the street, I once again pass the alleyway that leads to the stupa without noticing, reach the junction for Sahid Park Road and turn right. The road angles to the northeast, so I'm thinking, *Finally, this must be the way*. Tara Goan Park on the corner is now a tent village for people still displaced, 18 months later, by the earthquake of 2015, and the road is even worse than Boudha Road. There's still no sign of the stupa that I've noticed, and although it hasn't been all that far, it has been hard riding, so I pull over for another map and water break, thinking the Great Boudha Stupa is proving an elusive goal for this first bicycle outing. I should have chosen something simpler, like Tibet maybe.

Sitting at the single table set up out front of another takeaway shop, I take the time to have a few cookies and read up on my destination. Even if I don't stumble across it, at least I'll know something about it. Boudhanath is the largest stupa in Asia, and whereas Durbar Square leans toward Hinduism, Boudhanath is decidedly Buddhist. There are a number of legends attached to the origins of the site, thought to date from around AD 600, and to the various restorations since then as well. The current structure is from the 14th century, when its predecessor was destroyed by invaders.

My favourite of these stories comes from the official World Heritage Site pamphlet and deals with how the site was chosen in the first place. A widow named Ma Jhyazima wanted to make an offering to Buddha and approached the local king for permission. Permission was granted, provided the land used didn't exceed the size of a single ox skin. Undeterred, and with a bigger plan in mind, the widow cut the skin into thin strips and laid the strips end to end to encompass the area now recognized as one of the most important places in Buddhist culture. Tibetans in exile live in the surrounding neighbourhood, and pilgrims visit from all over the world. It is one of the few places where Buddhist practice and teaching on this scale is not interfered with. It sure would be nice if I could find it.

As I'm reading up, children from the grade school next door begin to wander past. Walking with their parents or in groups of twos and threes, they are shy with their *na-mastes*, but when the older age group lets out, everything changes. They're from the Progressive English Secondary School and are about 12 years old. Within seconds, 15 of them descend on the shop for cookies or candies. Two of the bolder boys immediately snap up the available plastic chairs and tuck in right next to me on both sides. That's when the questions start flying in scattergun fashion. *Where are you from? What do you do? How long will you be in Nepal?* Their English is quite good, far better than my French was at that age, and we fall into an energetic, if at times halting, conversation.

"I am from Canada," I say, and one of the boys standing at the back of the group jumps in.

"Canada is the second-biggest country in the world."

I'm impressed. I had no idea where Nepal was when I was 12, let alone any details about it.

"Yes, it is. Can anyone tell me what the biggest country in the world is?"

Four or five voices answer in unison: "Russia."

These kids have been doing their homework, and I find the exchange so interesting that I want to get some of the details down in my notebook. They find this to be incredibly interesting. The two brave ones leap up immediately and lean in over my page, eyes riveted on every word. It's a strange experience: they report back to the group what I'm writing, and I figure after a couple of quick notes they'll lose interest, but as long as I write, they watch intently. After I put the notebook away, we discuss the merits of school on Sunday and what their favourite sports are, and they confirm that yes, the stupa is just up this road and to the right.

Like I haven't heard that before.

Eventually, I do find the stupa, down what turns into a fabulous flagstone alleyway with tons of historic charm. As was the case with some of the buildings in Durbar Square, the stupa itself is undergoing earthquake repairs and is covered with scaffolding but is still worth a visit. The surrounding courtyard is busy but quieter than Durbar Square somehow. The very stone and brick radiate Buddhist calm. Monks with shaved heads and maroon robes complete the scene. It reminds me very much of Jokhang Temple in Lhasa, Tibet, somewhere I have not been in almost a decade.

There is an energy that permeates places like this: they are felt as much as they are seen. I do two koras (mindful circles), desperate to yell, "You're going the wrong way!" at tourists travelling counterclockwise. Then I sit on a bench for awhile to just take it in. A dog has come to lie down next to my bike, and an aging monk is prostrating past on his own slow kora. It is perfectly acceptable to walk around the stupa, but the most devout show next-level commitment by lying face down and extending their arms over their heads, marking the spot, and only then stepping to that spot to repeat the process. It is a practice for the truly dedicated, and I give him some rupees in exchange for a photo. When dark, rumbling clouds appear on the horizon, I realize it's time to go.

Out on these little day trips, I have found all the monuments and temples and stupas in the city worth exploring. They are imbued with a lengthy history someone born in North America can find difficult to comprehend. Grasping the religious significance of these sacred places also requires an open-mindedness that contradicts the straight-line and self-centred thinking prominent in the West. But it's in the spaces between the landmarks that you get a feel for everyday life in Kathmandu as you walk or bike through them.

Making my way back to Thamel was a disaster of navigation that I don't want to talk about, and I didn't make it to Pashupatinath today, but I'll get there. What's important is not checking destinations off my list but developing a deeper understanding of this crazy place with all its layers. It's so great. I love it here.

4.

DRAGGING MY FEET

Every honeymoon ends. After nearly ten days of exploring, reading, writing, eating, resting and generally being
a human being instead of a human doing, I'm having a
clunker. The world of to-do lists and timelines I left behind in North America has made an appearance, unwelcome and unbidden, and no matter how hard I try, I can't
shake the feeling of unease that has descended. My old
broken patterns are here, right where they don't belong.
To be fair, I'm fighting it. I've been fighting it all morning
but am at an impasse. I don't want to go out and jostle my
way through the crowds and the smog and the noise, but
I don't want to stay in either. There's too much space here
for my mind to get away from me.

Actually pack up my things, check out of the hotel
and hit the open road? Forget about it. The sudden monsoon downpours are still too frequent, and, to be honest, I haven't quite found courage to leave the comforts
of Kathmandu. For a time, the quirkiness of being in a
foreign land is distraction enough, so I concentrate on
those details. For example, the light switches are on when
flipped in the down position, and off when flipped up. For
the life of me, I can't ever remember that. Seeing as the
ceiling fan and most of the lights are on the same four-
switch box, I flip everything every which way whenever I
enter or leave the room.

My favourite "you're not in Kansas anymore, Dorothy" quirk of the room, though, is the bathroom: a completely tiled-in, all-in-one sink/shower/toilet set-up that allows me to wash my laundry, myself and even my bike at the same time, with acres of space to spare. Brilliant.

Channel surfing, once I figure out the correct power source, has never been so weirdly entertaining. Programming in Nepali, Hindi and Chinese, where you have no idea what's going on, except in some of the ads where tag lines or select phrases are randomly switched to English, is the norm. Cheesy action movies and music videos appear to be an Indian specialty, and this morning there is also a Chinese film dubbed *and* subtitled in English. One English-language, hour-long drama also has English subtitles, just to be sure. And then there's cricket and soccer, of course. Full-game replays, highlight packages and panel talk shows. All day, every day, it seems. I now know more about India's Kerala Blasters than I ever would have thought possible.

These idiosyncrasies can only distract for so long, however, and the things I need to do linger. I need a Trekkers' Information Management System registration card ("TIMS card" for short), and a permit for Sagarmatha, the national park where Everest is located. There are a few precautionary meds from the pharmacy I forgot to pick up in Canada that need collecting, and informing the consulate of your plans is recommended in many of the guidebooks. And, and, and ... The fussy details of travel are creeping around the back of my mind, which only punches my "I should" button hard and fast: *I should get all this done today; I should hit up more points of interest before I move on; I should be training more in preparation for the hike, doing more stairs and taking longer bike rides.* My favourite obnoxious internal summary of the situation: "I'm not getting enough done!"

It can be easy to fall into the trap of sightseeing like a Westerner. Like travel is some kind of competition to be scored or judged. The question is, where the hell do I think I have to be, anyway? This town isn't going anywhere, the trek isn't going anywhere and I've got lots of time. Relax, dude, geez ...

Okay, fair enough, but I can't stay in the room, despite the top-notch entertainment radiating from the small screen. Unable to find the energy for a stupa or temple complex, I settle for another low-intensity exploration of the neighbourhood to try and shake off the cobwebs. This is going to be a mindful walk, urban-style, dammit – if I can manage it.

My boys at the taxi corner are used to me now and don't show much effort anymore, and for the most part the casual wave-off is sufficient as long as I stay in Thamel. I am familiar here, which allows me to be a little more attentive to the details of this place without interruption. I can't help but be amazed that I enjoy the chaos, the hustle and bustle in the squares and around the temples, the crowded streets in Thamel and all the noise everywhere. It isn't like me to be so engaged. I don't normally thrive in an urban environment. I find people interesting. Crowds? Not so much. I should be out in the mountains already, but I'm having a hard time pulling myself away. I am a fly on the wall. Content in my role as voyeur, even if I do occasionally get sucked in against my will. The distinction can make all the difference in how you view things. Charles Dickens once wrote, "Thus I wandered about the city, like a child in a dream, staring at the British merchants, and inspired by a mighty faith in the marvellousness of everything."

I suspect there are similarities between London in the 1800s and modern Kathmandu that might not spring to mind immediately. Both are places of rapid population growth, coupled with limited access to resources for the average person. A lagging infrastructure is an inevitable consequence of development, and rapid expansion of urban areas carries with it certain challenges in any era. Air quality, water quality, the reliability and quality of lighting at night and working conditions for labourers are often compromised as part of the awkward struggle toward modern living.

Here, the attempt is obviously foreign to my experience. The faces, the language and the manner of dress are all different from what I grew up with, which in turn are different from what Dickens witnessed, of course. But there are similarities too. I was in Toronto recently, and I wonder how different Durbar Square is from the square at Yonge and Dundas streets. Not much, once you get past the initial impressions. There is a cultural component here that is not as pronounced in Toronto, but you still get the working-class folks trying to get where they need to go, the street performers, the restaurants and shops on the fringes, the tourists, the hustlers, the bums, the drop-outs. The backdrop is more polished and obviously much more expensive in the Big Smoke, but the crazy dance that goes on is similar. Except for the occasional cow joining the scene, of course.

My attention is drawn to the shops lining all the streets in this neighbourhood. I have always been curious about what people do as part of their daily routine when I travel. I can't help but watch them as they go about their business and try to figure out how they make a living out of it. Somewhat more challenging is trying to figure out if they enjoy the work they do. We are not our jobs and we are not our careers, yet we spend an awful lot of time and energy on them. Why, when there is so much to see and do out in the world?

The easy answer is that in the West there isn't the time, and in the developing world there isn't the money. That's a simplistic observation, to be sure. This system we've created seems hell-bent on suppressing the wandering impulse for some and restricting it for others, but I sense it all goes much deeper. Today I want to get my head around the consequences, at least a little bit. I've come all this way. I want to understand.

According to the website Statistics Times, Nepal had the world's 18th-lowest gross domestic product per capita in 2014. The first 16 countries on the list are from Africa, and, at just over US$698 a year, the average Nepali makes more than the average citizen in just one other Asian country, Afghanistan, which ranked 17th-poorest. The average Canadian makes more in a single two-week pay period. Stats can deceive, of course, but no matter which way you look at it, Nepal has a long way to go to achieve economic parity with the West. The situation is better in Kathmandu and the trekking regions, where most of the tourist dollars end up, and you sure wouldn't know there's trouble here economically if shopping is the measure. Roads and infrastructure, okay, there are obvious and glaring issues, but shopping – well, it looks like the national sport.

Outside the tourist district, in areas targeting locals, the scene makes Thamel look like a church social (complete with casual conversation, cupcakes and coffee – or, in this case, underlings sent to get steaming cups of milk tea). I'm not sure who's fronting the money for all this, but an incredible amount of inventory is carried by hundreds, if not thousands, of independent retail outlets in this part of town alone. Some are little more than holes in the wall, with a hundred square feet of floor space or less.

Last night I walked down a long alley consisting exclusively of pashmina shops, one after another after another. Down another, shorter alley, it was housewares – pots and pans and pots and pans, as far as the eye could see. It is the start of the tourist high season, and Dashain, the largest festival in the country, is also about to start, but still. Prices are low and inventory is high. In the popular Thamel restaurants, there are always five waiters on shift when two would do. I can't figure out how anybody makes any money.

I've watched a lot of people doing a lot of different things: bricklayers, rickshaw drivers, cab drivers, policemen and soldiers. Deliverymen dropping off chickens and eggs and produce and beer on bicycles and motorcycles; tanker trucks of water on Chaksibari Marg every morning to service the hotels and restaurants; 35-pound canisters of cooking gas being dragged around. There are a lot of people working hard, some for very little reward. But hang out in a neighbourhood long enough, and this is what you begin to see: what's happening in the background. You witness what working life is for people, and what needs to be done to keep things going. Some of the people appear perfectly content in their efforts, others not so much. When it is not so busy, employees revert to that ubiquitous time-killing technique: surfing their cellphones.

I, of course, sympathize with this effort to get ahead, and the challenge of actually doing it. I'm clearly not fond of being hustled, but I can still appreciate it when someone is willing to put his or her head down and do the work. I have tried to do it too. Tried to figure out how to make a proper go of things without losing my mind. Like so many the world over, I had to, I needed the money, so I got stuck in and made every attempt to be an exemplary modern consumer soldier. Make more money in order to spend more money – that's the heart of the modern capitalist model, right?

In hindsight, there was no way any "job" was ever going to be good enough for long, because being that person punching the clock was ultimately the wrong thing for me. I knew it, I have always known it deep down, but we all have to do something in exchange for money. That's how our society works. Precious few of us find that thing that not only pays us but also fits our core values and beliefs. I love to write and take pictures, but I have made the majority of my income in the service industry. Bringing people food and drink is my occupation. I have dutifully put "bartender" on my paperwork for most of my life. I was professional in the truest sense of the word. I went to work, did the job and got paid but was not exactly pleased that it appeared to be my lot in life.

Then, somewhat miraculously, I got a promotion, and everything that goes along with it. A raise, more to think about, more to do, and at first I thought the upward mobility would bring change in my attitude, in my perception of the experience. And for awhile I was so busy trying to figure out how things worked as the boss that I was distracted enough to get through it without complaint. Then, almost imperceptibly, my efforts at work became all about the money. I had no real passion for the job and no enthusiasm for doing more than was necessary, and that made me unhappy.

It was exhausting, and it was all I could do to keep up. By the end of a 45- or 50- or, occasionally, 60-hour work week, I had no energy for anything else. Early on, I had ideas about reshaping things and making improvements that would, in turn, make my work life more interesting and fulfilling. I wanted to put my mark on it, I wanted to be really good at it. But that never happened. I thought about taking a course in professional development and aspired to improve as a manager of people but could never get around to doing any of it. My job was all about putting out fires and keeping the machine rolling. And there certainly was no opportunity to have a life outside of work. There was simply no time.

Then, a few days before my 46th birthday, I had what I now see was the beginning of an epiphany. It was the birth of a profound observation, happening in slow motion. Not a crash-and-burn, all-guns-a-blazin' kind of defining moment that would have sent me straight to an airport, but a subtle, deep-seated sense that without eventually finding another way, I was as good as dead. I might be alive for another 46 years, but I wasn't going to live that life to any meaningful degree. I would simply be working through it with my bad knee and sore hip, not to mention the spare tire around my middle.

Dietary and lifestyle adjustments were called for. The situation was growing desperate. I needed help and took that common first step. I went to see my doctor for some advice.

"If you want to lose weight quickly, cut out bread and pasta for awhile," my doctor said as I sat there in his examination room, wishing for some kind of magic bullet that would effortlessly remove my pain (and miraculously make me young and fit and handsome again, of course).

I was looking for an instant fix; all he was giving me was practical advice. But, like I said, I was desperate.

"And now that your blood pressure is creeping up again, cut down on your salt intake as well," he said.

My doctor was a whippet-thin outdoor sports enthusiast who had helped me muddle through the accumulated physical issues associated with middle age. He also knew what I did for a living and saved the most challenging of the required dietary changes for last.

"You should also cut back on your alcohol consumption. Don't you have something like O'Doul's at the bar?"

"Well, sure," I said as blithely as I could manage, "but that's not nearly as much fun."

"True," he said without missing a beat, "but a heart attack or a stroke isn't very much fun either."

He did have a point there.

And so the journey back to Nepal began – innocently enough, I think. I needed a reason to keep plugging away, I needed a goal besides money to make the effort worthwhile and I needed something to dream about. I thought the ideal would be to drop everything and go trekking again, but I was in no position to just walk away. I was trapped in a vortex of bad habits and debt that can be difficult to climb out of, and attitude and dietary changes alone weren't going to get me where I wanted to go. The money part of the equation aside, I needed to deal with the chronic pain, which was slowly but surely getting worse.

So there I was a few weeks later back at the doctor's office, ready to splash out some cash for an experimental treatment not covered by Alberta Health or my private health insurance. Durolane is a stabilized form of hyaluronic acid thought to aid in lubricating and cushioning joints damaged by osteoarthritis. But the procedure works better for some people than for others, and at 300 bucks a pop, it's an expensive experiment.

Getting down to business, my doctor infused his voice with a calmness that was barely noticeable in tone and volume, yet remarkably relaxing at the same time – probably a good thing, seeing as he was getting ready to approach the general area of my genitals with a needle over three inches long.

After saying something like that, I feel I must explain in more detail.

The hip joint is relatively easy to find on the average human being. Stand up, let your hand drop directly at your sides, bend your elbows slightly outward and feel for the hard, bony lump in among the fleshy mass where your buttocks and thighs meet, and there you have it, the ball and socket set-up of the modern hip joint. Stick a needle into your body anywhere around that region, and all you're going to get is a broken hypodermic for your troubles. Access to the joint capsule is through the uppermost part of the front of the thigh, perilously close to body parts nobody wants stabbed under any circumstances. There I was, staring at the fluorescent lights on the ceiling, with my underpants hiked up to expose my upper thigh, while a guy I barely know leaned in and said, "This is going to pinch a little bit."

Yeah, right, doc.

To be fair, the local anesthetic was more uncomfortable than the giant needle, and at no point was the procedure painful. Watching an equally numb left knee get injected a couple of minutes later, I was amazed at how resilient the human body can be as he jiggled the needle around to distribute the artificial synovial fluid evenly throughout the joint. My instinct was to cry out, but in the end I never felt much of anything.

Unfortunately, the procedure didn't help. This wasn't the magic bullet I was hoping for. In the end, most of the progress I imagined that day was theoretical. The days drifted into weeks that turned into months as I floated in a steady state of repetition. I would go to the gym once in awhile, or commit to cutting down the alcohol and TV consumption. Nothing stuck. Nepal was a far-off dream. Happiness remained elusive. I settled down and struggled through, as we so often do. Without motivation, a purpose and a point for your actions, it seems, anything can get tired fast, and the cage you're in doesn't need bars to be effective.

But through it all, I kept dreaming of wandering around a tiny corner of Asia with no strict itinerary and no mindless duties to uphold. I had a desperate wish for a splash of wonder that I didn't know how to find anymore, but I was looking for a way to get there at least, and that was something.

What I wonder now is if anyone I've seen over the last few days dreams of travel to distant lands as they're surfing their phones or hauling water or laying brick or standing around looking bored in front of government buildings while holding rifles. We Westerners take our mobility for granted, and I suspect financial restrictions are only part of the challenge for Nepalis. Obtaining a foreign visa is probably not as easy as stepping to the customs counter upon arrival and laying down some cash, which is the current procedure for visitors coming here. But Canada is a beautiful country. I would recommend it.

• • •

Today I'm up early. This is a disturbing trend. After two weeks, I'm thoroughly over the jet lag but can't manage to stay awake past 8 p.m. and am up by 5:30 a.m., like clockwork. This is not like me at all. I am a bar person, a night owl. Resigned to the situation, I read and then check my social media to see what my friends with day jobs, who are just finishing up their workdays back home, and my friends with bar jobs, who are just starting theirs, are doing. Mostly I'm just killing time. Breakfast at Hotel Mandap doesn't start until seven.

Out on the street, it is eerily quiet. Even the man who owns the convenience cubbyhole next to the guest house isn't working yet. Taking the little S-bend tight on the corner on the way to Chaksibari Marg, I am brought up short by a young cow, who obviously has somewhere to be, because she doesn't even break stride and expects me to give her the right-of-way. Cows are sacred to Hindus, and on the books in Nepal it is still a crime worthy of jail time if you kill one. This young miss has already figured out who the boss is around here. Sidestepping to the right, I give her a little pat on the shoulder and let her pass.

After breakfast and some writing, I head back to the guest house to collect my bike, with the goal of finding Pashupatinath firmly in mind. With a little experience under my belt, I manage to get across Kanti Path with only a minimum of fuss and am actually headed in the right direction. Pedalling along at pace with the rest of the traffic is thrilling, as is tying to avoid the occasional wide-open storm drain that could easily swallow my front wheel without a second thought.

The route is not always straightforward, however; there are twists and turns and forks in the road that defy the inherent logic of a grid system. A city that has grown rapidly and is essentially a patchwork of neighbourhoods can't be expected to be plain sailing, but this is ridiculous. Before long, I am lost again. Somehow I have gradually veered north, and only realize to what extent as I pass the U.S. embassy for the second time in the span of a few of days. A development that inspires surprise – "Hey?" – followed by a flash of recognition and understanding that comes all at once: "What the fuck? Seriously?"

But at least I know where I am, and from here it's easy going, on a route I've recently used. Turning right on the Ring Road, I encounter a different set of dogs and a different set of cows, but the traffic is lighter, so I am able to make good time. I take a left onto a steep exit from the main road that leads quickly to a small temple on a bend in the Bagmati River. By my rough and quite possibly erroneous calculation, it is not far upriver from Pashupatinath. Two families are here already, so I try to be as inconspicuous as possible as I push my bike past them and settle in a short distance away, on the stone steps leading down to the water.

Every foreign culture has its own word for us whiteys, often derogatory but not necessarily menacing – a term used in peer-group social situations, often in the face of minor intrusion. The one I have heard on previous visits to Nepal is *Meek-karu*, which translates as "eyes white," but that is a Sherpa word used mainly in the Solu-Khumbu and other regions where that particular ethnic group has settled. The Sherpa people were more intrigued by the eyes of early foreign visitors to the Everest region than by our comparatively pale skin, oddly enough.

The equivalent word in Nepali is *kuire*, which means "fog eyes," and after the initial awkwardness of this *kuire* showing up at what is clearly not a tourist attraction, nobody pays me any mind, except the occasional monkey. Rhesus macaques are a fixture at many of the holy sites in the Kathmandu Valley. The protected habitats around these temples and shrines are oases of trees in an otherwise congested metropolis. By extension, the monkeys are also protected, by faith if not by law, but it is an uneasy alliance. The macaques associate humans with food – handouts and garbage – but they are wary and territorial by nature, which makes them unpredictable.

Thankfully, most of the local troupe is across the river, preoccupied with the complicated workings of their group dynamics, and this suits me fine. Every once in awhile, a single monkey or a group of two or three will come by where I'm sitting. Generally, they give me a wide berth and a sideways glance, and I make sure nothing I do could be misread as aggression or confrontation. Because when a rhesus macaque is having a bad day, it is a terrifying display of screeching and biting. When they fight, it's like rabid raccoons tripping out on meth. And the adults fight a lot.

The juveniles, on the other hand, spend most of their time playing. When they're not busy eating or grooming, they are usually engaged in a non-aggressive form of wrestling that has a distinctive game-of-tag component. This behaviour prepares them for the relentless territorial battles of adulthood, and they engage in it everywhere: on the ground, in the trees, on temple steps. Here at the bend in the river, a favourite pastime involves three or four young monkeys chattering and swinging in the tree canopy before the bravest launches himself into the water from what looks to be an insane height. He is immediately pursued, with apparent delight, and the whole group dog-paddles to a convenient point outside the main current. After shaking off the water and wrestling around briefly, they take off up slope into the trees to do it all again. It's amazing to watch.

Eventually, the adults move farther up the hill to another part of their territory, and the rest of the group follows. This is disappointing, but the show is over, so I gather my bike and do the same. It has been a peaceful interlude in the crowded city, but I do have a destination in mind, and I'm not quite there yet.

Shree Pashupatinath Temple is sacred in the Hindu faith and an important traditional site for cremations. The ornate collection of roughly 500 temples and shrines, some of them off limits to all but a specific group of devotees, sits on the banks of the Bagmati River, also considered sacred to Hindus and Buddhists. What is immediately notable to a visitor, though, is not the wide array of interesting architecture but the funeral pyre platforms pressed right to the river's edge. There are ten of them in total on the western bank of the river, below the footbridge, and currently two fires are burning.

The cremation process catches your attention immediately because it is so public. Death in the Western world is largely hidden. A loved one gets put in a box, and in some traditions an open casket is viewed at some point, usually at the wake or during the final service. After that, the deceased is hidden. My father was cremated after he passed, and as a preteen I found the whole thing confusing. Ostensibly, his spirit was there, but he was also gone, and only a vague sense of his presence was reinforced by those who came to pay their respects. In the end, it is a box or an urn that gets put in the ground; strangers see off the actual body. Here things are different. This is very public mourning, and the family is much more involved in the proceedings.

Depending on who has died, a specific set of traditions must be followed, but there are some basic universal procedures. The body is placed on a stretcher, and then family members carry it to the assigned platform, where the head and sometimes feet are washed with river water to purify the deceased. Bodies are wrapped in white, orange or red cloth, and sometimes all three. Strings of marigolds and colourful powders are also often placed with the body. Only natural elements are allowed, so straw and wood are used for the fire and clarified butter is used as an accelerant. Watching from a distance, I'm not sure if this is a better or a worse way to mourn the dead; it's just different.

Seeing my father burned down to ash might have been too much for my fragile young psyche to handle. Or it might have helped with closure. Who knows? Hindsight rarely helps with these kinds of questions. As the oldest male child, however, I would have been responsible for performing the final rituals and touching the flame to his corpse if I were Hindu – and the head is the traditional ignition point. That, I admit, might have been a little too much to deal with.

The Bagmati River is about 25 metres across here, and at first I can't bring myself to get too close to the proceedings. It feels intrusive, so I sit about 50 metres downstream on the opposite bank from the pyres and leave my camera in my bag. One of the cremations has just started, and another is nearing its conclusion, so I take up a space on some steps leading to the river and try and be as unobtrusive as possible, but I am also very curious about the process and how the families here deal with death. As the advanced fire burns down, an attendant with a long pole begins pushing still-smouldering logs and ash straight into the river.

Although sacred, the Bagmati is also just a river in a land without adequate waste treatment facilities, so it also channels excess waste water downstream, and trash floats by at regular intervals. In among the food offerings tucked into tiny banana-leaf rafts there are paper plates, newspapers, candy wrappers and the occasional Head & Shoulders bottle. On this side of a small sandbar, where the water is only a few inches deep, a 10-year-old boy saunters by in the slow-moving current with magnets tied to a string. He's trolling for coins.

After about 20 minutes, I am growing a little more comfortable. Two new pyres are being set up, so I decide to move farther up this opposite bank toward the main temple complex. This is not as ghoulish as it sounds. Important temple for Hindus, active cremation site, tourist destination, bathing site, public park: this place is all of those, and more. Just upriver from the pyres, a dozen Nepalis (or perhaps Indian pilgrims) have peeled down to their underwear and are washing in the river, and half a dozen Western tourists are sitting on the stone steps right across from the ghats. Most notably, the walkways on both sides of the river also serve as thoroughfares. People who have nothing to do with the proceedings casually walk within a few feet of the grieving families and the wrapped bodies lying on stretchers. No one even bats an eye.

As I said, this is nothing like how things work at home.

On the pyre closest to me now, the men from the family have picked up the stretcher and are moving it onto the platform. They perform three clockwise circuits of the carefully arranged logs and then lift the body off the stretcher and place it on top of the pyre. Shuttling up and down the steps to the river's edge, they gather cupped handfuls of water and place them on the now-exposed head, ritually cleansing the body. There is much burning of incense, and the occasional discussion about procedure, and in time an older gentleman lights the fire on what I assume is his wife's body. The family shows strong emotion, and I cry along with them. As all this is going on, two more pyres are being set up and decorated with strings of marigolds.

The complete burning of a body takes a couple of hours using these old-fashioned methods, and after a time it does begin to feel morbid to be a voyeur to such an intimate family moment. When a dozen tourists show up on the steps near my perch, that signals it's time, so I return to my bike ride in a sombre and reflective mood – a state quickly replaced by my fervent attention on not getting lost again on the journey back to Karma.

5.

THE FRIENDSHIP HIGHWAY

I don't want to go. I don't want to go! I. Don't. Want. To.
Go.

Okay, that's not entirely true, I've been daydreaming
about this adventure for a long time. I've planned for it.
Saved for it. Worked hard to get to this point. The thing
is, I'm having such an interesting time, a part of me doesn't
want to leave the city. It has been almost three weeks of
puttering around Kathmandu and writing and seeing the
sights, and I'm comfortable. I've settled in. This is a dangerous state for an adventure to be in. It's going to be hard
work out there, and I'm used to the casual pace of my day
trips. I like my simple breakfast and Nepali tea to start the
day, my late-morning naps, my afternoons of exploring
and my beers and fabulous dinners in the evening. But it's
time.

Picking my way through Thamel and the major thoroughfares at the heart of the city by bike, I find my way
eventually to Madan Bhandari Road and the Araniko
Highway, which travels northeast past Bhaktapur and carries on all the way up through the mountains to Tibet. I
tried the route out of town on one of my day trips, so it
has been easy to navigate, and the difference today is that
Dashain, the country's biggest and most widely celebrated
festival, has begun, so the roads are practically deserted.
Half the city has gone back to their home villages, so I can

bob and weave all over the place without consequence. It's great fun.

There is a minor traffic jam at the Ring Road junction as buses jockey for passengers who've not yet escaped the city, but the dual carriageway to Bhaktapur is wide, with an actual shoulder, so this is also easy going.

Pedalling along at a comfortable clip, I get an occasional *namaste* shouted from the roadside, and at intersections where traffic is backed up near Bhaktapur, conversation is easily struck up with motorcyclists. Solo motorcyclists are not the norm in Nepal as they are in North America. Quite often they have a passenger, and sometimes two or three. What's remarkable about this is that passengers never wear a helmet. The driver does, but his buddy, or his girlfriend, or in some cases wife and small children, do not. They want to know where I'm going with so much baggage strapped to my bike, and I oblige them with a short-version explanation. I want to know where their helmets are but am too dumbfounded to ask.

After Bhaktapur, the holiday-travel tone changes. Traffic doesn't increase so much as condense. Road improvements have not reached this far, and the highway turns into a single lane of traffic in each direction. In most places the road is just wide enough for two cars, and not always wide enough for two buses or two trucks. Inevitably, someone has to give way. With no real shoulder, that can turn into an interesting game of chicken. In some places there is a gravel and dirt verge that kicks up a cloud of dust when a vehicle leaves the blacktop, but that is by no means universal, and more often than not it is a rough exit from the pavement. A two-, three- or even four-inch drop into a pothole is common. In a few spots, the entire road is only four or five feet wide – the potholes have eaten the rest. But these challenges don't slow anyone down much, which makes for nerve-racking riding.

It turns out this part of the route isn't just a passage to China anymore, not a path to an unknown and exotic destination – it's a commuter link in a rapidly growing part of the country. The threat of traffic has distracted me from the bigger picture, and it has almost escaped my notice that the climbing has begun. It is not yet steep, but I'm painfully slow, and the tight inside turns where there is no shoulder are a real concern. My bike is wide with the panniers attached, and drivers here habitually cut corners, leaving me with nowhere to go. Without any momentum, it takes a long time to navigate the more hazardous sections. When I look forward, the worry is that someone will appear suddenly, cutting the corner. Looking back to gauge traffic is an exercise in endless calculations, with permutations and possibilities shifting constantly as new sets of cars and trucks and buses enter the equation. No matter how hard I push on the pedals I, … can't … manage … to … go … any … faster to escape the danger.

Even as I spend parts of the morning with my heart in my throat, it turns out the most exciting part isn't wondering whether someone is going to run me down from behind, but wondering if they'll run me over from the front, while passing.

This culture is so laid back in so many ways. The power has been out in Thamel for 18 hours? Oh, well, it'll get fixed eventually. The flight to Lukla has been cancelled because of cloud cover at the notoriously dangerous airport? I guess we'll try again tomorrow. The ATM that accepted your card Tuesday wants nothing to do with your business today but might work again tomorrow, maybe; nobody knows for sure. Not much you can do about that.

But the relaxed approach to problems and delays does not translate to the road. On the highway, all bets are off, and patience is exempted from its traditional place in the collective consciousness. Passing in the middle of villages and in the middle of intersections? Not a problem. Passing on turns, passing uphill, passing uphill on turns? Sure, why not. The whole experience is deeply unnerving when you are at the bottom of the vehicle pecking order. The only thing you can do is keep moving forward and hope the road improves soon.

Entering another highway town at the end of a long, slow climb, I wonder if this might be Dhulikhel, my destination for the day. I've already passed through Sanga and Banepa, so I must be getting close. I have not noticed much municipal signage so far (surprise, surprise), so I've taken to reading the address posted below the business name on most of the bigger shops, which usually includes the village or town and sometimes the district. It's a pleasant surprise to find out I'm here already.

I don't know exactly how long I've been on the road, and even though it's only been 35 kilometres, I expected more climbing, longer climbing, steeper climbing. I'm not sure what length of time I was expecting, but it seems like I've gotten here relatively quickly. As a result, there's no rush to find the guest house, and it's still too early for lunch. I've packed enough snacks for a full day, and after standing in uncertainty for a few minutes, I have decided I just need to sit down and have something to drink.

Off to the side of the main road is a rutted dirt access that runs parallel. It's hard to tell if this is a designated service road or simply a series of front yards – in need of some serious landscaping – of businesses facing the highway, but it is nice to get off the bike. At the near end, a small restaurant has plastic deck chairs set up out front in the dirt. Leaning my bike on the wall, I settle in with a 40-rupee (about 50-cent) glass bottle of Sprite that reminds me of childhood trips to the corner store, and watch the traffic pass.

I thought maybe my perceptions of the morning's experience were overblown, but after five minutes there is no doubting the mayhem is real. At the crest of the hill that marks the middle of town is a major T-junction. At the top of the T is a regional bus stop. The Nepali driver handbook must clearly state that the appropriate response to coming upon such a situation is to speed up and honk lots, because that's what everyone is doing.

I can't help but wonder: What would inspire me to bicycle in this madness?

But I don't have to face it for the rest of today, so my attention moves on to other things. There's a young girl, maybe 4 years old, hanging around, and she is curious about my bike and panniers and pack but is wary of the big white guy sitting in the chair nearby. Clearly, this is the proprietor's daughter, and eventually he comes out and has a seat, which emboldens her to explore the straps securing my gear, then the pedals, and finally the helmet hanging from the handlebars.

The proprietor is only a few years younger than I am, and we fall easily into a genial conversation about how I came to be here and where I'm headed. I explain my ultimate destination and ask for directions to the string of hotels and guest houses that are, by my map, located just out of town but off the main highway. What I don't do is seize the opportunity to practise my Nepali.

With over 100 indigenous languages spoken across the country, Nepali acts as the national language, and as such is a common communication tool in the seven provinces, which are further divided into 75 districts. It is estimated that 35 million people in the immediate region speak Nepali, which is closely related to Hindi, and 50 per cent of the population uses it as a second language. The problem is, English has gained a solid foothold wherever urbanization or tourism is prevalent. Even if I were more rigorous in my study of the Lonely Planet *Nepali Phrasebook & Dictionary* I've packed, it hardly seems essential. The truth is, beyond *namaste* and *dhanyabahd* (thank you), I haven't been practising at all. This will become my private shame as the trip progresses.

After I say my goodbyes and head off in search of my guest house, it's clear that travelling in this fashion is going to be an adjustment, and not just to the language. One of the drawbacks of modern automobile and air travel is that it has dulled our instinct for distance. We measure distance in time, not miles or kilometres. Speeding up the experience of travel has changed how we view each trip. Movement becomes about the intervening period to the destination, and the ground covered loses significance. The focus is on being here and getting there, and the details simply pass us in a blur. Through experience, I have come up with a formula that helps moderate the modern warping of distance. Most trips that can be done in an hour by car take about a day by bike. And if it takes an hour by bike, then it's going to be about a day on foot.

The revised perspective allows for an experience of the surroundings that is more natural. More in tune with the pace set over the course of human development – when I am able to relax into the new timetable, adjust expectations and focus on the terrain, that is. It is only in the last 100 years we have created the ability to rush, and we are addicted to it. In the next two months, I'm not going to be going anywhere quickly. I find that realization intriguing – alluring, even. I *can't* hurry. Not really. If I hustle, and I mean really put in an effort and skip lunch, I might be able to get to one of the destinations up the road or trail a little bit quicker, but overall the trip is going to take the time it takes, and I can't overcome that. It would be impossible for me to repeat a huge effort day after day. I'm too old, for one thing. I'm not motivated to try for another. I want to enjoy the nuance of this place, not speed through it.

This change in attitude does take some getting used to. Ever since I landed in Kathmandu, I have been fighting off the urge to do more and go faster. Once, on the Canadian prairies between Saskatchewan and Manitoba, I covered 188 kilometres in a single day on my bike. That part of the country is remarkably flat, and there was a ferocious tail wind to help me along. It seems a tremendous coincidence – not to mention some kind of adolescent taunt – that my biggest ever single day on the bike is the exact distance from Kathmandu to Jiri. Taking the more challenging nature of the terrain into account, I have given myself four riding days this time, just to be safe.

If I remember the formula and don't get too worked up about the slower pace, I'll get there. Eventually. I hope. In the meantime, I shouldn't forget to enjoy the stops along the way. Otherwise, what's the point?

● ● ●

The town of Dhulikhel turns out to be an unexpected treat. Once I escape the hardscrabble centre of the town proper, the way to my hotel is the kind of classic country road cyclists dream about: meandering, devoid of traffic, full of local charm and picturesque. Booking online can be a crapshoot, but the guest house – a family-run place with fresh food from the garden – is more than I could have hoped for at less than $20 a night, and the room is outstanding. Okay, that might be a slight exaggeration, but the room is perfectly fine for the price. It's the view that's outstanding.

A sweeping panorama greets me out the windows on the north and east sides of the room, and a small balcony with two plastic patio chairs wraps itself around the corner of the building. As is common in the foothills of Nepal, the building is nestled into the slope so that the front appears to be two or three storeys high, while the back soars impossibly high above the valley. A couple of cows graze in terraced fields directly below, and small houses dot adjacent hillsides. The main valley appears lush and fertile, and a succession of increasingly large, tree-covered hills march off into a blue-green haze in the distance. The Himalaya remain hidden, engulfed in puffy white clouds.

It proves impossible not to stay an extra day at Himalayan Sunrise Guest House to try and get a better feel for the exceedingly pleasant setting. The surrounding hills and the valley below are the antithesis of the hustle and bustle of Kathmandu, and I want to explore it. I can still feel the call of the road – the urge to press on and try and keep a four-day pace to Jiri is nearly overwhelming – but I also want to see a little bit of the country that is not pressed up against a main highway.

The other factor in the decision is that I've got too much weight for the bike but don't know what to do about it. Spreading everything around the room on the first afternoon after checking in, and continuing with the project after breakfast the next morning, I can't come to a consensus on what could or should be left behind. Biking gear and tools, clothes, hiking boots and a pack, camera equipment and batteries, toiletries, first aid – it all seems essential, and yet a little too much.

After a couple of hours of fretting, I arrive at the obvious solution: ignore the problem. On the advice of Anish, my front desk clerk, waiter, local information specialist and brand-new trip advisor, I set off for the pilgrimage site of Namo Buddha and the Thrangu Tashi Yangtse Monastery. It's a challenge, but certainly doable, to ride without all the gear along what can best be described as a deteriorating Jeep track. At the junction with the B.P. Koirala Highway, a newly paved side road proves to be nothing if not steep, but it's a relief to find I can ascend a really big hill without being forced to walk. The intermittent rain throughout the day is refreshing after a hot and humid morning, not to mention dramatic to look at from the lofty ridges that mark the route to the monastery.

The monastery itself is peaceful and serene, as these pilgrimage sites tend to be, the sprawling complex spread out along a ridge in a way that encourages casual exploration and mindful reflection. I spend two hours wandering among the temples, statues and stupas.

On the way back to the guest house, I stop for lunch and end up having a lovely, if linguistically challenged, chat with a group of young guys from a nearby village who are sitting at the next table. As I gaze off the covered deck at the latest cloudburst to come rolling past, it occurs to me that a steaming plate of *dal bhat* at a little roadside restaurant where I'm the only non-native present is my secret little pleasure. *Dal bhat* is a staple dish in this part of Asia. *Dal* are lentils, traditionally served in a soup poured over the *bhat*, or cooked rice. The exact spice combinations vary, and every cook will also have a unique take on the accompanying curried potato and vegetables. Some foreigners find it boring to eat rice every day, but I'm always intrigued by the flavours that come out of each individual kitchen. It's never exactly the same twice.

After the rain has stopped and the clouds break apart, I'm hoping the main Himalayan range is finally going to come out from behind the bank of clouds that extends for hundreds of kilometres across the northern horizon. It never does.

• • •

This morning is a little better. The clouds part enough to hint at the seemingly endless string of mountains ahead. It's hard to imagine the exact route except to understand there will be very little level ground from here. The expectation is to climb, of course – this is the Himalaya – but, except for the traffic, the trip from Kathmandu to Dhulikhel was not as taxing as I anticipated. Moving north means moving in the direction of the highest mountains in the world. After that, travelling east toward the trailhead at Jiri will require crossing over the drainages via huge ridges. There are bound to be some challenges in that.

Straight out of Dhulikhel, however, it's down, way down.

Rejoining the main highway after a pleasant warm-up along the secondary road to town, I encounter very little traffic, which is a good thing, because the highway gets even worse than it was on day one. It's perfectly fine, then perfectly disastrous, then perfectly fine again, all within the space of a few hundred metres. Lack of maintenance is only partly to blame; even in the best of circumstances, it would be difficult to keep up with repairs here. The hill is so steep and the space for a road so narrow that the natural tendency is for everything to slip down into the valley below.

In the shadows of the hillside, it remains cool this morning, and the potholes are a very real threat to my rims. As I may have mentioned, I'm carrying too much weight. While that makes any incline in the road a little more difficult, it makes a descent like this way too easy, which makes it hard. I don't have to pedal at all. Point the wheels on a downhill vector, and within ten metres enough momentum has built up to make potholes, hairpin turns and the occasional landslide debris field dangerous propositions indeed. To make matters worse, all said weight is concentrated over the rear wheel. I'm not sure the rack supporting it all will be up to the challenge for long.

On the plus side, the cars and trucks that are out already can't travel all that fast because the road is so winding and steep. It's fun for awhile: it's not every day you get to bomb down a slope that appears endless. But eventually my thumbs start getting sore from keeping the bike steady and pulling hard on the brakes to hold momentum in check. Occasionally, a heart-stopping view from the outside lane presents itself – heart-stopping for both its beauty and its terror. One lapse in concentration or a misjudged turn and ... Well, I shudder when I think about the consequences.

After the steepest parts of the descent from Dhulikhel, the road eventually begins to level out, and the traffic insanity returns as everyone gets back up to speed for the final few of the 12 kilometres to the village of Panchkhal, where I expect to finally climb for real. Crossing over a minor ridge, I'm ready for it, but before too long it's down again, this time more gradually along a river, for another eight kilometres. There's hardly any traffic, and it makes for very nice riding. It's probably the best riding of this trip so far, because the road has gotten so much better.

As a result, I'm not constantly picking a path through potholes, calculating possible collision points with rapidly moving vehicles or worrying about falling off a ledge. (Sometimes the drop from a ledge would have been three metres; other times it was more like ten. Once in awhile it was much more.) Being clear of all that is enough to inspire a few words of appreciation, shouted out to the largely uninhabited valley.

Coming eventually to the town of Dolalghat marks a change in feeling as much as orientation. This is where the commuter link ends and the Araniko Highway begins in earnest. I draw a crowd by parking my bike and having a snack outside a small shop across the street from the bus park that doubles as the local fruit market.

Now the climbing will finally begin. I'm trading the downstream flow of the Cha Khola and Indrawati for upstream travel along the banks of the Sun Kosi. The Araniko Highway was built with the help of the Chinese in the 1960s on an old yak trail trading route and is named after Araniko, a 13th-century Nepali architect whose designs spread to Tibet and China. At the border it becomes China National Highway 318, but it also has another designation, one that I prefer, and that's the Friendship Highway. This informal handle appeals to my sensibilities not as a genuine attempt at cross-border unity or international diplomacy, but as a clever jab at Chinese propaganda, a little tongue-in-cheek if you understand the geopolitics of the region: "We'll help you build this road, no problem. It will improve trade and bring our countries and our cultures closer together. Don't worry that we would swallow you whole if given half a chance. It's not so bad, just ask Tibet."

Political motivations aside, the road from here is an impressive and improbable achievement. It climbs from 625 metres at the bridge crossing the Indrawati to 5050 metres at the crest of the Thang Pass in Tibet. Bicycle touring companies that operate trips in the opposite direction, from Lhasa to Kathmandu, claim it's the longest descent in the world. If this is true, and I were so motivated (and had an impossible-to-get Chinese visa that permitted solo travel), I could conceivably attempt the longest road climb on the planet, starting from this very spot.

I'm crazy, but not that crazy. Fourteen thousand five hundred vertical feet seems ambitious, so I return my glass bottle to the vendor and content myself with the gentler opening section to the epic climb. For the most part it's a gradual uphill with nothing too steep to contend with, but it is still an incline, of the type that slowly drains away your energy without your even noticing. The surrounding hills begin to crowd the river a little more with every kilometre that passes under my wheels, and evidence of previous landslides becomes more common. I feel as if I'm moving from a valley into a canyon.

At the junction to the Swiss-engineered highway, about 40 kilometres from the Chinese border, is the frontier town of Lamosangu. Perched right on the river, it's a dusty, shabby outpost that I doubt has seen better days. I suspect it has simply always been like this, at least since the road reached this place. The valley is quite narrow here, and the long main street does not hold many charms. With no sidewalk, the three- and four-storey buildings are right against the road's edge and appear to loom, giving the street a slightly claustrophobic air. Power lines criss-cross overhead, and the single string of prayer flags does little to enliven the scene. If I didn't know any better, I'd say this place bordered on menacing in its initial impressions.

One of the remarkable accomplishments of this country is that, despite the economic challenges the average person faces, and the rapid urbanization common in developing societies, aggression is rare. I noticed this when I flew into Kathmandu. It was dark and I was exhausted and alone in a foreign country where I didn't speak the language, but, at the same time, everything was fine. Despite being the perfect target for a hustle, or something worse, I felt safe and secure, if a little disoriented.

The bigger towns and cities of Nepal may be threadbare and dusty, and after the earthquake the whole place looks even more beaten up than before, but I feel comfortable here. Despite the vast discrepancy in income and lifestyle, I never feel threatened or resented. Sure, I am always on guard, worried that someone is trying to take me for a few extra rupees, but for the most part I am just another person trying to make my way in this world. I may look different and I may talk differently, but that doesn't make me a target. Lamosangu is kind of giving me the willies, though. It could also be I'm overly sensitive because I'm tired.

Past the bridge over the Sun Kosi, the big hill that marks the start of the Jiri road starts immediately. Just looking at the steep beginnings where it reaches up and out of sight, I realize I can't face the idea of *that* right now, tired or not. It's been 50 kilometres so far today, and who knows for sure how far it'll be before I can find food and shelter again. The trouble is, the main street through town was too dire to contemplate. Besides, I didn't notice a single sign in English for a guest house. Google the keywords *guest house* and *Lamosangu* and see what doesn't come up.

But there has to be something here somewhere. I suppose I could go back to one of the beach resorts I passed around lunchtime, in Balephi. They exist because rafting is a popular entry in the things-to-do-in-Nepal catalogue, and they looked quite welcoming, but the last one was five kilometres back, maybe ten, maybe more. Sitting on a rock by the side of the road at the base of a giant hill, trying to figure it out, I wish I had been paying more attention.

After walking over to a food stall across the road to ask about a place to stay, I am surprised to be informed the building next door is a guest house. I wouldn't pick it out of a brochure, but it's a guest house, apparently. The manager, a retiree with a limp, confirms this improbable development and leads me all the way to the top floor, where the rooms with attached baths are. It ain't exactly the Ritz, and for 1,000 rupees I'm being ripped off for sure, but I don't have the energy to haggle with the old guy. I just want to have a shower and lie down for awhile.

It takes two trips downstairs to collect my gear, and when I get in the shower, I don't want to put my soap down for fear it will get infected. Three previous guests apparently felt the same way, because their bars of soap have been left in, on, and around the sink. This discovery has forced me to take a good look at my surroundings, and one of the pillows and the blanket is now headed straight for the floor. The second pillow will do if covered, and I have to give a quiet shout-out to Jocey for reminding me to bring my own pillowcase for just such an occasion. Sleeping on top of my sleeping bag will keep me off the sheets and mattress – which, I admit, are not the absolute worst I've ever seen.

Standing in the middle of the room, I've towelled off and am already dripping wet again, with sweat now instead of water. It's incredibly humid, and, of course, the fan fixed to the wall doesn't work. I'm not even going to bother trying the 13-inch LED TV bolted right next to it. It'll only make me crazy. Lying in bed and listening to the traffic go by just outside the window only makes me miss my corner palace with the tremendous view high above the valley in Dhulikhel, but eventually I do sleep. Quite peacefully, all things considered.

• • •

Adventure is difficult to define absolutely; it is a fluid thing, influenced by individual interpretation and outside expectation. Mark Jenkins, in a short piece in *Outside Magazine* titled "The Unguided Route," said, "Adventure means embracing both serendipity and disaster." So true: there are elements in any experience that can help define it as an adventure if the circumstances are right, and words that give it shape. Words like *excitement, thrill, risk* and *danger* ramp up the adrenaline. *Exploit, deed* and *feat* speak to expectation. *Stimulation* and *uncertainty* suggest a lower-octane strategy.

After the short nap, I start to feel better again and realize this is also part of what adventure looks like. It's not always stunning views and dodging traffic and engaging with strangers in a foreign land; sometimes it's just boring, everyday observations about the weird world you've stumbled into. Staring up at the ceiling, I notice this room is not exactly square. Not even close. And that is a bit disconcerting when you're lying three storeys above the street in an earthquake-prone country. But it isn't long before that legitimate worry is overtaken by a somewhat less serious observation, one related to refinement, not structural integrity: the love of pink paint in this country.

I've seen it in public spaces, as well as hotel rooms and hallways all over the place. It's like someone down at the factory mixed up a huge batch of red that didn't quite have enough pigment to get there, and they were forced to sell it at a deep discount in order to move it from the warehouse. One thing is for sure: pink is no longer just for tacky time-share condos in Florida or the rooms of prepubescent girls. It has found a home in Nepal.

By the time I head back downstairs, the afternoon has slipped away to happy hour, and I order up a beer and settle in to the open-air dining area with my map, notebook and guidebook. A TV is on in the restaurant, but I'm not interested. The manager slips into the dining room from time to time to watch a few minutes of the news but spends most of his time in the kitchen, where, by the sound of things, unnecessarily industrious activities are going on. Unnecessarily industrious only because I am the only guest here, as far as I can tell.

As the last of the afternoon bleeds away, I begin to wonder about dinner. The matron of the establishment eventually comes out of the kitchen, and I catch her attention. Forget that I probably would have ordered another beer about 20 minutes ago if given a chance; my stomach has now taken priority. This is a local-traveller guest house, so she doesn't speak much English, but she manages to explain it will be *dal bhat* on offer this evening. I indicate as best I can that this will be perfectly fine, preferred even, and settle back into my guidebook and maps, thinking I've successfully ordered. After nearly an hour, it becomes obvious I haven't. Even though it still sounds busy in the kitchen, something has been lost in translation. I don't know if she's forgotten, or if staff and guests simply dine at the same time, i.e., whenever it is ready.

The matron reappears briefly, but before I can confirm, she's gone again, sucked into a world of rattling pots and whistling steam.

In the interim, two Nepali guests arrive, and one heads to town almost immediately. The other sits down at an adjoining table for the spotty Wi-Fi and to wait out dinner. Shortly afterward, the owner of the guest house shows up from town (and the local *chhaang* house, I'm guessing), and any misunderstandings over the evening meal are rectified. The *dal bhat* is ordered, and my bike, which is leaning up against the far wall, is examined in detail. And it isn't long before some homemade hooch is offered to accompany the long-awaited second beer.

While *chhaang* is more closely related to beer, another common homebrew in the Himalaya is *raksi*, which is made from millet or rice. It's clear like vodka, and I am expecting something with a moonshine-style kick, but this is much smoother and reminds me of Japanese sake. Whatever it is, it would be rude to refuse.

The next two hours turn into a long and enjoyable cultural exchange. English lessons are at the heart of things, but as so often happens, I end up learning a little more about this wonderful country. I also get to share a little bit about my home, a place these two men will probably never get a chance to visit. My fellow traveller and interpreter is a devout Hindu and doesn't drink, but my glass is persistently refilled. The owner, who I now realize must have spent the whole afternoon at the *chhaang* house, is now more restrained. He gets half measures to my full cup.

I only hope the homebrew isn't too strong. I've got a big day tomorrow.

6.

THE CLIMB FROM HELL

The first expeditions to Mount Everest approached from the north side of the mountain, through Tibet via India. George Mallory, perhaps the most famous of these pioneering climbers, never saw Nepal except for the view from along the northeast ridge down into the country. He was the one to name the Western Cwm from somewhere along that elevated vantage point. Mallory and his climbing partner, Andrew Irvine, fell to their deaths during the 1924 attempt at the summit. Whether or not they made the top is a matter of some discussion to this day, but they did manage to name one of the famous features on the Nepal side without ever setting foot on it.

In 1950, Mao Zedong, chairman of the Communist Party of China, initiated a campaign to exert Chinese sovereignty over Tibet. The "liberation" of Chamdo effectively ended Tibet's control over its own affairs, and the 14th Dalai Lama, Tenzin Gyatso, eventually fled to Dharamsala, India, where a government-in-exile was set up to promote Tibetan interests. Not surprisingly, climbing from Tibet was suspended and the borders were closed to outsiders. It would be decades before foreigners made another attempt on the north side of the mountain.

At about the same time, Nepal began opening its borders, and mountaineers began the search for a southern route up the mountain. The catch was that they had to walk in from Kathmandu; such was the lack of infrastructure at the time. There were no roads through the Middle Hills, only footpaths. The Swiss expedition of 1952 took 23 days just to reach the area around Base Camp on foot. Slowly the roads expanded outward from the capital, to Banepa by 1963, Dolalghat in 1967 and Lamosangu in 1970. The Jiri road further altered the approach beginning in 1980, when you could drive to Kirantichhap, and now the journey from Kathmandu to the trailhead at Jiri is 188 kilometres by bus or four-by-four. After that you still have to walk.

The last time I travelled this road was in 2009, in a rented four-by-four complete with driver. It was a tight squeeze, with myself, Jocey, my mom and dad, our guide, our porter, the driver and all our gear, but there was no way I was taking a public bus on a remote mountain road as long as there was another option. I had tried that with Jocey and our friends Neil and Joyce in 2007, on the way to Langtang National Park, north of Kathmandu, and to say it was a terrifying experience would be something of an understatement. I'm surprised we survived. One bus ride in rural Nepal is more than enough for a single lifetime, thank you very much.

The southern border of Langtang National Park is only about 30 or 40 kilometres from the Kathmandu Valley as the crow flies, but the access road to get to the trailhead at Dhunche is far from straightforward, travelling northwest out of Kathmandu on the way to Trishuli Bazaar before swinging more directly north, for a total distance of about 115 kilometres. Amazingly, the journey takes eight hours. That's how good the roads are beyond Trishuli Bazaar.

Much of the early part of that journey was innocuous enough, the road decent (by Nepali standards), with enough room for two vehicles to pass each other without too much trouble. It was slow going, however, as all mountain roads tend to be. There were government checkpoints, with soldiers packing rifles and checking papers (this was at the tail end of the Maoist insurgency that had thrown the whole country into chaos, and still had lots of people on edge), and long, grinding climbs followed by steep descents that would occasionally wring a plaintive squeal from the tired brakes on our bus.

A key element in keeping the road from eroding prematurely along this part of the route, however, was an open concrete ditch, approximately two feet wide, set on the inside edge. It was designed to channel rainwater to various creeks and culverts along the way. The ditch was squared off at the edges, and as we were lumbering along, I thought it looked perfectly capable of sucking up a vehicle right to the axle. In fact, it appeared designed for that purpose, and sure enough we did eventually pass a large truck that had drifted too close and was hung up. A handful of men were standing around, trying to figure out how they were going to get the darn thing off, but we were able to squeeze past.

Beyond Trishuli Bazaar, the road was less accommodating to multi-vehicle traffic as it began a long climb up into the mountains. I found myself sitting in the window seat on the river side of the bus as the road became single-track, and the burnt-out, mangled remains of trucks and buses that had miscalculated on what had become a treacherous and narrow dirt path were remarkably common. Disturbingly common. There were also plenty of occasions where the amount of space between the rear wheel of the bus and the edge of the drop was six inches or less, and there were no concrete ditches to catch an errant vehicle.

In one particularly hairy moment, we were passing another bus coming in the opposite direction, and I could not see any solid ground out my window no matter how hard I pressed my face to the glass and looked down. There was only open space, and busted-up vehicles dashed on the rocks below. Even the usually unflappable driver's assistant – who stands at the passenger exit door and collects fares, shouts instructions on how to jam one more person into or on top of the bus and communicates with the driver in a series of whistles and coded messages slapped on the side of the vehicle – lost his nerve.

The bus lurched into gear after making way for an oncoming vehicle but seemed to hang in space for a moment, rear wheels catching the edge of a slab of rock beneath us, but just barely. My man – and you have to understand, this is a guy accustomed to hanging off the side of moving vehicles over drops of 300 metres and more – slapped the side of the bus three times in a decidedly panicked fashion, and shouted the equivalent of "Go, Go, Go" to the driver in no uncertain tone. The bus gained purchase and lurched along.

I don't think most of the other passengers had even noticed we just experienced an *oh, shit* kind of moment where we could have ended up at the bottom of a gorge in a flaming heap. I looked around, wide-eyed, but everyone seemed preoccupied by his or her own personal discomfort. It was hot and crowded, and we had been on the bus for six hours at this point. I decided not to relay the experience to my travel companions until dinner that evening.

Needless to say, I never, ever, want to repeat that Langtang bus ride, or anything remotely like it, again, which is why I'm about to find myself bobbing and weaving through traffic on a bicycle instead, along a similarly dilapidated roadway. Maybe not the smartest move, but I'm not quite ready to start walking yet. After crunching a few numbers while planning this trip, I realized walking the full route from Kathmandu to Everest Base Camp would take two extra weeks at least. I may be a dreamer and a seeker at heart, but I do also have a practical side. That's just too far, and that much walking through the hot, steamy foothills would become redundant after awhile.

Sir Edmund Hillary himself complained about the trials and monotony of slogging back and forth over these hills on the way to and from the Khumbu. Naively, I thought riding would be a lot faster, not to mention easier. As I'm about to find out, I was only partly right.

• • •

Thankfully, I'm not hungover this morning, but my bike is making life difficult. Somewhere around midday yesterday, the gears began slipping again, with renewed enthusiasm. This is a continuation of the problem that started all the way back in Kathmandu, but up until now it hasn't been severe enough to keep me from using the lowest gears available. It has been an annoyance, not an issue, and I chose to ignore the problem because *that* always works out in the end, right? Now I can't get to the last gear at all, and the second-last slips around like a freewheel every ten pedal strokes or so.

Fiddling around with the rear derailleur after breakfast only results in a minor improvement, and draws a crowd. The guest house owner, his wife, the old guy who checked me in yesterday and my interpreter from last night have all taken an interest in the project. None of us, me included, actually knows anything about bicycle repair, so it's largely an exercise in futility, but every time I make an adjustment and go for a short test ride up the first 20 metres of the hill, there's an air of hope among my pit crew. Every time I pull back in the driveway, they're expecting an enthusiastic thumbs-up. After a few attempts, I expect everyone to lose interest. They don't. I think they're just waiting to see if I can make it up the steep hill ahead with all my travel gear loaded on the bike. I'm kind of wondering the same thing myself.

Turns out I can – to start, anyway.

Getting on and off the bike has been awkward these last few days. Swinging my leg up and over the saddle is within my skill set, but the added few inches required to get my foot over the hiking pack strapped on the back with bungee cords is at the outside edge of that ability. The pack isn't any higher than the seat but does extend far enough that my foot has to rise to a similar level as my knee on the swing over. To make matters worse, I have no front rack. No equipment strapped there means a back-heavy load. Upset the balance in any way, like with the clumsiest ballet move of all time, for example, and the front end tries to buck up and away from my body while the back end dives straight for the ground at my feet. I've almost fallen a few times. The bike has fallen twice.

I wave goodbye over my shoulder after finally getting my act together. Lamosangu can't get in my rear view quickly enough. These early roadside stops have not been the quaint villages and pretty little towns I had in my mind's eye. The progress, convenience and opportunity that new roads promise to remote areas aren't always delivered as advertised. Around here, roads also mean grime, diesel fumes and litter. My preoccupation with escaping this particular dustbin has made it easy to underestimate the challenge ahead. I'm not an engineer, so I can't comment on the grade required to make a road possible in these circumstances, but it is quite a hill, one that goes forever up switchback after laborious switchback.

With the equipment issues temporarily under control, the riding isn't too bad at first. I'm fresh and eager, and in the shade cast by the mountain I'm about to climb, the temperature is bearable. It remains cool for the first hour as I make my way back and forth up the switchbacks, simultaneously trying to figure out which direction the road is eventually going to go so I can get a handle on what I'm up against. As I struggle along, views up and down the Sun Kosi Valley are particularly inspiring. On the one hand, it doesn't feel like I'm getting anywhere significant, yet, on the other, the bottom of the valley is gradually falling away far below with every pedal stroke. The first hour passes with this constant changing of perspective.

As it tends to do, the sun eventually begins to win the battle with the slope and is gaining ground on this sheltered side. Whenever it breaks through the trees, I instantly turn into a giant, greasy, sunscreen-and-sweat-covered mess. Every 15 minutes or so, I can wring out the front of my T-shirt as if I have just come out of a pool. The morning continues in this slow, sweaty fashion, but the homes and small farms dotting the surrounding hillsides form a tranquil backdrop. The overall effect is to make the area around Lamosangu appear a little less grim. From a distance, it looks positively picturesque. Only the road intrudes on that tranquility.

The original construction of this road was something of a marvel. Heavy machinery was not used, even though it was available. Envisioned by the Swiss, who organized and funded the project as a way to bring economic benefit to the area, this entire 110-kilometre stretch was completed by hand in the late 1970s and early '80s. Rocks were broken using picks and sledgehammers, and earth was moved using shovels and wheelbarrows. The large rectangular wire baskets filled with broken stone to support the roadbed and prevent erosion were all woven by hand, and at the height of construction, 9,000 local labourers were on the job.

Even after travelling a relatively short distance on this terrain, I can see why it took 11 years to complete the road using these methods. It's just too bad nobody has bothered with significant repairs since.

This was once the gold standard of Nepali road building, but the seams are beginning to show. Huge potholes are common, and significant sections of the road have worn away at the edges to make it ridiculously narrow. There are also ten- to 20-metre sections where it has deteriorated to nothing more than a gravel driveway. Old landslides have been tamped down by vehicle traffic in places, and it's important to remember that strategically positioned rocks are often makeshift traffic cones, warning of landslip and the erosion of the underlying roadbed. Areas where the ground has simply sagged create an undulating surface that even a four-by-four can navigate at no more than a few kilometres an hour. It's a miracle there are any vehicles in this country more than five years old, considering the beating they take on a daily basis.

On the plus side, this highway is only one lane wide. Not one lane in each direction, mind you, but one lane total. At first glance, this wouldn't appear to be a good thing for a cyclist, but the tight, blind turns, steep aspect, and deteriorating surface all contribute to slow traffic flow. This is also where the Nepali obsession with the horn comes into its own. The *beep beep*s of cars and motorbikes are a welcome courtesy, but you can generally get an impression of the size of the vehicle coming up from behind by the sound of the engine. The ahooga-style horns of the trucks and buses, on the other hand, are a charming combination of *Dukes of Hazzard* and ocean-going freighter, and you can hear them from a mile away.

With this consistent early-warning system, it's pretty easy to pick out escape routes to little islands of safety on the inconsistent roadside shoulder. Before long, I'm pedalling on whatever side of the road is least dangerous, but with two directions of traffic forced into narrow chutes created by the hill pressed to one side, and a long drop on the other, everybody is kind of all over the place anyway, so it hardly makes a difference.

This system isn't perfect, however, and every once in awhile I do have to perch on the very edge of the drop to get far enough off the road to avoid being hit. Two buses passing in opposite directions take up an awful lot of room, and sometimes I'm pinned against an ancient cement barrier. In places, the barriers have been swept away by a vehicle that didn't quite make the turn. In other spots, there just isn't that much land available, so there never was a barrier to begin with. It's not always a precipitous drop, but it would almost always be an uncomfortable fall. Damaging to equipment and body alike.

After a few hours of travelling in this methodical if exhausting fashion, it feels like I have to be getting close to my lunchtime goal of the village of Mude. Yet every crest proves a false summit, and every switchback is followed by another hairpin turn set off in the distance. Occasionally, I catch a glimpse of something flashing through the trees almost directly above, only to realize it's a vehicle farther up the impossibly steep grade, two or three switchbacks overhead. Sometimes the flash is on an adjoining slope where a truck or a bus is suddenly visible. It takes a moment to remember this is the only road in the area, so eventually I'll have to make it all the way over there, only to find more of the same when I arrive. There continues to be no visible peak from this low angle, and no pass a road could sneak through on the way to the next valley.

It's just up. Forever.

As I begin to tire, the realization comes to light that I can't ride the steepest parts of this hill. The walking starts innocently enough, a couple of dozen metres up an abrupt length of road where the picks and shovels and sledgehammers weren't up to the task of levelling the grade, but those short sections are getting longer and longer as the morning creeps toward noon. It gets to the point that I've probably walked a quarter of the way so far, and the heat, the dust and the trucks are slowly demoralizing me. To make matters worse, the equipment problems are not a thing of the past, as I had hoped. The gears are still fine, but now my rack is bobbing and buckling under the strain.

Never has the decision to forgo a complete gear assessment before leaving Canada been so obviously a mistake as it is right now. I should have packed the whole lot up and taken it out for a weekend trip. Not only have I dramatically misjudged the accumulated weight, but this is also the wrong bike for the task. Unburdened, it's great. In the city, it's nimble and agile and quick, but now that it's fully laden with two months' worth of clothes, toiletries and other supplies, those qualities have been overwhelmed. More importantly, the rear rack was a last-minute purchase, bought in haste when I realized a previous model I owned didn't fit this bike. I installed it for the first time in the hotel room in Kathmandu. Now I'm stuck with it.

The problem is, it's a mountain bike rack, designed for lighter loads, fatter tires and disk brakes. My hybrid bike is intended for street and light trail riding. It's not designed for heavy touring, but the upright-seated position is more comfortable for an ageing body. The rack is simply a poor purchase, one predicated on sizing and not the task at hand. If I stand up on the pedals to try and inject a little more power into the effort, the load wobbles. If I push on the pile of gear, it wobbles. If I hold the bike upright and give it a little shake, everything wobbles.

Pulling up to an old roadside storage shed for repairs, I am grateful for the rest, if nothing else. The shed has a covered front porch so I can get out of the sun, and there's a convenient post holding up the tin roof to lean my bike against. I want to avoid unloading the whole thing, so after a few sips of water, I end up lying down and peering under the back end to try and figure out what has gone wrong. A couple of local kids spot me from across the road and come over to check out what's going on.

The only tourists these guys likely see are through the windows of buses, and the language barrier is evident. I try to chat with them, but they seem happy to just watch as I unload all the gear and pray I've got the correct Allen key for the bolt that has come loose. It's an awkward repair (not to mention the dumbest design ever), as I have to reach through the spokes to get an inside angle on the rack, and it's probably a good thing these kids don't speak English – in true repairman fashion, I use colourful language to help the process along.

It is interesting to note the differences in how people watch others across cultures. When I want to observe someone's behaviour or habits, I generally sit on a patio with a coffee, or hang out at a park or historical monument and scrutinize from a distance. These kids just walk right up and stand and stare. It's weird, not to mention difficult to get used to, but I have heard the practice is even more pronounced in India. I can barely imagine it. One man's intrusive is another man's curious I guess.

• • •

Repairs completed, I have little choice but to continue the slow process upward. As I gradually move across the landscape, the people will change as surely as the scenery does. Nepal is a confusing collection of ethnic groups and castes, greatly influenced by the Indo-Aryan heritage from one side of the Himalaya and the Sino-Tibetan heritage from the other. The Newar are long-established inhabitants of the Kathmandu Valley. They have their own language, and their influence extends far beyond the capital because they have become a dominant part of the merchant class. It is entirely possible many of the shop owners I meet along this road will be Newar, even though I'm moving ever farther into the Middle Hills, home of the Tamang. The Tamang tend to be farmers and porters, and, like the Sherpa, have their ancestral roots in Tibet as opposed to India. Brahmans are defined by their caste rather than their ethnic group, and although the caste system is not as strictly adhered to in Nepal as it is in India, Brahmans continue to benefit from the class structure, dominating jobs in government and business.

After I leave the road behind at Jiri, the religious undertones will continue to shift from Hindu to Buddhist, and a scattering of Rai villages will give way to a dominantly

Sherpa influence, although a large number of Rai do live and work in the Khumbu. It is a complicated mosaic, and the blending of classes and cultures and religions is by no means seamless, but it is a largely peaceful mix.

It isn't until two o'clock that I realize I haven't had lunch yet. By now, my thinking brain has shut off and a kind of stubborn determination has taken over. "It can't be that much farther now. It just can't be," I say to myself over and over again. "I'm having lunch in Mude, dammit, I can make it."

This declaration is not based on any evidence; I have no idea where I am in relation to the top of the hill, where I assume the village is perched. So far there have been plenty of small homes and snack shacks peppering the roadside, but nothing that would be considered a settlement, so short breaks for chips or chocolate or candy are all I have managed, along with water filtered from the small creeks cutting across my path at regular intervals. My map is largely useless because distance and time have become a muddled mess, and I'm operating with the addled mind that comes from excessive heat and fatigue. Rational planning and problem solving have disappeared completely. Life is just blind effort now.

But something else is at play here as well. It's not simply that I'm pigheaded or that I've tapped a hidden well of determination. The truth is, I can't question this climb or I'll cave. I'm afraid to stop for lunch because I might not start again. I can't think about what I've taken on. I can only trudge forward. If I give up on this hill, it's quite possible I'll quit altogether. Flag down the next four-by-four and get to the next big town and rejig the entire journey. More than anything, I want to find a quiet, shady place to sit down and lick my wounds. Then maybe I can face reality and try to figure out an easier way to do this.

This is a bad idea, of course, because there isn't an easier way. This is the route, and the intervening topography is unavoidable. Kathmandu sits at 1400 metres. Everest Base Camp is at 5300 metres. There is nothing but mountains of varying heights in between. I might not find a day more challenging than this one, but there are bound to be a few that are equally so. I'm still trying to ride the bike, but I'm mostly walking now. Putting one foot in front of the other, taking turns pushing from both sides of the bike so my back begins to ache equally, I don't think about it; I just struggle slowly upward. I find I'm not determined so much as resigned.

Eventually, the road crosses over the hillside through a small pass to the opposite face. There's a short, delicious downhill stretch leading to a proper village, and I almost weep with joy. I'm not what you would call a religious person, but I do tend to give thanks in these kinds of situations, in my decidedly idiosyncratic way.

"Thank God, thank God, thank God. Thank fucking God!"

It can be argued idiosyncrasies have consequences, and karma is a bitch. My appreciation is short-lived, as the road leads through town and then snakes off to the right and begins to climb again. In time, it moves back over the ridge to another small settlement that is not Mude, and I am forced to pull over at the local general store for a proper rest. I'm hungry and I'm thirsty and I'm desperate for this to end.

Sitting in the shade, stuffing my face with chips and fruit and Sprite, I watch the locals come and go in a steady stream, and a little bit of energy returns. They barter for goods and chat amiably with the proprietor and are largely indifferent to the foreigner sitting off to the side. From here I can see, in the near distance, the only obvious guest house on the street, and it looks worse than where I stayed last night. This is depressing, because I wouldn't need much of an excuse to call it a day. After refuelling, I pedal up to it just to be sure, mostly because that's where the road leads anyway.

Up close, it does look a little too rough for my liking. Truth be told, it looks like a flophouse. There also appears to be a thriving metal shop operating in the front yard, and nowhere obvious to lock my bike overnight. Besides, there is hope in the distance. For the first time all day, I see actual evidence of an end to this folly. There's a low point in the surrounding hills, one with three important characteristics:

1 – The saddle between mountaintops is not that far away.

2 – It's also not that far above.

And 3 – The road shifts back to the right side of the main ridge, indicating that this rough highway leads that way.

This is more than enough to lure me forward, so I return my pop bottle, execute another awkward ballet move and actually manage to ride again for a short time.

Increasingly, I am finding it difficult to judge people's age here. In Kathmandu, the young urban types look very much as they do everywhere. Often well dressed, and raised on a diet lower in processed foods and animal products than ours in the West, the 20- and 30-somethings are easy to identify. But life can be hard in rural areas, and the wear and tear begins to show in the older generations. Someone could be in their mid-40s or early 60s, and I would have a difficult time guessing which it is.

According to Statistics Canada, the average life expectancy for a male in my country in 2016 is 79 years. For a female, that number jumps to 83. Data published by the World Health Organization in 2014 gives numbers a full decade lower for Nepalis: 67 years for men; 70 for women. The reason I bring it up is that I've been walking for the last 15 minutes in the company of a couple from a local village, and I am amazed by their resilience, in light of the fact they appear to be about 60. I noticed them when I was sitting in the last village, and I wondered how far they were going to go with what appeared to be a heavy load of supplies. I certainly didn't expect to see them again.

Yet here they are on the road ahead of me, obviously headed for the pass. I've been slowly gaining on them, but this is hardly a race anyone would pay to see. We are blundering along against the steepness of the hill and taking frequent breaks to catch our breath. The loads are cruel and the heat is oppressive, and every once in awhile a bus rumbles by to kick up a choking cloud of dust. I have been using them as the world's slowest pace car, but before I can catch them, they veer off on a small side road and the highway swings left and continues upslope. I've been fooled once again. The saddle in plain sight is *not* the escape from this valley.

For all my foggy thinking at this point, there is an important lesson to be learned, one that might come in handy during the hike. Once you're in trouble – or, more precisely, once you *realize* you're in trouble – it's often too late to remedy the situation in a sensible way. I have badly misjudged this hill, and I didn't have a backup plan. It never occurred to me that I might have to walk today. I never thought about anything other than making it to the top by lunchtime. It never even crossed my mind until after lunchtime had passed that this would be impossible. As a result, the only option I would consider once my brain stopped operating was to keep going. Physical limits do need to be explored once in awhile, but consequences should always be kept in mind. Mountain climbers refer to this irrational behaviour as "summit fever," where the mind convinces the body, "We've come too far to turn back now!"

I've got the fever.

I suppose I can always flag down a ride in a pinch; cars are not as common this late in the day, but they do still pass occasionally. And even if this place were completely deserted, the worst that would happen is an uncomfortable night out. I am almost out of food, but I have enough snacks that it's unlikely I'll die out here, and I do have access to water: streams and springs continue to be a common feature. I can also easily go down to that last village if it comes to that. The only thing stopping me is that I don't want to have to do this last bit of climbing all over again in the morning.

So, for now, time has ceased to exist. It's just me and the hill and the hope of getting where I'm going before darkness falls. For about three hours I have been dreaming of what my guidebook called "possibly the only pleasant place to stay en route." Reading about it last night while waiting for dinner, I figured it would probably be my lunch stop. After about four hours of relentless climbing, expectations changed, and I imagined it would be a reasonable final destination for today. Now I'll be happy to reach it at all. My ass has officially been kicked. I gave up riding an hour ago and am only pushing the bike 20 or 30 metres at a time before taking a break, so I'm more than ready to be done.

In a small clearing on the valley side of the road, a pair of water buffalo are grazing near a sign for the resort. An old man is slowly herding them upslope. There's no indication of where the resort itself is, just a phone number on the sign, but up through the trees to the left are hints of something perched on the ridge, something substantial – a collection of buildings, perhaps? I don't want to get my hopes up, but please, please, please let it be so.

Twenty metres farther up the road, there is a proper sign. It's faded but clearly sports an arrow pointing in the direction of a small stone driveway. It has taken me almost nine hours to travel 28 kilometres, but I have not died. I have made it to heaven.

That said, it could be that my Cicerone guidebook is a little out of date.

7.

Make no mistake: this resort was once truly grand. But time has not been entirely kind, and my options are limited. I'm exhausted, and my back is killing me, and the actual village of Mude is still a good 20-minute walk up the road. I'm simply not up for it. I park my bike at the gate by the deserted guardhouse and climb a few dozen steep stone steps up to the main collection of buildings. At the top is a wide flagstone terrace with a few outdoor tables and a group of four young, hip-looking Nepalis having tea. Apart from that, the place appears deserted.

Stepping into the dining room, I'm greeted almost suspiciously and half expect to be asked the question, "Hey, buddy, are you lost?" But when I inquire about a room, I'm assured there are some available, at 2,000, 4,000 and 7,000 rupees a night. I'm a little too tired for math, but quick mental calculation gets me to about $25, $50 and *give me a break*. On the other hand, I'm almost tired enough to justify a splurge based on the day's effort, so I do entertain the more expensive options before eventually coming to my senses. My room is a bit musty, but the bathroom is clean enough, so I head back down to my bike to collect the rest of my gear.

I am, of course, immensely grateful to be here, and not just because the climb from hell is over. Every day is a victory in this odd, awkward journey I've taken on, even when I don't get very far. It wasn't all that long ago that I couldn't even walk, let alone ride a bike up a giant hill. It wasn't a dramatic fall or catastrophic accident that involved ladders or motor vehicles or icy sidewalks that put me on the sidelines. It was age. I wore out a joint. I experienced a slow accumulation of damage that eventually grew beyond my ability (and pharmacology's best efforts) to cope with it. The Durolane experiment didn't work, so I decided to take advantage of that miracle of Western medicine: joint replacement.

In the days leading up to my hip replacement surgery in 2015, I was anxiety-free, at least in the sense that I had little to no anxiety about getting a part of my leg lopped off and replaced with a space-age combination of titanium and ceramic. I was limping more often than not and was in pain nearly every moment of every day. It had become a quality-of-life thing, and I couldn't keep putting it off. I was going in and getting the procedure done no matter the risks, however minor they are these days.

In a coincidence of timing, the pay period at my job lined up well with the schedule for my surgery, and it made sense from a business point of view to work through the last Sunday of our biweekly pay period, tie up any loose ends and apply for unemployment insurance on Monday, take time Tuesday to wrap my head around the idea and then have surgery on Wednesday morning.

Unfortunately, winter never really came to the Rockies that year. Snow was thin in the valley bottom, and temperatures were rarely below freezing. Shoulder season was nonexistent in the food and beverage industry, and naturally we had a busy weekend on my final days, when all I wanted was to drift off into the hazy bliss of unemployment and good prescription drugs. The gritty details are unimportant now, but we were short-staffed, and the weekend was filled with stress and pain. Babysitting staff and dealing with the everyday bullshit of the job were killing me.

With everything going on in the lead-up, it didn't occur to me until sometime on Tuesday afternoon that I should probably get my affairs in order in case something did go wrong on the operating table, and I sent off a hasty email to all concerned, explaining how I wanted my meagre assets divided up in a worse case scenario. By the time I checked into the hospital, I was officially burnt out. My brain was still whirring with the leftover energy of an over-stimulated mind, but I had no nerves or concerns or excitement. Life was happening around me, and I was a passive bystander. All I had to do was show up and hope for the best.

In the sterile, bright, somewhat chilly holding area outside the surgery suites, I finally had a moment to think about everything that was happening. Only one other patient was waiting for surgery: Ivan, a roughly 70-year-old gentleman with a strong Eastern European accent, was in for what appeared to be a second or third procedure on a stubborn tumour on his lower leg. He didn't seem particularly concerned about his situation either. I found it comforting, and odd. I wasn't frightened or lonely or anxious. I wasn't anything. Like Ivan, I was resigned to the situation and realized with little more than a passing interest that if this was the end, if I was that unlikely statistic and succumbed to some unforeseen complication, that was okay too.

I simply didn't have the energy to care.

Going into the surgery suite, I remained strangely detached, but coming out of it a couple of hours later, I was genuinely happy to wake up, even though waking up appeared to have happened a bit early. Having been put on general anesthetic for hernia and knee surgeries in the past, I didn't look forward to the groggy, nauseous fog of the recovery room. When offered, I opted for a spinal this time. It was a decidedly different experience. After drifting off on a mild sedative (it could have been ten minutes later or three hours, for all I could tell), the first thing I heard was a strange voice from somewhere "out there" in the conscious world.

"Try not to move," the voice said.

I had been wriggling around in the unconscious realm, like you do when you known you're having a bad dream and want to get out. The voice helped give me context, and I did lie still for a moment as my senses came back in a more organized fashion. That's when I realized I was cold, and shivering uncontrollably, negating any attempt to be still. I was also unsure if I was meant to be awake at all, but decided to deal with one thing at a time.

"Umm," I said to the anesthesiologist sheepishly, "I'm feeling really cold."

He immediately piled warm blankets on me, and the effect was instantly comforting but only led to the next question on the list.

"So" – a short pause, for effect – "should I be awake already?"

The reason I asked was that the surgery was clearly still in progress. I was lying on my left side, with a sheet draped across my midriff, so I couldn't see anything below my chest. I don't know how long I'd been out for, but the buzz of activity in the room indicated we weren't finished yet. The conversation between members of the surgical team was direct and professional, but the activity surrounding those interactions seemed out of context somehow.

When I think of surgery, I think of a delicate act, sharp scalpels and other specialized tools wielded with the utmost care, but this wasn't brain surgery, as they say. This was a pivotal load-bearing joint being removed and replaced with titanium and ceramic. Not much delicate about that, as it turns out. The closest comparison I could come up with was a bunch of guys out in the shed banging some pipes together, and the pipes weren't quite the right size to fit. I couldn't feel a thing, but every improbably violent adjustment shook my entire body, making me anticipate a pain response that never came.

"There's 10 or 15 minutes left to go," the anesthesiologist said. "I can put you back to sleep if you want, but you'll end up spending more time in the recovery room that way."

Since I couldn't feel anything, I decided to ride it out. It would be a good story to tell, if nothing else. That is one of the pleasures of being a writer – no matter how strange, uncomfortable or disgusting life gets, there's always a part of you that thinks it could be used in a story someday.

Apart from the brief interlude with the boys in the tool shed, that first day with my new bionic hip proved exceedingly pleasant. After months of working myself up at work (sometimes justifiably, sometimes not), I was suddenly deposited in a shared room with an elderly roommate who spent most of the time sleeping behind the curtain that separated our beds. After my visitors came by to make sure everything had gone well, and between occasional visits from the nurse to check my vitals, I was left alone for the most part, and it was glorious. Forced to take a break I badly needed, I embraced the quiet and relative isolation.

Sure, the pain medication helped (oxycodone is a wonder, believe you me), but choosing a spinal instead of a general meant there was no nausea, no dizziness and no disorientation. Chronic pain can be extremely demoralizing and mentally draining. To spend a day without pain after months of coping was beyond relief. It was a revelation. Hospitals can be depressing, depending on your prognosis, but after I got up to stand with the help of the physiotherapist only a few hours after surgery, and nailed the first of what would be a long list of rehab exercises, things were looking up.

Mainlining oxygen during the first 48 hours resulted in a satisfying collection of power naps, and I couldn't have been happier. In hindsight, my two and a half months off during recovery were among the happiest in my adult life. I mean, really, how often do you get a chance to take a break and re-evaluate everything – your hopes, your dreams and the future? More importantly, I was forced to live exclusively in the present while I focused on the little things necessary in getting better. The small victories and minor achievements that are normal and largely taken for granted become important again when you have been forced back to square one. Putting on your own socks and shoes, managing a flight of stairs without stopping and sitting on a toilet that doesn't have a booster seat attached are all major accomplishments on the road to normal mobility. But even making a new movement without pain or extending your range of motion by a couple of millimetres is noteworthy.

Along the way, I also rediscovered a sense of humour I'd thought was gone for good. I was carefree in my puttering. I had no aspirations, no responsibilities, only a humble effort to get better. My daily activities were greatly simplified. When I grew tired, I had a nap. When I was hungry, I ate. When I had even a minor improvement on the path to full fitness, it was cause for celebration. When you don't know for sure that you are ever going to be able to cross your legs again, it is an emotional moment when you do finally manage it.

I know this all sounds incredibly Forrest Gump of me, but that part of the process was wonderful. I loved it.

• • •

A year and a half later, the hip is great. I wasn't entirely sure it would stand up to an extreme beating when the chips were down, but not a single twinge or complaint is coming from anywhere near the six-inch scar down my side. My body as a whole is another story altogether. I drained the tank dry on the ridiculous hill yesterday. I may not ache specifically, but there's no way I'm going anywhere. After such a big day of exploration and effort, you want everything to be easy and comfortable and perfect. You want to find a hidden gem, that little corner of the world you never want to leave, that special place to remember. When you're travelling, it's common to want to love a place. This is almost that place.

The devil is in the details, as they say, and this is where perfection has fallen short. Nepal goes through distinct seasons, and the wet summers are a challenge for buildings without good ventilation. Central heating systems are rare, and proper insulation practices have not caught on in the building industry, especially in poor districts. At higher elevations, it is often chilly or damp inside unless the weather outside is perfect. My room has proven to be the latter. As a result, there are a few corners, especially in the bathroom, I'd rather not examine too closely.

The table in the main dining room is also not up to intense scrutiny. A growing trend in hotels and guest houses on the tourist circuit is the use of cloth napkins and placemats. It's a nice touch, especially farther up the trail, where the surrounding environment is both challenging and harsh. It is a scintilla of civilized in places that are still decidedly wild, but spend a bit of time in these remote outposts and you quickly realize laundry facilities are not always readily available. The napkins in this guest house are paper, so it's not an issue today, but the placemats have been turned over so many times I'm surprised the accumulated food stains haven't simply worn off.

But it is also unmistakably groovy in here. The haphazard collection of styles blends seamlessly into a pleasing mess. Iconic landscape paintings of the Himalaya, of the type I would expect to find at my grandparents' home, hang around the room. Rattan furniture and a low glass-top table create a makeshift lounge area near the large stand-alone fireplace, and naturally there is the familiar clocks-on-the-wall, times-of-the-world motif. New York, Tokyo, London, Mude. Every traveller in the world has seen a version of this in a hotel or hostel somewhere.

Furthering the jumble, the hanging light fixtures are encased in the familiar Asian paper lampshades, some of which are covered with the omniscient eyes of the Buddha. The walls are especially unique. Extra effort was put in to raise the mortar edges to create a sense of texture. To accentuate the effect, the raised edges are painted black, and the inset stone is whitewashed. There's also a small shrine in the corner by the door, filled with all manner of masks, figurines and statuettes, complete with a proper office chair for those who prefer a more corporate form of worship.

The space is what it would be like if Elton John, Shiva and the Buddha shared a clubhouse.

After the lukewarm introduction yesterday, it turns out the staff is nice enough, but sometimes you just don't click. I've been incredibly fortunate so far. For the most part, hotel and restaurant staffs have been capable, helpful and professional in their duties. Where competence has been lacking, agreeability has made up the difference. Everyone has been, almost without exception, incredibly nice. Here, it's taken me a little while to figure things out, but something different is going on: these guys appear bored and are simply going through the motions. It occurs to me this is not a family-run place, or even an established entity with committed long-term staff. This is a business, with employees, and the attitude shows. The slightly unpalatable details I've stumbled upon arise from the disinterest of uninspired wage earners as much as wilful neglect, and one thing you get over in a hurry in this country is being squeamish. Still, I resist the urge to peek in the kitchen, just in case.

Even though I'm not going anywhere today, it does seem prudent to check on my bike, which I hope is locked up down by the guardhouse. I was so tired yesterday, I don't even remember chaining it to a railing. It is a relief to see I did.

The journey back up to the resort complex is not without its challenges. I was worried my legs would be lead, and the equivalent of three storeys of stone stairs are awkward to navigate in my current state, but I'm not injured or otherwise permanently harmed. I should probably get going this morning but can't face the idea of anything more than exploring this hilltop haven, warts and all. Besides, it's still early in the trip, and there's a long way to go. It appears that a good night's sleep has given me a little perspective.

Combine the side trip in Dhulikhel with yesterday's long day covering a short distance, and I'm way behind schedule. Theoretically I should be in Jiri by the end of today, but so what? I can always get back at it tomorrow. Right?

Walking up past my room, I pass a separate building where the more expensive guest rooms are located, as well as a large conference room set on its own in yet another outbuilding. An outdoor clay badminton court looks to be in pretty good condition, even though it doesn't appear to have been used in ages, and the entire complex is on multiple terraces, with intricate stonework everywhere. It is all quite stylish, but a fresh coat of paint would go a long way. Up on the slope above the conference room is the Nepali version of staff accommodation, and in among the small collection of shacks, the maintenance manager has let loose a gaggle of extremely territorial geese, who all but chase me past a lovely garden and onto the flat open space at the back of the resort.

From there the view due north and down toward the southwest is sublime. The main Himalayan range is fronted by solid hills and a deep valley filled with billowy clouds. Above the range, wispy clouds feather the skies just above the snow-covered peaks in the distance. I'm firmly in the Middle Hills now, somewhere around 2500 metres at a guess, and the unusual cloud formations, with clear skies at the centre of the view, allow a sightline all the way down to the Annapurna range, 200 kilometres away. It is a picturesque panorama.

Even as the day passes in a largely pleasing manner, there are little blips in my psychic radar that I fight off with grim determination. Every time the anxiety of not moving relentlessly toward the end goal rears its head, I take a deep breath and hammer the impression down with a big metaphorical stick. "Relax, relax, relax. Don't panic. There's always tomorrow. You can beat your brains out against the side of a mountain again then."

It all works out pretty well, with a few simple pleasures; a hot shower, a short nap and a small pot of milk tea with lunch. Until it starts to rain and everything comes apart, with startling swiftness.

There was no hint of this change in weather this morning, yet here it is, and with every hour that passes, a misting drizzle gains momentum. The tin roof on the main lodge building is an excellent sounding board, and by the time dinner rolls around, the rain is pelting down, creating a considerable racket. What is remarkable about this is not that it's raining, but that it's been raining for hours. When the monsoon finally pushes off at the end of the season, it doesn't stop abruptly but sputters to an end in fits and starts. There have been mini-cloudbursts for weeks, lasting anywhere from ten minutes to a couple of hours. The racket outside is different; it's showing signs of real staying power.

This makes me mad. I know it sounds irrational, but I'm suddenly angry at the weather, and these hills, and the boredom I'm suffering as a result of both. I'm stuck either in my room or in the main dining room, and I don't like it. There's no Wi-Fi and no TV and nothing to do. Worst of all, that Nepali adage "tomorrow, no problem" might be a problem. If this keeps up, I won't be going anywhere. The popular saying got me through the early anxiety of taking another day off so soon, but now I may be stuck here indefinitely. This is not good.

I can feel the spiral coming. I'm going down the rabbit hole, and there's nothing I can do about it.

• • •

Nearly every technological advance is seen by the younger generation as just that, an advance. Older generations can be more cynical and view this new "progress" as a waste of time and money, or in some cases as the end of the world as we know it. All three could be true at the same time; reality is simply a function of how you view it.

What should be of concern regardless of opinion is how much more rapidly change comes about these days, because it appears to be altering us in fundamental ways we haven't even begun to understand. Change may be inevitable, and nature does not operate in a static state, but *hyperactive* change is the new normal, and that might not be such a good thing.

Michael Harris, in his book *The End of Absence, Reclaiming What We've Lost in a World of Constant Connection,* points out that the rate of penetration for a technology – i.e., the amount of time it takes for 50 million people to adopt it – has sped up exponentially in the last couple of decades. After its introduction in the 1920s, radio took 38 years to reach that mark. Before that, the telephone took 20 years for 50 million people to get on board with the idea, and television took a mere 13 years to reach the magic number. By comparison, the World Wide Web took four years, Twitter took three, and iPads only took two.

It is important to note the global population has also grown significantly in that time, so while our appetite for the "next new thing" may have increased, so too has the number of people with the hunger for it. In the late 1960s, the world population was 3.5 billion. It is now 7.5 billion. With that in mind, 50 million in this context is not as big a number as it used to be, but it is still a big number.

Nepal has fumbled around in this technological surge.

Cellphone coverage is widespread, but satellite TV is only now gaining a foothold in rural areas, and the Internet is widely available but can hardly be described as reliable. Even in Kathmandu, Wi-Fi is a dodgy proposition. Bandwidth is low. The frustration quotient is high. The feasibility of it all is easy to question, but if you had said to me as a teenager that you were going to take away my cable television, my cassette-tape Walkman (yes, I'm that old), and the newly affordable long-distance air travel that made the whole world accessible – well, I would have fought you tooth and nail.

These developments, as quaint as they seem now, became part of how my friends and I connected to the world and how we received information. Even today, I can't live without a heavy dose of music streaming from my TV on a satellite music station, or off a playlist burned to my laptop from a huge pile of compact discs tucked away in my closet. The question is, is my generation going to be the last to at least ask, "Is all this technology and connection doing us any good? Does any of it make me a better person? Smarter? More worldly?"

Or is the tech revolution now simply part of human evolution? Are distraction and the inherent inefficiencies of multi-tasking the new focus? Is this who we are?

I'm not sure, and I have a natural impulse to resist.

Cellphones are a particular sore point for me, right there next to my opinion that cars are the ultimate sucker bet. Slick salesmanship has created a market that *appears* to be essential. Who would *die* if they didn't have a cellphone complete with data plan? (Or couldn't own a personal vehicle, for that matter – but that's a separate argument; check out *Lost and Found: Adrift in the Canadian Rockies*, page 122.) By the time each new generation figures out phones are not pivotal to human existence but remain a luxury item, it's too late. They're hooked. Now everyone *has* to have one. There is even a stigma attached to not being part of the gang. Having a fancy car can be seen as a status symbol; so is having a full-service personal communication device. The more bells and whistles attached to it, the better.

I am part of the last generation who didn't have personal phones when we were kids, or even as teenagers. A phone had a rotary dial and was attached to the wall in the kitchen, period, end of story, and I still haven't adjusted to the change. Sure, I had to get a cellphone when I got promoted. I needed it to communicate with staff, touch base with vendors and (the only use that I found truly valuable) deal with emergencies. The problem is, it was always there, vibrating away dozens of times a day regardless of whether I was up for it or not. What began as pleasant expectation soon became a stress reaction: "Oh, goodie, someone wants to talk to me," transformed very quickly into "Dammit, now what?"

Part of the problem was that it was impossible to know the content of the message (at least with the archaic model I had at the time), so all the messages sounded the same. When I had my hip replacement, I was in the hospital for three nights, and by the middle of that first full day I began having anxiety attacks because I'd left my phone at home. I was on medical leave, you understand, and so had zero work responsibilities to attend to but had been so manipulated by my ring tone over the previous three years that I was like Pavlov's dogs, figuratively salivating at this 21st-century version of that experiment's simple bell every time a cellphone went off on television.

Even these uncomfortable warnings don't seem to deter

us. Harris's book notes that the first cellphone call took place in 1973, and now there are 6.8 *billion* cellphone subscriptions worldwide. That's close to one subscription for every person on Earth. When you take into account how many children under the age of 10 are presumably not yet using cellphones, then, practically speaking, we may have reached a one-to-one ratio already. We are connected to an unprecedented degree, but traditional face-to-face interactions are suffering as a result.

This sentiment is reinforced in the March 2015 issue of *Outside Magazine*, in a small piece called "Tame Your Phone," by Alexander George, who cites a UK study that found that having your phone handy (which is the whole point of a mobile cellular phone) could have "negative effects on closeness, connection, and conversation quality."

No shit. Clearly, I'm not a fan, and I have tamed my phone in the best way I know how. It's been on airplane mode since I boarded a plane at the Calgary Airport 26 days ago. I only brought it with me for the handy apps. The camera, voice recorder, compass and calculator are nifty gadgets packed into a small space. I do suppose it would come in handy in an emergency, provided I can get a signal, and it did give Jocey some peace of mind that I brought it along. The theory is that if I get into trouble wandering around on my own in the middle of nowhere and something bad happens, I could try and get help.

The thing is, I never bothered getting an Asian SIM card. They're cheap and available just about everywhere, but I couldn't bring myself to buy one. For some reason, the idea felt like an assault on my adventurous spirit, an intrusion on my independence, a slap in the face of my can-do, need-to-take-a-break-from-technology attitude.

Right about now, I wish I'd gotten over that bravado.

So it seems that I have, like so many adventurous travellers, grossly romanticized the simple life of a rural villager. Coming from a culture steeped in stress and hyperconnectivity, it's appealing to imagine a simpler life with fewer responsibilities and expectations. This outlook is fine and dandy when you're just passing through a place, content to spend an evening, chat with a few locals and then move on. On days like this, with no access to the outside world and nothing to do, you realize it would be hard, not to mention boring as hell, for this to be your day-to-day reality. Who wouldn't embrace every gadget available in this situation, if only to break up the monotony?

• • •

I was up half the night fretting about the conditions, but the rain has persisted, and for all the encroaching psychic darkness triggered by the situation outside, one inescapable truth persists: I am warm and dry. This resort may be overpriced and slightly disappointing, but the weather can't get to me. This is not always the case for the people who live in this country.

A small group of aid workers checked into the resort yesterday, three Nepalis and a man from Switzerland. They are in Mude following up on a school reconstruction project with SOS Children's Villages Nepal, and the national director, Shree Shankar Pradhananga, is the epitome of Nepali grace. He is friendly, outgoing and kind. We chatted briefly at dinner last night, and I liked him immediately. We are the first up for tea this morning, and the rain is pounding down on the tin roof.

"Are you going to delay your departure?" Mr. Pradhananga asks as he sits down at the large dining room table and glances at the ceiling.

"I think so," I answer, resigned to it even though I really, really want to get out of Mude. "There's no point going out in this. Everything will get wet, and you can't see anything."

"True."

The situation outside is nothing short of torrential. It has a ferocity that is impossible to downplay. I am officially storm-stayed, even though the brunt of the monsoon should have dissipated by now.

"This is a bit unusual, isn't it?" I ask, just to be sure I haven't gotten the month wrong.

"Yes. This is like the rainy season. It should be a little bit of rain once in awhile, not this."

When rain is notable to a Nepali, you know it's coming down.

The others have yet to appear for breakfast, so I take the opportunity to ask a question I've been wondering about since coming back to Nepal. The aid group reconstruction effort is earthquake-damage-related, so Mr. Pradhananga will likely know the details as well as anyone.

"With the challenges Nepal normally faces – the monsoon, landslides and some very old buildings – how much of the construction going on is still earthquake-related, and how much is normal construction and renovation?"

"Mostly earthquake."

"It's been a year and a half."

"Yes."

By Mr. Pradhananga's estimate, of the 600,000 people displaced in April and May of 2015, 5 per cent are back in their homes. This is amazing to me, even in a country known for doing things at what one might call a leisurely pace.

"Why? It's been so long."

Mr. Pradhananga makes a gesture that is a cross between dealing cards and the universal cash money move made with the thumb and forefingers. "Distribution of funds. The government promised 300,000 rupees to every affected family. First instalments of 50,000 were just made. Maybe a month ago."

Slightly over $600 Canadian of the promised $4,000 per eligible household has been distributed. This should surprise no one, and I can't help but be snide. "Sounds like government."

"Sounds like government in developing countries in Asia and Africa, yes."

Wow.

It would be naive to think this kind of thing doesn't happen everywhere, in one form or another. In just about every country in the world, the titles "politician" and "public servant" have been operating on opposite ends of the reality spectrum for a very long time, but this is next-level stuff. It can be argued that corruption, incompetence and greed have a more direct impact on the populace in poorer countries because the offences can be more blatant and the victims more vulnerable.

In the article "Man-Made Disaster," which appeared in the April 25, 2016, edition of *Time* magazine, Nikhil Kumar noted that damage from the earthquakes was estimated at $7 billion, and that over $4 billion in international donations had been pledged. Not enough to rebuild the country in its entirety, but enough to get most people out of tents and sheds and other temporary shelters. Kumar writes: "Instead of focusing on reconstruction, Nepal became consumed with a protracted political battle over the new constitution that had been in the works since the monarchy was abolished in 2008."

It's easy to be critical from a distance, and it's nothing new for a government to be unable to prioritize a to-do list and allocate resources. It is regrettable but not necessarily criminal, or even wilful. But, among Nepalis I speak with directly, another overarching theme has emerged in the discussion of government, and that is greed. Chatting with the young men in Durbar Square, or at lunch during the day trip to Namo Buddha, I hear simple frustration at the incompetence, but the real agitation – the bitterness and the feelings of hopelessness – comes from the perception of theft. The sentiments are not always overt. From my impression as a visitor, Nepali people are generally too restrained, too polite, to express it outright, but there is an underlying belief that anyone who rises to power is not interested in working for the good of the people but is only there to take a turn dipping their hand in the cookie jar.

If you are in a position of power, this is a dangerous view for the young and educated segment of a population to have, because eventually they're going to get motivated to find out the truth. As a cynical Westerner, accustomed to shady financial dealings and a culture of cronyism in business and government, my first question is always "Where did the money go?" Followed by "Why isn't there more transparency in the system?" These questions are gaining traction here.

I suspect anyone who has ever been to Nepal is happy to donate what he or she can in the face of such a devastating event. It's a way to give back for so many memories. Stories of misappropriation of funds, vague accounting and incomplete status reports tarnish that giving. That frustration is nothing compared to what the people of Nepal suffer under such greed and ineptitude, of course, but it still makes you mad as hell. I can't imagine how someone living under a tarp or in a tin shed for over a year feels about it, and I'm amazed this country isn't in a perpetual state of civil war.

The conversation with Mr. Pradhananga is just getting interesting, but as the rest of the group comes in for breakfast, the focus shifts to the day's schedule. They have a construction site to visit and another project on the agenda that is half a day's drive away. There's so much I want to follow up on, but there's still plenty to think about as the group heads off on its mission.

Unsurprisingly, the rain continues to fall outside, but somehow it feels a little less oppressive, and the conversation has buoyed me. Good people are trying to fix things, and I am contributing to the local economy in a small but important way, by visiting. I'm feeling hopeful. I have a renewed optimism that the rain will stop and I'll be able to get back out on the road to continue this journey. Borrowing the house phone to check in with Jocey makes me feel even better; it's a minute and 22 seconds of reassurance and positive energy that couldn't come at a more opportune time.

Whenever I begin to lose my bearings, the message from her is always the same. Whatever minor setback or insignificant detail is getting me worked up, whatever expectation I have let get out of control in my mind, I am reminded to "shake off those Western *shoulds* and soak up what Nepal has to offer." The advice is as unwavering as it is sage. Sometimes you need someone half a world away to help put things in perspective for you.

Back in my room, I notice the cicadas have come out this afternoon in full voice, which means the rain has finally stopped, but the mountaintop the resort is on is still enveloped in dense cloud. One of the trees out my window is barely visible, not 30 metres away. A ghostly figure cast in an ocean of grey and white. The cloud cover, oppressive only a few hours ago, is now just part of this slow, and hopefully transformative, experience.

Sitting under my sleeping bag with my feet on the coffee table, I must accept that resting, writing and watching the fog drift past are just as important to this adventure as pushing up and down these huge hills. In this place, the decision to go or not to go isn't entirely up to me; the weather and the landscape also have a say. I only participate in the process. Ultimately, we come to an agreement and then see how things play out.

Somehow, I've got to find a way to make this okay with me.

8.

After the unplanned extra day off, I'm happy to be able to get out and ride today. It's not raining this morning, but the clouds have also not peeled away. There's always a chance it could start up again at any moment. The village of Mude is barely visible up in the distance, and the road continues to be steep, so I have to start off on foot. This has the effect of making me feel very stupid, especially when a car comes past and the occupants look over with a mixture of surprise, sympathy and bewilderment.

In Mude I'm able to get on the bike again, and it isn't long before I reach the final crest of the Hill That Just Won't End and begin traversing down the slope at the other side. I'm sure the views are spectacular from here, but I can't see a thing. There is massive road construction along the entire Lamosangu–Charikot corridor, but with Dashain still in full swing, I have yet to witness anyone actually working, and today is no exception.

It was curious passing parked road-improvement equipment on the climb from Lamosangu, but I was so preoccupied with the task at hand that I didn't think much of it. Clearly, the plan is to widen the road to two lanes and presumably resurface the entire 50-kilometre section, but they have only gotten as far as pulling down parts of the inside slope with giant backhoes. The dirt and rock have been roughly graded where work has begun, but the rubble sits two feet above the adjacent roadway, narrowing it further. Once the work is completed, this journey will be much easier to navigate, but the most difficult, dangerous and dusty sections so far have been where "improvements" are underway.

It also doesn't take much of an imagination to envision things getting even more treacherous once there are two smoothly paved lanes, because then everyone will just drive like maniacs.

Up in the fog, after so much rain, the road is now a muddy swampy bog anywhere the adjoining slope has been peeled away. The occasional vehicle or motorcycle looms from out of the distance with headlights on, but after it passes I get the feeling I could be on the moon. I can't see the valley below, or the mountains in the distance, or much of anything at all. I don't know how far it will be until I begin the steeper part of the descent to Charikot, or what I might find in the interval. It's eerie and unsettling.

After the small settlement of Aahaldanda, the descent begins in earnest. While climbing these hills is a difficult undertaking, coming down is pure joy. Slipping out of the clouds is a gradual transition from a bleak and disorienting landscape into a picturesque rural utopia. I never have to pedal, except at the awkward stream crossings, where the water is diverted over a designed dip in the roadway, and the most demanding task is keeping my speed under control. The rack does continue to be obnoxious, but I'm not surprised. I have to stop every few kilometres to tighten the bolt that caused so much trouble on the way up, but this provides repeated opportunity to step to the edge of the valley and soak up the beauty spread out below. A good chunk of the morning passes in that perfect vision of the Middle Hills I had in my mind's eye.

After finally reaching the bottom of the drainage and crossing a more substantial creek, the road begins to contour upward again. This is a surprise. I imagined it would be a day of descending. I am fairly fresh and so don't suffer the indignity of pushing my bike often, but there are moments when gravity wins, and near the village of Makaibari I suddenly get the strange sensation I'm being followed. Out of the corner of my eye, I spot a weird figure over my shoulder, one my brain can't process because I haven't heard anything coming. Even the quietest motorcycle announces itself in some way.

Turns out it's another cyclist, a Westerner, which is amazing, because not even Nepalis bother riding a bike around here.

Jeremy is from California and has pedalled all the way from Pakistan in his flip flops. He's organized and tough. His bike might be an old beater, but he's got a front rack and has properly distributed his load. He's obviously camping en route, and I am immediately jealous of his determination, not to mention his ability to stand up on the pedals and overcome the steepest bits with relative ease.

Despite his superior abilities, he is humble about his efforts, and we chat for a few minutes about the rigours of bicycling in Nepal: the giant climbs, the insane drivers and the cloudy or hazy conditions that persist at nearly every decent viewpoint. A shared favourite is when someone shouts *hello* or *namaste* from somewhere away from the road. It's a friendly and encouraging gesture, but what do you do? A wave seems insufficient reply, and a *namaste* in return only elicits follow-up questions, "Where are you from?" and "Where are you going?" primary among them. While climbing, you don't have the breath to respond, and on the way down you don't have occasion to answer. By the time you hear the question, you're gone.

Once we start drawing a crowd of curious locals, we decide sharing the road would be a nice change to our solo travel agendas, but Jeremy drops me pretty much right away, and I am left alone again with my awkward uphill struggle.

• • •

By first impression, Charikot is a lot like Lamosangu, only bigger, and positioned on a ridge instead of tucked in a canyon. It's not exactly somewhere to enjoy a day off, but I just want to stay for awhile and read and write. I simply don't feel like doing more than that. Perhaps predictably, there is resistance to the realization. It's somewhat ironic: in Mude I just wanted out; now I just want to hang. As the kids like to say these days, WTF.

Robert Louis Stevenson, in *Travels with a Donkey in the Cévennes*, wrote, "For my part, I travel not to go anywhere, but to go. I travel for travel's sake. The great affair is to move; to feel the needs and hitches of our life a little more nearly, to get down off this feather-bed of civilization, and to find the globe granite underfoot and strewn with cutting flints."

What is remarkable about this quote is not necessarily the content of it but the date to which it is credited, 1879. These days, the "feather-bed" has grown plush beyond our wildest dreams, to say nothing of its wastefulness, and for some the inclination to resist the subtle trappings of modern life never goes away. There's a primal instinct that says we aren't meant to be so pampered, that there needs to be an element of struggle incorporated in our existence. If it isn't there, we will go out and find it, but that impulse alone isn't enough. Paul Theroux, in *Fresh Air Fiend*, wrote, "Travel, its very motion, ought to suggest hope. Despair is the armchair; it is indifference and glazed, incurious eyes."

As I've gotten older, my travel is about hope as much as effort. I hope for different. I hope for interesting. I hope for better. And I have a growing sense that these concepts overlap. I have often been inspired by the idea of all of those "cutting flints," but something has been missing in my single-minded approach. There has been an element of dissatisfaction in simply going and doing without taking the time to experience the experience. There's a sweet spot between lazy and frantic where attentive lives; I just haven't figured out where it is.

When I do manage to stumble upon it (or get rained into it), I can't wait to scamper away like a startled mouse, afraid I'll be caught doing nothing.

Tim Cahill, in his *Outside Magazine* article "Professor Cahill's Travel 101," gets to the heart of why developing a relaxed view of the world is appealing in "Rule 5: Boredom greases the cogs in the machinery of marvels."

Is simply participating in these marvels my greatest aspiration? It could very well be.

So I'll settle for a walking tour of Charikot today, because as Cahill informs us, idle boredom is good; and, as Jocey suggests, this is also Nepal. Bustling cities and road-side towns with dusty, litter-strewn streets; quaint and tidy villages away from the main roads; historic and culturally significant landmarks; hefty Middle Hills and jagged, snow-covered peaks. It's all part of the confused whole. I want to experience this part of what Nepal has to offer a little more keenly, and forget about (or at least try to forget about) my weird performance anxieties.

In an interview he did after writing *The Fearful Void*

in 1972, Geoffrey Moorhouse said, "One reason I did this book is that all the books I've read about rough journeys, from Fuchs's *Crossing of Antarctica* to Thesiger's *Arabian Sands*, do tend to exclude the soft, weak, feeble, nasty sides we all have. They all seem to be bloody supermen. You think, 'didn't they ever cry, or do something really shitty?'"

I wonder, didn't anyone ever come to the conclusion they weren't super-travellers? That they were curious more than driven? That they were eager and enthusiastic but somewhat lazy as well? Could it be that my urge to travel is rooted in a search for a better understanding of myself and of the world around me, and I've been distracted all this time by larger ambitions? By bigger goals concocted to justify the attempt?

In his book *The Art of Travel*, Alain de Botton explores this notion in chapter 4, titled "On Curiosity." He compares (quite cleverly I think) the experience of his own modern-day trip to Madrid with that early German explorer Alexander von Humboldt's epic journey to South America in 1799. It's a big leap to make, at first glance, but de Botton manages to bridge the gap in time and location deftly with a reasoned argument that the nature of physical exploration of the world around us has changed, and our expectations of what can be achieved by venturing "out there" needs to change as well.

Humboldt was a go-getter, no question. Just reading a brief summary of his achievements and discoveries during his five-year mission is exhausting. By contrast, de Botton is attempting to explore a modern city unknown to him but meticulously mapped and described by others. The task appears pointless, and he has great difficulty warming to the idea, until he realizes he's looking at the problem the wrong way. There are very few blank spots on the map anymore. The world has been measured and surveyed and studied to a remarkable degree. Modern transportation makes almost every place accessible to a properly motivated individual. One could say it has all been done before, so why bother?

In de Botton's account, it was Nietzsche who first coined the term "life-enhancing" as the logical progression from the pursuit of the cold, hard scientific fact that was a big part of early travel and exploration. Nietzsche argued that the pursuit of fact alone was a sterile endeavour, and to have real merit, the individual had to use facts to enhance life, effectively saying that any trip is worthy when the goal is to expand understanding. Even if something is already known to others, it continues to be important to learn it oneself, if only to enhance one's own being. One of de Botton's revelations on the subject reflected on Humboldt's accomplishments: "Instead of bringing back 1,600 plants, we might return from our journeys with a collection of small, unfêted but life-enhancing thoughts."

I cannot think of a better outcome than that, or one more worthy of my attention.

• • •

The last day on the bike proves tremendous. Travelling in the early morning down 17 long switchback-littered kilometres, through pine and rhododendron forest with cicadas trilling everywhere, is peaceful and exhilarating at the same time. Unfamiliar birdsong accompanies me as the road dives past isolated homesteads and small settlements, with old men sitting at roadside stalls having morning tea. Increasingly, the forest shares space with terraced fields, and as I near Tamakoshi Bazaar, the first morning buses from Jiri begin to appear.

Tamakoshi Bazaar itself is a sight to behold. Located in a tight part of the valley and clustered around the western side of the bridge crossing the Tama Koshi, it is a crazy, congested little stop on the route between huge climbs. Trays of fruit and chips and pop are for sale through bus windows to travellers unwilling to get off during the driver's short break, and the small central square is a mash of horns and engine noise and shouting. The small bus park hardly seems big enough for all the people and vehicles crammed into the small space, but as I sit here having a snack, buses come and buses go and not once does someone get run over, which seems a minor miracle.

Climbing away from the river promises to be another soul-sucking effort, but at least I have an idea what's coming. It isn't long before I fall into the familiar routine of riding for awhile and then pushing the bike up the obnoxiously steep bits. Coming out of the shadow of the hill while travelling east, I start to get hot, but I'm resigned to it. "One long, uncomfortable day, and I will be in Jiri," I keep thinking, "where part two of this adventure begins." It will be six months before I read Goran Kropp's *Ultimate High: My Everest Odyssey* and learn that the man who bicycled from Sweden to Nepal, climbed Everest without supplemental oxygen and then biked all the way back to Sweden also had to push his overloaded bike uphill around here. This information would make me feel better about my own efforts if I knew it now.

Taking a break for some water and to reapply sunscreen after about six kilometres, I am feeling the effects of the toil when a family of four, on a tractor pulling a trailer loaded with fine gravel, stops to ask if I want a ride. I decline at first – it would be contrary to the spirit of the trip, after all – but after a short debate I think, *What do I have to prove?* So I throw my bike and gear on the pile in the trailer and jump in on top. It's the easiest four uphill kilometres of the week. In a way that I could never properly articulate, I *enjoy* rumbling along with no exertion on my part. I would even go so far as to say it's more exotic and adventurous than simply cycling up the hill. Bouncing along, I can barely keep the smile off my face.

Energized by the lift, I find the subsequent riding good, but I'm still travelling very slowly. As I approach the small hamlet of Namdu, a Jeep slows to ask if I need any help. Part of me wants to muddle through the rest of the climb, while another part wonders, *Is this my lucky day?*

Stubborn and *determined* win out, at first. "No thanks, I'm fine. It's just steep," I say.

"I'm picking up tourists from Britain. We are going to Jiri. We can put your bike in the back."

"No, it's okay. Thanks."

"My name is Shyam. My village is just up ahead. We will wait, if you change your mind."

Lucky day doesn't want to be left out of the conversation entirely.

"How far is it to Jiri from here, anyway?" I ask before they pull away.

"Twenty-five, 30 kilometres."

"Mostly up?"

As if I have to ask. From the edge of Namdu, you can see the ridge ahead, and it's obvious there's no real low point to the pass. As I make my way through the last 500 metres to the village, the debate rages in my head. This part of the trip was ill-conceived, no question about it. I've got too much weight on the bike, and I'm not strong enough to pedal the steepest parts of these hills fully loaded. It is demoralizing, not to mention a blow to my ego. This is not a country for cycle touring unless you're a masochist or in training for King of the Mountains at the Tour de France. Lesson learned.

On the other hand, I committed to doing this, and doing it in an unusual fashion was part of the appeal. I can't just jump the last 25 kilometres, can I? Can I?

In the end, I feel I've done enough hard work to still respect myself in the morning, and I reason I am on an adventure, not some kind of hybrid forced march. I accept the lift, stubborn pride be dammed.

In Namdu, Shyam's son Sachim expertly ties my bike in the back, and we're off. Shyam insists I take the front seat, and he gets in back with Darryl and Jo, from England. Darryl is another Nepal veteran, with three previous visits under his belt, and he and Jo are on a brief honeymoon. Any reservations I had about the decision to accept a ride quickly disappear as we compare notes on what a wild, weird place Nepal is. As Sachim drives in silence, Shyam interjects on occasion with his expert advice on the area, and I realize that except for a few minutes with California Jeremy, I haven't had a proper conversation with a Western traveller in a month. It's nice to get another perspective on this place and hear stories about parts of the country I've not yet been to.

Travelling those last few kilometres of the infamous Jiri road, I think about this section of the trip. This was supposed to be about roughly retracing the steps of the early adventurers to this region, those hardy and daring souls who passed through on the way to confront glory and tragedy among the world's tallest peaks. I imagined endlessly hard work as I moved up and down these formidable hills, with a final goal firmly in mind.

That's how I planned it, anyway, but it's not turning out

like that at all. This realization just keeps coming back to me over and over again. Like a part of my mind is persistently trying to resist a change in attitude, but the new reality refuses to be denied. The hard work is there on the days I'm ready to face it. Throwing myself against that labour day after day after day, however, doesn't seem to be the point at this point. As I'm about to continually find on the trail ahead, this place is crawling with go-getters, eager to push the limits of their will and endurance. It turns out I'm not that guy anymore. It could be that I never was. I am equally content sitting in a hotel room, punching out words on my keyboard, or wandering a village or the backstreets of a burgeoning city with no real idea what I might find. I have discovered at the heart of things a much more laid-back person than I ever would have thought existed, one who is fighting the addiction of action. I want to see where it leads.

Getting to Jiri before noon, I am shocked to be standing wide-eyed in the small bus park in the blazing sunshine. I have milk tea with my new fast friends in a rundown tea shack, then quickly recover my bearings, check into the Evergreen Hotel & Lodge, right on the creek, and for ten bucks get a great corner room overlooking Main Street that's painted a fabulous shade of Nepal-hotel pink.

Here I spend a contented afternoon, drinking beer and looking out the windows at Jiri's midday commotion while listening to tunes and organizing all the shit I won't need to haul uphill anymore. The bike and all the related paraphernalia, along with any extra anything, is being left behind. From Jiri, it's just boots and a pack. For about a minute, I feel a twinge of guilt about skipping 25 kilometres of the planned itinerary. It feels like cheating somehow. Then I have another swig of beer, pick another song from the playlist and get over it.

9.

THE WORLD AT FIVE KILOMETRES AN HOUR

It is not entirely clear what fluke of evolution moved us, as a species, along the path from simple ape to a more advanced form of hominid, and then eventually to modern human. Even now, you may be surprised to learn, we are 98.4 per cent identical, genetically speaking, from chimpanzees, our nearest living relative. Theories abound about when and where we stepped away from our hairy cousins and became us. The development of speech, a dramatic increase in brain size and the appearance of the first primitive tools are all part of the complex puzzle that is our prehistory.

What happened, and in what order, is a book in itself, and a subject hotly debated among academics and anthropologists for decades. The literature is rife with theories about how and why it all went down, and after plowing through a small fraction of it, I can't even begin to figure out what the key factor in our transformation to fully modern human was.

Part of the puzzle that does seem plausible, however, is this: at some point in the distant past, the isthmus of Panama rose from the sea. That changed the flow of warm ocean currents and precipitated a dramatic change in global weather patterns. The continent of Africa began to dry out, forests gave way to open savanna and, while that was happening, a small creature from somewhere on our evolutionary timeline came down out of the trees and learned to walk upright. From there we eventually grew a big brain, developed speech, made stone tools, learned to farm and built cities, and in time invented Internet porn. But before we managed any of it, we, along with our fellow early hominids, walked.

Given the state of health and fitness in the developed world, and the ubiquitous nature of the internal combustion engine in modern society, it is hard to imagine walking as anything more than a means of getting to the bathroom during a commercial break on television. Some people still use it as a form of relaxation and/or exercise, but there was a time when it was a means of transportation. Once upon a time, it was the only means. Bill Bryson, in *A Short History of Nearly Everything*, explains that the colonization of the planet occurred by putting one foot in front of the other over and over again. He writes that "sometime well over a million years ago, some new, comparatively modern, upright beings left Africa and boldly spread out across much of the globe."

It is even possible the expansion progressed at a pace of 40 kilometres or more a year, across a landscape that was every bit as daunting and challenging at ground level as it is today.

While we may take the act for granted now, walking remains at the base of our being, arguably as important to us as a species as any other factor that led to becoming human. Some of the more recent arguments even go so far as to suggest it was *the* key factor, the idea being that freeing the hands literally allowed early *Homo sapiens* to think about other things, namely the challenges they faced in what was a very large world around them. Whatever the catalyst is beside the point: bipedalism has been going on for a long, long time.

Even with this distinguished history, and the inherent simplicity of the act, the art of walking has been largely misplaced in our modern routine. Walking still has a purpose for an adult, but much of the pleasure of it is gone, lost in the distraction of getting to a destination, or overlooked by a preoccupied mind that is concentrating on other things. As I have written about in my previous book, the automobile has simply removed an untold number of trips from the equation. Cable television does a good job smothering the will for it.

So, while walking sounds like a simple enough request in this life, and indeed it is a simple enough task for most, the magic in it has proven elusive to me lately. Sure, I walk at work all the time. I walk more at work in a day than many people walk in a week, but that effort doesn't seem to get me anywhere, it just takes me around and around in circles. The trouble is, at my core I'm the type of person who needs a destination at the end of the road to keep all that effort from becoming stagnant and pointless in my mind. I would walk to the ends of the earth with the right motivation but get bored easily, and delivering plates of food, clearing glassware and slinging drinks hardly seems like a noble pursuit, no matter what kind of spin you put on it. My work life has become an exercise in mindless repetition, with no final destination and no discernible purpose beyond executing my job and collecting my paycheque – which, as it turns out, is not a great way to live, no matter how much money you make.

A busy day of work involves walking from the bar with an armload of dirty dishes to the dish-pit in the kitchen, then over to the pass-through, where fresh meals have been plated and are ready to go out to the patio. Forgot to ask for extra dressing for that salad? No problem, more walking. Want another beer now that your food has arrived? No problem, more walking. Ready for your bill? No problem, more walking. Occasionally, a trip to the office is required for some mundane reason or other, and I'll hide in there for a few minutes during slow moments in the serving cycle, but that's basically it, hour after hour on rapid repeat in the summer months, when all I do is walk.

I measured it once on an average Friday day shift, using the health app on my phone, and was surprised to learn 7.5 kilometres is an easy amount of ground to cover when you're not paying attention. One sunny day later the next week, I covered 14 kilometres in a single nine-hour shift. On the Saturday and the Sunday of an August long weekend, the number was 19 kilometres each day. That's back-to-back 27,000-plus steps to nowhere.

It remains a somewhat demented fact of life in much of the Western world that we continue to aspire to a "lifestyle" that requires such a sacrifice of our time, energy and ultimately our health. In Canada, if you are a company man, you get two weeks of paid vacation a year for the first five years of employment. After that you can tack on an extra week. A 40-hour work week is also part of the labour laws, but if you are motivated to get ahead, sticking to those 40 hours is a pipe dream. A 50-hour work week is likelier as you strive for the "good life" everyone keeps talking about.

The irony is, it isn't even the "good life" we're chasing; we're more just trying to survive the pressure of holding up our end while fighting off the exhaustion that comes with the effort. It can be a subtle and insidious grind. Somehow I survived the madness, for a few years, anyway. I'm grateful for the opportunity to make good money. I may be worn out and half-broken, but I honoured my commitments for as long as I could manage and saved up enough cash to be free of it for awhile. Now I will be walking in a completely different manner. Every day there is a new destination, and there is nothing complicated or pressing about getting there. It's so simple. This is what I will be doing now. Get up, have breakfast, walk. Stop for lunch, and then walk some more. Maybe take a few pictures, find a guest house, have dinner. Read. Write. Go to bed.

It's a wonderful change from an everyday life of stress and enterprise and worry. There's no organizing other people's schedules, no troubleshooting, no juggling staff personalities and abilities, no putting out fires, no faking a good mood. There's just one thing. Walking. The bike ride didn't go exactly as planned, but I figured out I'm here to see a little bit of the world, and perhaps more importantly be a part of that world, at a pace that might not make sense in this day and age. The average human moves across the landscape under their own power at a rate of about five kilometres an hour. The idea of that feels right. It feels natural to want to try. I think it's going to be great.

• • •

I think it's going to be great? *Great?* One of these days I'm going to have to look up the definition of that word. Perhaps when I think *great*, the term I'm really looking for is *interesting*. *Arduous* and *ridiculous* also work in a pinch.

Walking out of Jiri proves simple enough. The hotel owner was kind enough to let me lock my bike on the roof, and past the bus park the paved road continues on to the actual trailhead a few hundred metres away, where a succession of clay steps cut into the mountain leads straight up. When I walk along the level ground, my pack is heavy but not completely unreasonable. What's unreasonable is my camera bag. I have about five of them at home, each purchased in succession as limitations revealed themselves. They all work well enough in specific scenarios, but none are a perfect fit, and with a big backpack this is the best choice now: an oversized fanny pack swung around to the front. Did I mention the tether anchoring it to the shoulder straps of the backpack to keep it from bouncing off my thighs? No? Well, there's that too.

I look ridiculous. Porters will wonder why I haven't hired a porter. Locals will occasionally laugh.

This unconventional set-up aside, the long bicycle ride to Jiri was helpful. I'm not completely out of breath from minute one. The steep grade is manageable, not an unwelcome slap in the face, and before long there's a stretch of nice contour-walking along well-worn single-track. The way is even signposted for a time, but within the hour the path meets a road and things begin to get a little more complicated. I've been here before, so this is all familiar, but not that familiar. It's been a long time, and the finer details of the route have grown hazy. I'm on a ridge crossing, so pointing my feet in an upward direction is a safe bet, but beyond that it's anybody's guess.

Part of the problem is that the word *road* is a stretch by any definition. *Gravel driveway* is more apt, and although there are sections where a real effort has been made to create a viable avenue for vehicles, it remains largely impassable in places. Overgrown with vegetation and eroded by the elements. For a pedestrian, it makes no sense to follow it anyway, because it meanders all over the hillside in search of a reasonable grade, and it's impossible not to stumble across it and be drawn off course.

My Cicerone guidebook may have misled me in Mude, but a little tidbit in the Trail Note on page 97 remains wholly accurate: "Trekkers without guides will have to be vigilant in order to avoid taking the wrong paths, and should ask frequently or risk a time-wasting diversion."

Yup. Advice taken, but to be fair there aren't exactly people hanging around at every minor trail junction, and the sheer number of local footpaths means there is no obvious route. I thought I would be clever and dust off my orienteering skills instead of just following the road. How hard could it be?

How hard indeed.

As I travel up through the small farms, it's obvious I've lost my way at least a little bit. The trail is plain to see but not well trodden, and looks very much like all those small pathways that intersect at regular intervals. The only thing to indicate I haven't completely screwed this up is that the hilltop is drawing slowly closer. My map isn't detailed enough to positively confirm my position, and a progression of compass readings is roughly on line, but it could also be I've drifted slightly left.

What I'm not prepared to do is trespass across everybody's fields, hop waist-high stone walls and bushwhack through the forest that runs along the top of the hill. I'll get straightened out when I gain the ridge.

Near the top, the narrow band of trees is lovely. A mature stand of evergreens diffuses the light across the forest floor, and the temperature drops notably once I'm out of the direct sunshine. At the top there's a small Mani wall. This collection of stone tablets carved with mantras important in Tibetan Buddhism is the first I've seen so far, and it marks a T-junction at what I assume is the road from earlier. I have a vague feeling I should go right, but that can't be correct. It looks like doing so will eventually lead back over the ridge and down to where I've come from. There are also plenty of road cuts visible all over the adjacent slopes ahead that are not indicated on my map at all, which makes it difficult to get a proper bearing. Heading directly left would clearly be wrong, but this is turning into a series of educated guesses. So I find a seat on a rock nearby, break out some water and try and figure it out.

Even though this one might possibly be shit, I still do love maps. They are a source of inspiration and fodder for the imagination as much as a practical tool for navigation. Rosita Forbes once wrote, "That is the charm of a map. It represents the other side of the horizon where everything is possible."

Even more so when said map is of dubious accuracy. I don't need to imagine what might be over the horizon: I'm not sure what's going on right in front of me, which is as unsettling as it is interesting. Part of me still wants to go right, but a bigger part of me says *trust your eyes*, and, after taking three koras of the Mani wall for luck, I'm relatively certain I've chosen correctly and begin a slow descent along the hillside directly ahead.

Before long the terrain is wide open and the views are fine. As I traverse the slope, I can eventually see what I think is the village of Shivalaya, down at the base of an adjoining valley. Tomorrow's lunch stop, the village of Deorali, is clearly visible above it in the distance. As is the set of trails snaking up to the pass between the two. Standing on a small hillside spur, I take a moment to pull out my map and compass to confirm my bearings once again. All good.

In *Vagabonding: An Uncommon Guide to the Art of*

Long-Term World Travel, Rolf Potts writes about the huge empty spaces that existed on the earliest maps: "The more these unknown areas were explored, the smaller the terra incognita became, and gradually the physical limits of the world ceased to be such a mythical secret."

Now those empty spaces have been filled in, but so much of this world remains unknown to personal experience. In that way, the world can still be mythical and mystical and inspiring to the individual. Good travel is an education, and seeking out places not yet seen but often imagined is another step toward greater knowledge and better understanding. Even coming back after a long absence, it seems, can be that stimulating.

The road is forced by the contour of the hillside to meander instead of taking a direct line, and just as I begin to get nervous about the overall angle, fearing I'm drifting even farther left, I come upon another, larger Mani wall, where a prominent trail descends sharply into the forest below. It's an obvious viewpoint that I believe coincides with the one marked on my map, and there are even arrows scratched into the hard dirt, pointing down into the valley. This must be the way.

Nope. Wrong. Thanks for trying.

In the end, I have veered off course and should have turned right when I had the chance. Only blind luck keeps me from descending 300 metres or more on the wrong trail. A young Nepali man has appeared to set me straight at the most opportune time. I haven't seen another soul in over an hour.

Walking back up to the T-junction with my new friend is not so bad. I was only 15 or 20 minutes off course, and it's a lovely day. It's sunny but not too warm, with the hint of a breeze that keeps me fresh. Or at least keeps me from sweating all over the place. I do spend a lot of time try-ing to get my bearings, trying to reconcile the terrain un-derfoot with the map in my head and the map in my bag. The drainage I was about to go down does flow toward Shivalaya, so in my mind there has to be a connecting trail. There are trails and roads zigzagging everywhere, but my emergency guide is adamant we go back.

So we continue to walk together, and I drag my feet, hoping he'll leave me behind, but he seems intent on get-ting me to the Mani wall. I think he thinks I'm stupid, be-cause he keeps bringing up the correct route, using the distant visual cues. We'll have a few minutes of pleasant conversation about Nepal or Canada or his home village in this small district, and then suddenly he'll launch into it all over again.

"How did you manage to get lost? That's Shivalaya down there, you can see it, yes?"

"Yes."

"That's Deorali over there across the valley. Mali is along this ridge. You've got to go there first. Do you understand?"

Yes, yes. I understand. Can we talk about something else, please?

Upon reaching the junction, he practically pushes me in the right direction, and then descends through the woods exactly where I came up 45 minutes ago. He's headed to Jiri, so at least I got that part right.

In chapter 7 of *Solitude: A Singular Life in a Crowded World*, Michael Harris explores map making and the impact it has had on how we view the world around us. Mapping has evolved over the centuries as a way to un-derstand and navigate our environment. He contends that every map is "a straining to reduce enormous and uncer-tain surroundings into something legible."

Makes sense; we want to know where we're going. We always have. According to Amy Lobben, a professor at the University of Washington, way-finding is an inherited trait. "It is so important to everyday existence and is probably key to human evolution," she says in an interview with Harris in the same chapter in *Solitude*. "Our ancestor's ability to get to a food source and back, for example, would have been essential."

The landscape has not changed, but our perception of it has. The broadening of the collective horizon has coincided with an ability to get almost anywhere more easily. As a consequence, finding the neighbourhood grocery store is no longer a task, it's an errand, but the underlying instincts survive. Do we get disproportionally upset about not being able to find our way in a strange city because it triggers something at the base of our being? Do stubborn men refuse to ask for directions on a long trip because this is such a deep instinct? One we are not ready to simply let go of? I would argue maybe that's part of it, and will gladly cherry-pick one of Harris's conclusions in support of this: "If successfully navigating a mysterious landscape has always been an inherent part of our survival – if it has, in fact, allowed our ancestors to survive and pass on their genes – then to give up that skill is to give up on a part of ourselves."

So I got lost. Big deal. I feel silly about it, but I've also felt strangely alive these last couple of hours. I'm interacting with my environment in real time, trying to figure out where I am and where I want to go. In practising an ancient and hereditary set of skills not necessary in my everyday survival at home, I am tapping into something primal and energizing. It propels me forward.

Walking along the ridge toward the correct trail is easy

going, but the road is nothing like a simple rural walking path. In places it is exactly like you would expect, a double track of firm gravel with wild grasses and weeds growing up the middle, but in others the ground is not quite so solid. A clay-like mud dominates, one that has not dried out completely from the recent monsoon rains. It'll hold my weight, but not with any degree of certainty, and the last vehicles to pass this way have left deep ruts where wheels have tried to gain purchase. In the worst places, the bottoms of said vehicles have dragged along through the mud. There is no way a regular car would ever be able to make it through, which makes you wonder why they bothered making a road in the first place. If you're not going to lay down asphalt, a road here doesn't stand much chance against the elements.

At the village of Mali, the walking path finally becomes obvious once again, and I'm grateful to put the route-finding skills aside for awhile. It's a big descent to Shivalaya, through forest and field, homestead and tiny farm. By the time I reach the suspension bridge over the Khimti Khola, I'm ready to check in to the first guest house I come across, which I'm happy to report is only five paces beyond the far end.

No trouble finding that.

• • •

Despite getting lost yesterday, I'm still keen on avoiding an excess of company but will probably fail. It used to be everybody had to start their trek in Jiri, so when I only saw two or three Westerners all day, I figured I'd have the trail largely to myself. In the last few years, the main road has progressed all the way around the mountain I climbed, and group tours skip the first day of walking. Last night

at dinner, a large French contingent pulled up in a bus after the long drive from Kathmandu and checked into the
guest house next door. Now they're having lunch right
across the path.

Roughly translated, *Deorali* means "man-made structures on a pass," and true to the name, the village sits
astride the low point between hills. Bisecting the cluster
of lodges is the main trail, and running up the middle is
a series of Mani walls, five in total, each about 30 metres
long. Not many trekkers stay here, choosing instead to
fuel up for the descent to Bhandar. It was a tough climb
this morning, but there's no time to dawdle. After a bowl
of Rara noodle soup and some Coconut Crunchees cookies, I'm eager to get going. I want to get away from the
group as quickly as possible.

Individual trekkers are a welcome diversion out on the
trail – you can engage with them, or not, as the situation
dictates. It's easy enough to have a light-hearted chat, exchange information or simply say *namaste* and be on your
way. Couples are also decent company, for the same reason, but groups of four to six are much louder, more intrusive and more entitled, especially in the lodges. Big groups
are generally a nightmare to be around because they take
up space, talk over each other until the room is filled with
noise and slow the kitchen down to a standstill. My choice
of where to have lunch was predicated entirely on where
the French group decided to stop, and you can bet I didn't
eat with them.

At the edge of Deorali the trail descends immediately,
and without mercy. Amazingly, an attempt has begun to
extend the road into this valley, but it's so rough that only
a tractor can navigate it in the current state. The trail simply cuts across the switchbacks and plunges almost straight

down – and down, it turns out, is harder than up. Where the trail is hard, smooth dirt, it's steep and intermittently sprinkled with dust or pebbles, so you're never sure the foot you plant is going to stay exactly where you plant it, and the stone stairs, where they do exist, can be set farther apart than the average human stride.

If I slip here, I'm totally screwed. There's no recovery strategy that would work in time; I'm simply not strong enough to fight off momentum and gravity. Find yourself off balance – too bad. A stone moves underfoot – too bad. Tiny pebbles acting like ball bearings – too bad. This is an exercise in concentration: just put your feet in the right place and pay attention to that. I'm moving like a 90-year-old on a set of snowy steps, and it isn't long before my tired brakes wear thin and my knees and back begin to ache. But I'm not the only one picking my steps very, very carefully.

Another solo trekker has left Bhandar at a similar time, and our spacing allows a sense that we are travelling independently, but inevitably we come together at water breaks or pretty viewpoints. Our ongoing conversation begins with little jokes about the terrain and our slow pace, and eventually leads to a proper introduction. He's also Canadian, and I'm no stranger to his distinct accent. I'm curious where he's from.

"I'm Jamey, by the way."

"Norman."

"Where's home, Norman?"

"I'm from Quebec City. And yourself?"

"Montreal originally, but I live out west now."

It happens all the time: you travel halfway around the world to meet someone from a couple of hours down the highway.

Coming from the same home province is oddly comforting. It suggests familiarity and common experience. This, coupled with the slower pace we seem to share, makes it inevitable we'll spend time together over the next few days. Norman is travelling with his guide, Arjun, and his porter, Ram, both of whom look to be in their early 20s; although they're somewhat shy, my initial impression of them is that they seem to be nice kids. (It's troubling to have reached the point in life where people in their 20s are comfortably referred to as "kids.") After a month on my own, some regular conversation might not be a bad idea. It will also be nice to not worry about losing the trail again for a few days.

After the grinding descent, a break within sight of the village gives us an opportunity to pull out our cameras. Norman is also a photo buff, and this is one of my favourite valleys on the early part of this trek. What I find interesting about it is that instead of descending directly to the river, it has a large lip midway down the long slope, so the village and surrounding farms sit nestled in something of a large bowl suspended above the main valley. There is also a particularly attractive species of tree in bloom, adding little dashes of pale pink to the picture. It's all quite becoming.

We're in no rush now, and it's a nice enough day, overcast but warm, so there's no reason to seek out a guest house quite yet. Norman is giving the guys a hard time about the young girls working in a field nearby. He's encouraging them to go over and chat the girls up, but they're having none of it. Arjun and Ram are somewhat naive, and serious about their religious beliefs. Neither of them drinks alcohol or eats meat, from what I can gather. They may have opened up a little bit with me already, but never in a million years would they wander over to strange women and strike up a conversation.

Being shy does not necessarily prohibit a sense of humour, however.

As we're sitting there, a Nepali man is herding three old cows home after an afternoon of grazing. The pathway remains steep, and the cows don't appreciate the oversized stone steps. It looks like they could topple over at any moment, large bodies on uncertain legs taking a big leap of faith with every hesitant stride. Reminds me of someone I know. Leaning toward Arjun, I mention it in jest.

"Kind of looks like me."

"Yes," he says simply as he gets up to get us moving again. I'm not sure if he understands what I meant exactly, but there is a gleam in his eye to suggest he was thinking about the same dig. Either he's too polite to say anything, or I beat him to the punchline.

• • •

I reach the lodge first. Norman got caught up in his picture taking, and there has been no sign of the French since lunch. I heard from the guest house owner in Shivalaya that the group is booked at the Bhandar Guest House, so I check in at Shobha Lodge for some peace and quiet. It also happens to be where I stayed the last time through here. The lodge looks essentially the same, but this area did not fare well in last year's earthquake. The entire upstairs has been completely rebuilt, and the small, charming garden out back is mostly gone, replaced by a temporary shelter.

Geological time is slow time, ticking away at a pace that can be hard to relate to on an everyday level, but most of us can grasp the concepts. Reasonable people now agree we have mountains on Earth because of plate tectonics, an idea first proposed in the early 20th century by Alfred Wegener in a theory he called "continental drift." Acceptance was not instantaneous. Although short-sighted in many respects and slow to adopt new ideas that seem obvious in hindsight, the human animal is also curious, and over the last century we've figured out how plate tectonics works. We've come to realize the Indian Plate is bashing into the much bigger Eurasian Plate and is being driven beneath it at the leading edge. As a result of this slow-motion train wreck played out on an epic scale, the Eurasian Plate is being folded and pushed up at a rate of roughly one millimetre a year, while the Indian Plate is buried somewhere below the Himalaya.

The hitch is the natural world often ignores the averages. These faults don't slip past each other easily. The rough edges catch and grab and eventually lock up. Over time, the pressures build to the point of overwhelming the stalemate. The result is an earthquake, a powerful and destructive seismic event that can have devastating consequences. It is worth noting once again that the Gorkha quake killed over 8,000 people in Nepal. Nearly three-quarters of a million homes were damaged or destroyed. The disaster directly affected an estimated eight million people in one way or another. A year and half later, the country is far from fully recovered.

As I learned in Mude, the government has a lot to answer for in the debacle that has been the rebuilding effort, but people along these tourist trekking routes couldn't wait for assistance to arrive. They've taken it upon themselves to rebuild. Hastily and out of pocket, but what choice did they have? At least they have the means to do so. People in other districts don't have the same opportunity, and so they wait. According to the guest house owner on my first night out on the trail in Shivalaya, the entire village, with the exception of the recently erected police station, was damaged or destroyed. This lodge here in Bhandar is also not exactly as I remember it, but they are back in business as well. It appears the people here have done what Nepali people have always done in the face of hardship; they've gotten on with it.

• • •

In less serious matters, the group from France shows up before I even manage to unpack. Within minutes the other guest rooms are a symphony of clomping boots and bewildered voices trying to get settled in. There's a dozen of them, plus two or three guides, but their porters are housed off-site, so dinnertime does not completely overwhelm the kitchen. The proprietress is a tremendous character and keeps everyone in line and everything running smoothly in her spot-on Aretha Franklin–in–*The Blues Brothers* style. Amazingly, my food comes out first, and the French even share some of their stash of French liqueur, effectively destroying my grumpy preconceptions about what it will be like travelling in the company of obnoxious foreigners.

Mon dieu, who would have guessed *that* would happen.

10.

LA, LA, LA, LA, LA, LA

"I hate that guy."

It's an honest enough statement, and Norman has delivered it in perfect comedic deadpan. I hate the guy too. Arjun and Ram are off ahead, sitting on a rock somewhere, waiting for us to catch up, and a Nepali man in his thirties is practically running down the steep trail with a small backpack. He's skipping from boulder to boulder like a downhill skier navigating moguls, barely touching one before moving on to the next in an impressive display of balance, momentum and dexterity. The Canadian judges are giving him a 10 for execution, and a bitter 1 for artistic impression.

It wouldn't be nearly so annoying if he was wearing shoes instead of simple rubber flip-flops.

Norman and I have been struggling for about an hour now. Big stone steps, interspersed with an eroded and relentless trail littered with boulders, has sapped our energy, if not our sense of humour. I don't dare look at my map, but every small settlement in the region has the altitude scribbled on the various guest house signs. By my calculations, we still have about 300 vertical metres to go to the La. *La* means pass in the Sherpa language, and *khola* means small river in Nepali. At moments like this, what I want to know is why they have to be so fucking far apart.

We did the first half of this climb yesterday afternoon,

but the challenge of reaching the top of the Lamjura La is still considerable. Sete, where we stayed last night, is approximately halfway up from the start in the village of Kinja. It's over 1800 vertical metres from the river through the village to the top of the pass, and most trekkers try and break it up somehow, in Sete, or maybe even Dagchu, but no matter what you try to do to soften the blow, you can't win. Bhandar to Sete wasn't exactly a walk in the park. In the morning, it took us four hours to do what is usually a three-hour, largely downhill section, and it was nothing but uphill after lunch. This came as no surprise, of course; the Lamjura La is at a higher elevation than Namche Bazaar, widely considered the threshold village for where altitude acclimatization protocols should begin. The La is even higher than all but nine *peaks* in the entire Canadian Rockies.

According to *Trekking in the Everest Region*, by Jamie McGuinness, a walker going to Namche from the trail-head at Jiri will climb almost the equivalent of the exact height of Mount Everest. Because the valleys are so deep, the walker will also descend an accumulated height similar to that of Mount Ama Dablam, which is why most trekkers fly to the village of Lukla. They don't have the will for all that walking, or the energy – or, perhaps most importantly, the time. It's going to take me about ten days to get to Namche, instead of two had I chosen to fly. The part of me struggling with the concept of patience and attention, that workaday, check-the-items-off-the-to-do-list side of me, still bristles at this.

The realities of today's undertaking go a long way toward further tamping down any goal-oriented impulse. I can't do anything about it now anyway. It would be nice to report a second wind at some point, where I settle in and find a rhythm, but that would be a lie. It's simply one foot after another, and I try not to think about how much farther it is to the top. I find myself picking a spot higher up the route, a rock, a tree or a bend in the trail, and aiming for that. Whatever it takes to keep going. By the end of the morning, the pattern is 30 or 40 metres, followed by a 30-second rest. When I let the rest run on to 45 seconds, I just want to stand in that spot forever.

The village of Goyem is split up along the hillside, and the upper settlement is all but deserted when we finally get there. Over the last few days, I've been jealous of the passengers in the helicopters and planes flying overhead as they make for the more reasonable trailhead at Lukla, but a fog has rolled in hard and the flights have stopped abruptly. It's very quiet – too quiet. I've let the boys get out ahead, and this place has started to give me the willies, but the unease carries with it a little shot of adrenalin too. My senses are on high alert in the spooky surroundings. There's not even somewhere to buy a Sprite or some cookies. Goyem appears deserted, but is not abandoned. Muddy paths have not grown over; buildings are not falling into disrepair. There is even wood smoke coming from one of the tea houses, but everything is shut up tight, like there's a storm coming, or a plague.

Perched on a roof nearby, a giant crow, with his insistent croaking, is the only thing breaking the smothering silence. I can't help but wonder what he's trying to tell me, but I'm too creeped out to stick around and find out.

We skitter away from Goyem, and it doesn't take long to reach Lamjura, a small guest house community located 20 minutes below the pass. It's cold up here. Peeling off my sweaty T-shirt, I find changing my base layer is not enough – I have to pull out my puffy camp jacket for the first time. We've just missed the French group, it seems, but the owner is still cleaning up the aftermath. Since there are only four of us, our lunch is served in the kitchen, where it's much warmer than in the dining room.

In the kitchen we encounter a familiar family scene: an older sibling takes care of a toddler as Mom and Pop cook and continue to clean up after the last group. The scene is punctuated with a little rural charm as a large chicken wanders around, pecking at errant morsels on the floor. The dim lighting seeping in through the kitchen door and small windows is further dimmed by smoke from the cooking fire. Being familiar with commercial kitchens, I'm amazed at the dishes that can be whipped up in such a basic arrangement, but I'll stick with my go-to lunch of Rara noodle soup and some cookies, or maybe a chocolate bar. There is no time to waste on something more elaborate, as it's already well past noon.

• • •

Rebecca Solnit, in the introduction to *Wanderlust*, her book about the history of walking, describes the act in the most basic form. "Muscles tense. One leg a pillar, holding the body upright between the earth and the sky. The other a pendulum, swinging from behind. Heel touches down. The whole weight of the body rolls forward onto the ball of the foot. The big toe pushes off, and the delicately balanced weight of the body shifts again. The legs reverse position. It starts with a step and then another step and then another that add up like taps on a drum to a rhythm, the rhythm of walking."

Rhythm. I need to find *my* rhythm.

Walking is simple, yet remarkably complex. We take it for granted, until injury or illness interferes with the proper execution of any of the parts that make up the whole. We learn to walk as toddlers and barely think of it after that, unless we get damaged. It becomes an automated movement the mind ignores unless there's a slip or a trip. Walking is one of the first complex skills we master, and I've relived that stage of the process for the second time again recently. Now I'm in adolescence, where I find out what my limitations are going to be going forward.

After all that climbing, the thought of finally travelling down after the La is exciting, but it's not easy. Relentless switchbacks combine with large steps, loose stones and a steep aspect to make for a challenging afternoon. It is not as energy-intensive as going up, but it is more difficult because a misstep would mean a nasty fall. Gravity may be in our favour, but it's pulling hard.

As has become habit, I am largely separate from the boys as we walk. Arjun and Ram are off somewhere, sitting and waiting as usual, and Norman is just out of sight ahead, or sometimes behind, engaged in his own private battle with the terrain. I can often hear the clink of his trekking poles on stone, and occasionally catch a glimpse of him through the forest, but generally we find our own space on the mountain. Only occasionally do we meet locals travelling in the opposite direction up the pass. With time to kill, and desperate to think about anything other than the task at hand, I wonder: Even without a solid rhythm, is walking like this worth all the effort?

We shun walking in our hyper-speed commuter existence, but the benefits that can be gained from engaging in a little self-propelled travel can be surprising. In *Born to Walk: The Transformative Power of a Pedestrian Act*, Dan Rubinstein digs through some of the studies on walking and finds a plethora of benefits that far surpasses what you might normally attribute to such a – well, you know – pedestrian act.

Hundreds, if not thousands, of studies of the topic have been done, and the results are pretty clear: walking improves overall physical health. The risk of obesity, heart disease, stroke and diabetes all decrease if walking is part of an individual's weekly routine. Walking also improves bone mass, strengthens and tones muscles and improves the range of motion in joints. It's all fairly obvious, on the face of it: if you move your ass, there's less chance anything attached to it will let you down. What's remarkable is how little you have to do.

One of the survey studies Rubinstein looked at (a meta-analysis that pulled together the data on the health and well-being of 460,000 people over an 11-year period on average) indicated that walking reduced the risk of cardiovascular events by 31 per cent and cut the risk of dying during the study by 32 per cent. The benefits applied to participants who walked as little as five and a half miles a week, at a pace as slow as two miles an hour. The average adult walks at a pace of three miles, or roughly five kilometres, an hour. Imagine if your employer offered a 30 per cent increase in salary for two hours of minimal effort squeezed into your routine every week. If you make the average Canadian wage (in 2014) of $49,000 a year, that translates to $14,700, or $283 a week.

Few of us would hesitate. But if it's just our health and well-being at stake – well, then we find it harder to do for some reason.

Having been something of an athlete in the not-too-distant past, I find most of this information intuitive; it's a fairly obvious part of the overall equation when physical activity has been such a central part of your everyday life. Now that I don't compete anymore, I move less often, with less intensity, and have the paunch that is appropriate for that change in lifestyle.

What caught my eye in Rubinstein's book, however, was how effective walking was in the treatment of troubles not so easily measured. Depression is a subject that is getting more and more attention of late. An illness with symptoms less obvious than those of our physical ailments, it has been misdiagnosed and under-reported for decades. We are a go-go-go society, vulnerable to the idea that "sucking it up and getting on with it" is the best course of action whenever there is a challenge in our path. This approach is a close cousin to "just hanging on here." And, to be fair, these techniques are effective in "getting things done." The former is more efficient than the latter perhaps, but we are the cogs in the wheel that drives modern society onward, and these are the tools many of us use to keep going. There is a price to pay for that attitude, and we are only beginning to acknowledge it. Heart attack and stroke and hypertension get all the press, while the granddaddy of all First World problems, depression, continues to erode the possibility of happiness.

For a long time now, I have felt something isn't quite right about the way we do things, but that attitude has been something of a pet project. A personal vendetta against industrialization, urbanization, overpopulation, crooked politics and poor environmental stewardship that I broke out at parties when I was feeling feisty or exasperated, but that I felt in the darker corners of my psyche in a form I now recognize as depression. I thought, *If the human race is so great and everything is going to be okay, then why does so much of this dumb shit keep happening over and over again?*

167

A feeling of hopelessness is a symptom of depression, and nothing can feel so hopeless as taking on the world's bigger socio-economic issues with nothing more than a big mouth and a vague sense of indignation. So I was surprised to learn from Rubinstein that in 2012 the World Health Organization estimated 350 million people suffer from depression, and that it is the leading cause of disability worldwide. The information made me feel better immediately, because I no longer felt so alone. Granted, the causes of depression are varied and complicated; not everybody who suffers depression would check the box "because I think the modern world is a shiny shithole" as one of the contributing causes, but it was somewhere to start, and there, a few pages later in Rubinstein's book, was a simple way to help ease the symptoms.

You guessed it: walking.

A study done in the 1990s by James Blumenthal at Duke University showed that physical activity, including brisk walking, eased the symptoms of major depression just as effectively as drug therapy – a finding the pharmaceutical companies don't want anyone spreading around, I'm sure. I never imagined it was as straightforward as that. If you walk around a little bit, chances are you'll feel better. Obviously, there are other factors involved as well, but what I found even more interesting were the studies linking walking and brain function, and how walking can, according to Rubinstein, "promote new links between different parts of the brain, and to stimulate the growth of neurons and their ability to transmit messages."

In essence, walking "helps our brains navigate the intellectual puzzles of daily life" – an observation reinforcing the idea that maybe walking could be the trigger that spurred the development of a bigger brain in our ancestors. Walking might very well be what made us human, and it might also be one of the keys to helping us feel human again as we try and navigate the modern world.

It's amazing that a lifetime of making things complicated can be unravelled so simply. Scrolling back up the page, I'm struck now by Solnit's description of the basics of walking as rhythm. A rhythm that starts in the physical realm, but manages to then connect mind and body, and the surrounding environment, in a way that is balanced and natural. That sounds about right, and it appears I'm just starting to get the hang of it again.

Eventually, we manage to get below the clouds sweeping over the pass, and the hill relents a little bit. Coming out of the forest and into the fields near Tragdobuk, we stop for pictures and water, and as we traverse along the slope past the village, the end of the day never seems to get any closer. After I estimate half an hour of walking left to go, Arjun corrects the hopeful approximation to about two hours. For a time, the trail even levels out and it's largely horizontal travel, a little elevation gain here, a slight drop there – but we're tired now, so the pace remains slow. We've reached that point where you don't want to stop for anything, you just want to be at your destination. But I've got to take a piss, so I call a halt beside the most inconspicuous section of trail I can find.

There isn't much cover here, but a bend in the trail obstructs the view in each direction. We haven't seen many people all afternoon, so peeing here should be a harmless crime. A misdemeanour of trail etiquette. A gauche move by an obnoxious tourist seen by no one but the birds and the wind – and, you know, the Buddhist monks. Not two seconds into full stream, five of them come loping around the corner, and it's something of a miracle I don't soak myself in the attempt to tuck in and regain my composure.

They are junior monks, in their mid-teens, headed back to the Serlo Monastery, just above Junbesi. The irony is, they are deeply apologetic for the intrusion. I am mortified, of course, and convinced I'll come back in the next life as a slug or a dung beetle for this transgression, but they insist on mumbling apologies as they pass. A few of them even giggle in that embarrassed-schoolboy kind of way. Feeling stupid, I let them get far up the trail before finishing my business – and, as luck would have it, the senior monks in charge of the group also need to get home.

Needless to say, they are far less amused by the display.

As the light fades, we manage to reach the final bluff before the trail descends steeply once again into Junbesi. The views are normally splendid, but it is now so overcast and dark that we can't see anything, so we just clomp along without even stopping at any of the viewpoints. Rhythm, not to mention decorum, has been elusive today, but we have made a solid effort. Arjun and Ram have gone off ahead to secure us rooms, and finishing the day by headlamp is a testament to our stubborn determination, if nothing else.

There's a transition coming that is proving elusive, one that ideally would have happened already, but it turns out I don't have much control over it. My body is going to decide when it has adjusted to this new lifestyle of walking, and no cajoling, begging or pleading is going to change that. Somewhere up the trail from here, I'm going to be loping along, thinking about other things, when it will hit me: *I feel good. I feel strong. I feel connected to what I'm doing. I am present in this.* I haven't quite reached that point. There have been moments, but the real transition will come when I stop being a clumsy walker and turn into a mindful trekker.

I look forward to it.

11.

The Lamjura La is a significant physical barrier. Once over it, you experience a sense of accomplishment and relief. Not only have you overcome a major hurdle on the route to Everest Base Camp; you are also entering Sherpa country.

Sherpa is not a job, it is an ethnic group, and the distinction has been convoluted by modern mythology. The Western conception of sherpas, small *s*, as high-altitude guides, lodge managers, local trail information experts and conveyors of back-breaking loads is largely geographical in origin. It stands to reason that if your home is among the tallest mountains in the world, then when outsiders begin to explore your backyard in search of glory and adventure, they will enlist your help in the endeavour. Being exceptional at the task is going to earn you a reputation, but the average porter in this region is just as likely to be Tamang – guides come from all over the country in search of work, and nonfamilial lodge employees are often Rai.

Sherpa, big *S*, are the descendants of migrants from Tibet who settled in what is now Nepal over 500 years ago. They were farmers and traders who have since added hospitality, food and beverage and, most notably, mountaineering to their collective résumé. The Solu-Khumbu is their homeland.

The Solu-Khumbu district is what most Westerners

who have never been to Nepal might recognize, perhaps not by name but certainly by reputation. Mother Goddess of the World to Sherpas and Tibetans, Mount Everest sits near the top of a popular valley in the district and draws the curious and intrepid alike with her undeniable power. After Kathmandu and the Annapurna region, it is the destination most often visited by foreigners, but after the airport at Lukla was established in 1964, the southern, or Solu, half of the district was destined to be a footnote for most. Khumbu gets all the attention. The airport was originally meant to improve freight transportation in the development of schools and hospitals for the people of the Khumbu Valley. Sir Edmund Hillary, through his charity, the Himalayan Trust, was instrumental in making the airport a reality, but inevitably it has transformed into a shuttle for tourists as much as a tool for moving supplies.

In his autobiography, *Nothing Venture, Nothing Win,* Hillary himself predicted the danger to local culture the airport might pose but also noted the Sherpa people were already being influenced by foreign climbing expeditions. They wanted better education and health care as part of their quest for a higher standard of living. Hillary committed himself to making it happen.

Like climbing, trekking in the Solu-Khumbu also began within a decade of Nepal opening its borders in the early 1950s, but it hardly took off as a destination in the beginning. The first group that were neither scientists nor mountaineers arrived in 1955, and in 1964 only 14 foreigners visited the region. The development of international tourism coincided with this slow transformation but was in its infancy back then as well, so even if the borders had been open prior to the '50s, it is unlikely hordes of people would have made their way here.

It wasn't until 1974 that the first lodge specifically built for trekkers opened in Namche Bazaar, at a time when approximately 3,000 intrepid souls made the journey annually. Tea house trekking has become the norm since then, and a broad range of accommodation and restaurant options is available from Jiri all the way up to Gorak Shep, the last small settlement on the trail before reaching Kala Patthar and Everest Base Camp. That said, the words *accommodation* and *restaurant* remain open to interpretation, especially if you're judging by Western standards.

Before the spread of modern tourism, the people who called this place home kept a strong code of hospitality toward visitors. These trails were trade routes and pathways leading to summer or winter grazing, and the travel was arduous. The earliest tea houses were just homes at the side of the trail where the owner served tea or some other form of refreshment. As demand grew, entrepreneurs added meals and rooms to the equation, but even today, few of the tea houses would be considered hotels in the Western sense of the word. Although *lodge* or *guest house* does strike me as more appropriate than *tea house* these days, Westerners might compare them to hostels.

The rooms are spartan, no question. Two simple wood-framed single beds pushed against each wall, a single shared nightstand or small table between, and perhaps a row of hooks to hang your sweaty clothes on – that's all you can expect. There are no closets, and the shared toilet (or infamous hole-in-the-floor squatty) is either right next door, so you can hear what everyone is doing in there, or 100 miles down a hallway with creaky floorboards so everyone will be duly alerted when you're up in the middle of the night for a pee. Before you reach Lukla, where pressboard flown in from Kathmandu becomes the norm, the walls can be nothing more than single layers of pine slats that don't always touch the ceiling or the floor. Once, I jammed a pair of socks into an abnormally large knothole to keep from being able to see into the next room. Earplugs help with the noise in the busier guest houses, but, of course, I forgot to pack mine.

These quirky details aside, the price is right. Competition, combined with a community-implemented plan to avoid the bartering common in other types of transactions in Nepal, has led to a set price for rooms in much of the Solu-Khumbu. Two hundred Nepali rupees (equivalent to about $2.50 Canadian) is very easy on the travel budget. Western-style hotels, with Western-style prices, have opened higher up the trail, but I can't imagine shelling out $150 for a room after getting used to paying a few dollars a day, even if it does give me my own private bathroom.

Surprisingly, some of the basic lodges higher up the trail are also among the best, because they are the newest, and the feedback from six decades of travellers has helped shape the visitor experience. Here below Lukla, things can be more rustic. A fraction of the trekkers who visit Nepal take the long way these days, so many of the guest houses are much as they have been for two or three decades.

• • •

Norman, Arjun and Ram are continuing on this morning. I admit, it was nice walking with them for a couple of days, both to share the experience and for extra motivation to continue in the more difficult moments, but it will be good to go it alone again for awhile. At breakfast, I thought about getting my gear together and tagging along, but the rush of inspiration died quickly. I'm sore everywhere; even my traps have been cramping up in protest of my pack. Norman is planning the Three Pass Trek and doesn't have much wiggle room – twenty-eight days seems like a long time, but it's a challenging itinerary if you attempt it from Jiri. I don't feel at all compelled to keep up the pace. I'll settle for my day of rest. If recent history is any indication, I'm sure it won't be the last.

My guidebook breaks the trail up into sections between the bigger villages and offers an estimated travel time in days. Between the smaller villages are shorter sections; one or two of these take up roughly three inches on my map. It doesn't look like much, but three inches has proven to be ambitious, the meagre distance on paper translating into a long hard day in the real world. I've pulled it off until now, but after coming in near dark in Sete and after dark in Junbesi, I can see that the routine is going to get tired fast. There needs to be a new math. Maybe two inches on the map, instead of three, is a more realistic approach. Maybe if I'm not sitting down and eating lunch by noon, then I shouldn't take on an additional section. It'll be easier to manage physically, and I won't find myself slogging into a village at dusk, desperate for a guest house.

It's settled. Mornings are for walking. Afternoons are for tea, exploring villages, naps and writing.

Junbesi is a charming lodge village and a common off-day. It's the largest Sherpa settlement below Lukla, with a number of rewarding side trips in the area, including Thubten Choling Monastery. All of the options, however, involve going up, either on the way or on the way back, and some excursions would take three or four hours round-trip. I should go to Serlo, at the very least, and apologize for my trailside indiscretion, but I'll probably settle for the simple five-minute stroll down to the village to visit the school, founded by the Himalayan Trust in 1964, and the local stupa (or *chorten* to the Sherpa), located a few steps beyond. Later this afternoon, that is. Maybe.

After the boys leave, the lodge gets very quiet. All I can hear is the clock ticking on the wall, the occasional plane passing overhead on the way to Lukla and a little girl chattering away in the kitchen with her mother. She's working on her English and the Nepali version of her ABCs in what I imagine is a homeschooling session. At a guess, she's still too young for regular classes. In the relative peace and quiet, this guest house reveals itself as a fine example of the hospitality method at work.

In one sense, this is very much a commercial operation, with a large kitchen and dining room where 25-plus people can be accommodated for lunch or dinner. At the same time, to get to the dining room from the kitchen you must pass through the central space at the heart of the building, which happens to be reception, the TV room, the general family area and, I'm thinking, even the communal family bedroom, judging by the bed tucked under the stairwell leading to the guest rooms upstairs.

This kind of set-up is not uncommon in the smaller operations. In Shivalaya, all five family members slept in one small room adjacent to the dining area. It was strangely intimate, as the three young children prepared for bed behind a simple curtain between rooms, darting out occasionally to brush their teeth in the kitchen or take care of some important kid business before finally succumbing to the realities of end of day. It was adorable, yet intrusive. I felt like I should excuse myself and go up to my room in order to let them have their private family time.

Having a hot shower and taking care of my feet, which have thrown up a number of blisters, pretty much eat up the rest of my morning. As the afternoon settles in, I move my lazy day out to the sunny patio. There isn't much to report, but trekkers do pass by the lodge now and again – a husband-and-wife duo here, a solo walker there. What is interesting is about half of them are travelling without a guide or porter. This surprises me. Number two on the Cicerone guide pre-trek checklist is "Don't trek alone, if you have no companion hire a guide." But I can understand the decision to forgo the suggestion.

For a large group, guides are essential – somebody has to keep everybody on track, motivated and fed – but for independent trekkers, it is more a matter of preference. Having a guide does remove much of the uncertainty of travelling in a foreign culture, especially for a first-time visitor, but it also tends to reduce the interaction with lodge families. Food orders, local inquiries and similar exchanges are largely mediated by the guide. Personal contact is decreased. On the other hand, at snack stops I can see the wheels turning as shopkeepers make up a price on the fly for what they think I will pay for a Fanta Orange or a package of Coconut Crunches. And we don't really need to discuss getting off course straight out of Jiri, do we?

But guides are assigned through agencies that have sold packages with ambitious itineraries, and they are expected to usher the clients along according to the plan. A guide works for the client, pointing out the route, sharing local information, finding guest houses and acting as an intermediary in any number of daily transactions along the way. They even help serve the meals when it's busy. But they are responsible to their employers, and that can cause friction, especially when things don't go exactly right.

Norman and Arjun had a minor dust-up late one

afternoon over whether or not it would be prudent to send Arjun and Ram ahead to secure us rooms. We're slow, and Sete only has a couple of lodges, so Norman wanted to make sure we had a place to sleep. Arjun was reluctant to leave us, worried we might get lost. It was not an unreasonable concern, but Norman was adamant and eventually won the day. I could tell Arjun was uncomfortable with the directive and the prospect of calling his boss if something did happen to us.

It all worked out, but farther up the trail, the stakes get considerably higher. Strict schedules and high altitude are a dangerous mix, and more than once I've seen a guide physically assist a client to the next village, all but carrying them to the door of a guest house at the end of the day. Without doubt, there is pressure from the clients to continue in potential dangerous situations – summit fever is not restricted to actual summit bids – and a guide is also expected to deliver the itinerary promised in the brochure. Inevitably, a helicopter arrives first thing the next morning when the fine line is crossed.

None of this is my concern at the moment. I've got a room. I've got tea. I don't need to figure out the trail today. Acclimatization calculations are still a week away. The biggest concern is what to have for dinner. Maybe I'll grab a menu and start thinking about that.

• • •

Walking the short distance into the village, I make sure to stay on the main trail instead of taking the slightly shorter route that cuts to the right. I do this because I want to pass on the left side of the local chorten. *Chorten* (in Tibetan), or *stupa* (in Hindi), means "heap," and both cultures use these structures as places of meditation and worship.

There are subtle differences in design between the two that I haven't quite figured out, but the website Buddhanet describes the basic structure of a chorten as "a square foundation symbolizing the earth, a dome symbolizing water, and thirteen tapering steps of enlightenment symbolizing the element of fire. These steps lead to a stylized parasol, the symbol of wind, which is topped in the ethereal sphere by the well-known 'twin-symbol' uniting sun and moon, which is the shimmering crown of the Chorten."

Because it is custom to perform a kora in a clockwise direction, if you walk by any structure with religious significance, be it a chorten, stupa, gompa, Mani wall or giant Mani stone, you should keep the structure to your right whenever possible, even if you're simply passing by. It's a respectful gesture, and I find it remarkably uplifting to adhere to the custom. Even when it takes me slightly off route – up an otherwise unnecessary set of steps, for instance, or the long way around an enormous carved and painted boulder. Or, as has happened twice already, uncomfortably close to a copse of stinging nettles.

At the intersection in the centre of town, there are two choices: go down past the chorten to the river and across the bridge along the main trail, or veer left and head up-valley to a trail not frequently used by tourists, especially those without a guide. I take a right, but only after a moment of hesitation. I will undoubtedly be jockeying for position with the French and a new group of Italians this way, in addition to all their porters, but I'm not quite ready to challenge my route-finding skills again so soon after the adventure on day one, and that weighs heavily in the decision.

Just above the chorten, a group of four young guys with full packs are coming up the trail, which at this time of the morning seems a little odd. It's too early in the day to be coming out from the next village, and they have the vaguely disoriented look I have been perfecting over the last few weeks. It's kind of amusing when it's not you, but I can't in good conscience just let them wander off in the wrong direction, so I stop and strike up a conversation.

"Hey guys, how's it going this morning?"

"Not bad," one of them answers. "And you?"

"I'm good. Thanks."

There are nods of agreement all around, and another one of them asks, "Say, you wouldn't happen to know if this is the right way, would you?"

The assumption is we're all headed toward the Khumbu.

"Nope, it's not."

"Do you know the way?"

"I do," I say with a little more self-assurance than I'm entitled to. And with that, I turn them around, and we walk together down to a small footbridge, cross the river and start up the trail on the far side. To my surprise, they are not friends who came together to Nepal, but four individual trekkers – a Dane, a Dutchman, a Spaniard and an American – who happened to fall into lockstep over the previous days. As the trail ascends, steeply at first, our group of five begins to spread out, and conversation gives way to quiet, and then to increasingly laboured breathing, at least on my part. The American hangs out at the back for a time, and suggests I tag along going forward, but these guys are way too fit for me. It would be a struggle to keep up, and they would get increasingly annoyed at having to wait around at every water break, so I pass on the offer.

After they disappear up the trail, it gets very quiet and I fall into a steady rhythm for the first time. It's not as steep here as at Deorali or the Lamjura, because the trail contours slightly to the right instead of leading straight up over yet another ridge. I find myself walking for a decidedly uphill but still comfortable stretch before stopping to catch my breath and enjoy the surrounding forest. Then I repeat the process over and over again. The trail here travels east, and early in the walk the sun has not yet risen over the generous bulk of the hill. When it finally does, its light is filtered through a mix of tall pine and rhododendron. This is a good thing, because, true to form, I am already sweating profusely under the effort.

The occasional burbling stream, with the river a faint roar far below, eventually gives way to some open, terraced fields and warm sunshine that coincides with a levelling out of the trail. For a glorious stretch, there are no ankle-turning stones and no giant stone steps, only a hard-packed dirt path and some tremendous views along the surrounding slopes. A haze persists in the distance, but I would submit that contour-walking at 2700 metres should be ranked as some of the best hiking in the world.

The first good view of Everest from this part of the trail comes as a bit of a surprise – and a letdown, if you are even aware of what you're looking at. It is not the highest peak on the horizon, and not especially notable on top of that. It would be quite easy to stare right at Mount Everest without realizing it. Coming around the corner near Sallung, the trail veers slightly north, leading toward the main Himalayan range. Don't get me wrong: the overall view is enough to get the adrenaline pumping. It's a giddy feeling to realize it won't be long until you are in among the really big mountains.

A couple of rounded, tree-covered hills sit in the foreground, followed by a line of harder, sharper peaks with a dusting of snow; it's hard to tell where, exactly, the trail passes through. The scene all but beckons you forward. And tucked off to the left, poking out from behind a continuous line of ridges and peaks, is Everest, a dark, awkwardly leaning triangle in the distance with, surprisingly, less snow cover than the mountains in the foreground. There is little to give away the fact that it is the highest mountain on the planet.

It's hard to imagine what the earliest climbing expeditions made of the view. The most famous of those early groups, of course, was the 1953 British Mount Everest expedition, which included a beekeeper from New Zealand named Edmund Hillary. Born in Auckland on July 20, 1919, Hillary was an accomplished climber but remained low in the pecking order within the team. Many in the group had been a part of the Everest reconnaissance mission in 1951, as well as a failed attempt on Cho Oyu in 1952, so the trail was somewhat familiar to them. I'm sure they felt the destination was now within reach as they gazed toward the mountain, but I wonder if anybody honestly thought, *We are finally going to succeed where others have failed.*

Just as interesting would be what the locals would have made of the party itself. The villages along this route would have been tiny and remote in the early 1950s, and there certainly would not have been the infrastructure to accommodate such an ambitious outing. There weren't even any hotels in Kathmandu at that time, let alone anywhere in the Middle Hills. Led by Colonel John Hunt, the expedition was massive. The complement of British climbers, which numbered 13, was accompanied by *Times* correspondent Jan Morris and 20 Sherpas, including Sirdar Tenzing Norgay. Moving all the gear and food, however, required two large groups of porters travelling a day apart. The first group had roughly 150 individuals, and the second had closer to 200. I have no idea how to check, but I bet that's more people passing through in a couple of days than would normally have come by in a month back then.

Perhaps most amazing of all is that anyone could have figured out that the fairly nondescript lump in the distance was the tallest mountain on the planet, because at the time Everest was "discovered," nobody could get anywhere near the mountain. Both Nepal and Tibet were closed to foreigners, so all the surveying had to be done from considerable distance, in less than ideal conditions.

The survey of India began in 1808, with the goal of mapping the entire subcontinent and confirming what had long been suspected: that the Himalaya was the tallest collection of mountains on Earth. Kanchenjunga was believed to be the highest mountain in the range at the time (it is actually third-highest in the world), and it wasn't until 1856 that a clever set of calculations revealed that a mountain on the border of Nepal and Tibet was higher. What was clever about the measurements was that they were calculated from survey points that ranged from 108 and 150 miles away, a distance that required taking into account the curvature of Earth, along with a number of atmospheric conditions that could easily skew the results. "Peak XV," the original designation for Everest, was revealed to be 29,002 feet high, a number remarkably close to the currently accepted height of 29,028 feet. It was an impressive accomplishment.

Packing up my camera before hoisting my pack onto my shoulders, I take one more long look at the sweeping vista before me before beginning the descent to the suspension bridge over the Beni Khola. After the river crossing, there's one more big pass, followed by a collection of shorter, lung-searing climbs in the days ahead. It won't be until halfway up the infamous Namche hill that I'll get a chance to see Everest again.

12.

THE TREKKER SUPERHIGHWAY

I have finally made friends with the trail, sort of.

The long ascents have become a little easier as I've grown into them, but the never-ending descents continue to be difficult and awkward. In the charming courtyard of the Beehive Lodge in Puiyan, a little oasis of comfort presents itself, and I can't help but revel in some cautious optimism. Phakding is only a day away, and a day after that is Namche Bazaar, the cultural and economic centre of the Khumbu. When you fly to Lukla, the goal is generally Everest Base Camp or a scramble up nearby Kala Patthar, and nothing else matters; but when you walk in from Jiri, the goal feels more like the Khumbu itself. I'm almost there, and Kathmandu seems like an eternity ago.

Beehive is built directly onto the slope. The main building (with kitchen and dining room), the separate snack shack and the 12 small rooms in their own outbuildings all surround five levels of terracing in what amounts to a large horseshoe. The whole set-up creates a charming multi-level enclosed courtyard, with the main trail passing just below a small flagstone patio area where you can drink tea, eat Crunchees and watch the world (such as it is) go by. This is not yet a high-traffic area, but watching people come and go is still an interesting late-afternoon diversion.

Over the last few days, I've been travelling at pace with

a German man and his guide and porter. I don't see them on the trail often but do notice him in villages and tea houses along the route. He's a giant of a man and therefore hard to miss, and, like Norman, has his camera out often enough to mark him as another fellow photo enthusiast. Unlike Norman, he has rebuffed any attempts at casual conversation to break up the day. From my patio table, I can see 150 metres back down the trail, and eventually they turn up, the guide and the porter flanking the big man from a single step behind. They're walking in tight formation even though the trail is clear. It's just a bit weird.

A few minutes later, a pack train of horses appears with no one driving it, just to continue the weird. The horses seem to know where they're going and shuffle along at a casual pace, stopping every so often to graze on stray clumps of grass, the taller ones eating the flowers hanging over the top of the trail from the lodge's patio and first terrace. Trailing behind the horses is a single cow, clearly intrigued by the slow procession. Like all those annoying younger siblings from childhood, she just wants to be included in whatever it is that's going on. After about ten minutes, a Nepali man with a long bamboo stick shows up to move the animals along with gentle swats to the backside.

Near dinnertime, two American ladies from Vermont arrive on the way down from the Khumbu with bad news. It's busy up high. So far, the lower part of the trail has been something of a surprise. Early on there were more groups than I was expecting, and then an influx of independent trekkers surged onto the scene after the village of Ringmo, where the trail from the increasingly popular roadhead at Phaplu intersects, but overall there have not been as many trekkers as I was expecting. There certainly have not been enough to fill the villages along the route. Every stop seems to have two or three more guest houses than is absolutely necessary.

The last few days have been especially quiet – a dozen or so independent trekkers in small groups yesterday, a few more than that the day before. I haven't been entangled with a big group in almost three days, and there were chunks of time where I had the entire trail to myself. It was lovely, but all that is about to change.

According to the Americans, it's bordering on chaos up high; and according to their guide, with only a few days left in the month, October is shaping up to break the record for visitation in Sagarmatha National Park. The park encompasses 24,400 hectares, 69 per cent of which is the barren rock, snow and ice found above 5000 metres, so it doesn't take all that many people to fill the lower parts of the valleys. Midway through tomorrow, at the trail junction in Cheplung, I will trade what I've come to call the Horseshit Expressway (there have been far more pack animals than humans this week) for the Trekker Superhighway, and I'm not sure I'm ready for the transition. Under the circumstances, it is entirely preferable to look backwards rather than worry about what's coming.

• • •

The newly devised two-inch plan got me from Junbesi to Ringmo by one in the afternoon, and since it was also past the midday-meal deadline, there was no pressure to rush lunch. The gang of four had been waiting for their meals for an hour at the biggest lodge at the corner, and the French group was just heading up the trail toward the Tragsindho La, the last big pass on this part of the trek.

Taking a peek inside to see what the holdup was, I noticed the French porters were still in the kitchen, eating *dal bhat*. It was an easy decision to go across the path, order a small pot of milk tea and contemplate lunch at my leisure in the warm sunshine bathing the front lawn.

The next day started with a stiff uphill walk, and it was another spot where a road link has been attempted from the south. There was even a tractor parked next to the *kani* (a stylized decorative entrance gate) marking the top of the pass. Up the pass, the new road was ugly – cleared and graded but not paved and already deteriorating badly in places as a result of the elements. The trail sections, on the other hand, were not an obscenity. They were charming and challenging: stone cobbles or stone steps, an ancient pathway maintained against erosion and only damaged where it intersected the modern atrocity.

Clearly, I continue to be conflicted by the progress of these roads. On the one hand, I appreciate them. Mountain roads are fun to ride on (or at least fun to ride down), but I am growing to dislike much of the change they bring. In the big picture, they improve and simplify trade farther up the valleys, in addition to making personal travel more efficient, but it only takes one look at the squalid roadside way stations from Kathmandu to Jiri to see that prosperity is a fickle thing.

I expect some of the hamlets and villages along the route were once charming little stops along the trail. Now vehicle traffic passes quickly and doesn't necessarily stop. Foot traffic would be compelled to take a break for tea and snacks, or lunch, or dinner and a room for the night, because the distance covered on an empty stomach is finite. Once the asphalt goes through, the dynamic changes. Villages at key distances for vehicle traffic get bigger quickly, but the intermediate stops along the way suffer. The improvements promised by road construction come with less celebrated consequences. Charming and tidy can turn into rough, dusty and threadbare. Lamosangu and Charikot are perfect examples of the rapid-growth phenomenon, and you would be hard-pressed to find a small village along the road that wasn't, at least superficially, worn down at the edges.

Here is an imagined scenario, but one that is still entirely plausible. What I bet has happened around here is that someone got it in their head to "improve" the situation in these remote communities by pushing roads every which way. Impassioned speeches were likely delivered at the municipal level, and money was promised or even set aside for the project after much debate and political manoeuvring. Work was even started, but then something got in the way, as it so often does. The political landscape changed perhaps. Or a different project was deemed more important. The money was diverted, or misplaced (wink, wink, nudge, nudge, say no more, say no more), and the work stopped unexpectedly. Who knows if these dirt roads will ever get finished, or how far up the trail they might someday go. The haphazard approach reinforces the appearance that this is often the way things happen in Nepal. Nobody ever seems to know what's going on or where the money has disappeared to. Corruption and incompetence at the government level has been exposed to the world by the earthquake, where an immediate challenge to the well-being of the populace was handled poorly. It was an example of failure of power in the face of crisis. These slapdash road projects are a symptom of slow-moving rot.

I suppose it's possible blacktop was never part of the

equation, and dirt roads are all that can be expected, but that only exhibits a lack of understanding of the terrain and conditions. An unsealed surface will erode much more quickly. Whatever the case, the obvious plan is to continue these projects. This is a shame for visitors coming in search of a more traditional trekking experience. It's human nature to take the fastest route. The path of least resistance is an unfortunate compulsion. As these roads progress, people will continue to go by bus or by car as far and as fast as they possibly can. Already, as a result of improvements to the highway to Phaplu, saying you've come from Jiri often draws a blank stare among other trekkers. The classic walking route has already begun to be forgotten. I fear if a road is put in all the way to Base Camp, people will simply drive up. You can do it on the north side of the mountain already. The inherent acclimatization issues aside, I wonder: Where is the fun in that? Where's the discovery? The challenge? The accomplishment?

For now the landscape is spared, and it remains a footpath from Tragsindho onward. It's beautiful country, and the scale of this place continually amazes me. After descending to the Dudh Kosi, the trail turns up-valley over a number of mountain spurs, and hard, sharp, snow-covered peaks become a more common sight. The views down through the Middle Hills are also stunning, especially near sunset, when the horizon through every gap to the south appears to melt away toward India. The villages are prosperous, the terraced farms are becoming and the tranquility is never disrupted by the sound of a truck engine or bus horn. It's quite wonderful.

• • •

THE KATHMANDU VALLEY, SMOG AND ALL.

A COLOURFUL CHARACTER AT PASHUPATINATH.

NOT A LOT OF ROOM FOR A BIKE.

MAKING DELIVERIES IN BHAKTAPUR.

PRAYER FLAGS NEAR NAMO BUDDHA.

THE KATHMANDU "EXPRESS."

THINKING ABOUT ABANDONING THE BIKE TOO.

THE VIEW FROM THE HOTEL ROOF IN CHARIKOT.

SECURING THE BIKE FOR THE LAST MILES TO JIRI.

WRECKING A ROOM IN SECONDS FLAT IN JIRI.

A RURAL SCENE ON THE WALK IN FROM JIRI.

THE EYES OF THE BUDDHA IN BHANDAR.

ENDLESS
STONE
STEPS.

BREAKFAST IN SETE.

BABY GOATS HUDDLED NEAR THE LAMJURA LA.

A YOUNG SHERPA BOY NEAR LUKLA.

ALL IN A DAY'S WORK.

ROOSTER
AND BOOTS
IN NAMCHE.

NAMCHE BAZAAR.

A YAK NEAR THAME.

THE BHOTE KOSI VALLEY.

HIMALAYAN TAHR NEAR PHORTSE TENGA.

AMA DABLAM FROM THE VILLAGE OF MONG.

HELLO MOON.

GOKYO VILLAGE.

THE BASE OF CHO OYU.

EVEREST AT DUSK.

THE STUPA IN DINGBOCHE.

CHO POLU.

A PORTER
NEAR
DUGHLA.

THE AUTHOR'S MOTHER AT THE MEMORIALS
TO FALLEN CLIMBERS.

MOTHER AND DAUGHTER IN LOBUCHE.

GORAK SHEP.

A SCULPTURE IN ROCK, SNOW AND ICE. MOUNT NUPTSE.

JOCEY,
BRIAN
AND DENA
WAITING
FOR THE
SUNSET.

AMA DABLAM FROM KALA PATTHAR.

SUNSET ON EVEREST.

A TENT AT EVEREST BASE CAMP.

THE AUTHOR AT EVEREST BASE CAMP.

END OF THE
SEASON IN
NAMCHE.

I have a soft spot in my heart for the village of Phakding; my first trekking memories are here. For people flying in from Kathmandu, it is a popular stopover on the first day after landing in Lukla in the late morning or early afternoon. Lukla sits at 2850 metres, which is a full 200 metres higher than Phakding, at 2640. The short day of walking and the reasonable precaution of sleeping as low as possible on the first night in the hills is what makes Phakding such a popular place to spend the night, and the complexion of the village bears that out. It is essentially one giant guest house. Dumping my gear at Shangri-La and stepping back out, I am eager to get reacquainted.

I'm not disappointed. It's chockablock, just as I remember. The "main street" – a well-maintained flagstone path passing right through town – is the only thing separating the Shangri-La patio from the one at Khumbu Travellers, and it's only a few steps to the front doors of Tashi Taki and Everest and Kala Patthar. Up and down the strip there are easily 20 guest houses, and almost all of them have patios set up out front. Many also have combination coffee-house-bakeries attached.

At the moment it is not exceptionally busy. One of the things you notice immediately after getting up past Lukla is how obviously this path has turned into an avenue of commerce – with the significant distinction that this road does not feature heavy vehicles moving goods at breakneck speeds, or a gigantic train rumbling through town on iron rails at all hours of the day and night. This is a thoroughfare of yak trains, donkeys, sturdy horses and porters moving goods, with tinkling bells on the animals and muted voices occasionally coming from the porters.

It is a remarkably soothing background track, now that the flights to Lukla have stopped for the day and most of the trekkers have checked in to the various guest houses. They are either having a rest in their rooms or refreshments in their dining rooms, and right about now the first-time visitors are probably wondering what they've gotten themselves into.

On my first visit, in 2007, the short walk here was my first experience in the trekking culture, and everything was new. The altitude wasn't immediately apparent, but I did feel slightly winded on any minor incline in the trail coming from Lukla – though that might have been from travelling with a full pack for the first time in years, or because I hadn't done much preparation prior to leaving Canada. Whatever the complication, I was still happy to be travelling mostly downhill. Blundering along in the wonder of being somewhere new and foreign to my experience, I tried to take in the details of that transition between bouts of long, laboured breathing. The prayer flags fluttering here and there, the occasional yak and the Mani walls and intricately carved and painted boulders along parts of the trail were all absorbing, and I wanted to take pictures of everything.

But nothing catches your attention on your first day in the hills more than the porters and the crazy things they carry. Three or four full sheets of plywood piled one on top of the other, for instance; or cases and cases of beer stacked five high in oversized wicker baskets. You name it and somebody is hauling it: plastic deck chairs piled seven or eight high, metal roofing material, gas-powered generators. After a couple of hours you realize that if you sit at the side of the trail for long enough, just about anything you can imagine will eventually walk by.

Almost as amazing as what the porters haul around is how they do it. Whereas most Westerners carry backpacks with shoulder and hip straps to distribute the load, most porters use the more traditional tumpline, a strap designed to be worn just above the forehead, near the hairline, that directs the weight of the load down the spine. In theory, leaning forward slightly helps spread that weight across the whole of the back, but my neck hurts just thinking about it.

The walking sticks some porters carry are a clever bit of engineering. Made from a sturdy piece of wood, the handle is oversized and centred over the shaft so the whole thing looks a bit like a capital *T*. Most are much shorter than the Western-style walking stick, which is essentially just a ski pole without the basket at the tip. I found the shortness a bit odd, until I watched a group of porters stop for a break and use their sticks to support the cargo so they didn't have to put down their unwieldy loads. It was quite ingenious.

In the end, you never get used to it: whether it's the sheer volume of the porter's load or a creative packing job, there is always something new to amaze. Once, on the Langtang trek, I fell in behind a porter carrying sacks of rice. He was middle-aged and only about five-foot-four and couldn't have weighed more than 130 pounds. At nearly six-foot-two, I could see clear over his head down the trail, but I couldn't walk faster than he could, and he was carrying 20-kilogram bags of rice – three of them, to be exact; a load roughly equal to his body weight. To top things off, he was wearing cheap flip-flops but never missed a step on the undulating trail. I did also note that his calves looked like they were made of solid iron. Never in my life have I been so impressed by someone's physical determination.

If you fly, your first day in these mountains can be memorable even before you set foot on solid ground. For the record, it's worth pointing out that the flight in to Lukla is not for the faint of heart. It is obviously faster, but there are moments when you will question the decision to skip the walk. There is a famous quote from a veteran pilot with Nepal Airlines that goes something like this: "We don't fly through clouds, because in Nepal the clouds have rocks in them." Very reassuring. I find the small planes unnerving enough on their own. They are often ageing and distressingly creaky, are especially vulnerable to turbulence and crosswinds and are always loud, so reading that quote didn't help ease my mind. The flight path to Lukla is basically the same as the walk in from Jiri, and when you fly through the passes, the ground comes up remarkably quickly at times as you're looking out a side window. The Lamjura La and Tragsindho La are near the upper range of the altitude an unpressurized airplane should travel at, so the pilots are forced to shoot the gaps.

As you turn up-valley, the approach to Lukla is something to behold. One quirky detail of these small planes is the open cockpit, which offers a measure of forward visibility to the passengers. Sit in the front of the plane and lean into the aisle, and you can get a surprisingly good look out the front windows. What's out there is what has been described as one of the world's most dangerous airports. That's a sensationalized, Internet-generated designation – no sane authority would compile such a list publicly – but Lukla would certainly rate on anyone's Top Five Most Interesting Airports, that's for sure. Moving closer at 275 kilometres per hour, it hardly seems a reasonable target, a tiny strip of asphalt jutting out along a ridge on the north side of the valley. From ten kilometres away, the runway appears impossibly small.

The runway appears impossibly small because it is

only 527 metres long and so can only accommodate helicopters and small planes, and one of its unique characteristics is the slope from front to back. Incoming aircraft travel uphill at a gradient of 11.7 per cent after touchdown, which helps slow the plane. And that's a good thing, because the airport backs right onto the lower ramparts of Gonglha. Any plane that doesn't stop in time will simply bash into the side of the mountain. To date, this has happened only once, when a Sita Air plane lost braking control upon landing. There were no casualties, but the nose of the plane was damaged.

Outgoing aircraft use the slope in exactly the opposite way: after stomping on the gas, the pilots use the gravity aid to build up enough momentum to take off. It is a exhilarating thing to watch, because within metres of the end of the runway, the earth drops away precipitously into the valley below. It's not a cliff, exactly, but planes do essentially "jump" into the sky. It looks scary as hell, but there has never been a fatal accident on takeoff.

• • •

Phakding is much like the other stops along my walking route so far, only bigger. At the upper end, there are kids kicking a ball on the flagstones, using buildings as sidelines to their narrow field of play. Mixed in among the guest houses are a few stand-alone shops, including a tailor creating name-brand knock-offs on the spot, a couple of small general stores and a handful of Western-styled bars with pool tables front and centre as a draw. Reggae Bar and Sherpa Liquid Bar appear to be the most prominent options.

Ducking into Liquid, I'm greeted by Bob Marley on the rather impressive sound system and a pair of Brits playing pool with their guide, as yaks and chickens and trekkers pass just feet away on the "street" outside. Every single famous expedition that has ever attempted Everest from the south side has passed by here. Hillary, Norgay, Messner and Apa Sherpa, Anker, Ang Rita, Morrow, Krakauer and Lhakpa Sherpa, among countless other notable summiteers, have all hauled their packs past this very spot. Some of them have done so many times over. It's like a walk of fame, except the honourees have left only dusty boot prints that have long since blown away.

Apart from the small British contingent, Liquid is empty, and the afternoon bartender appears bored out of her mind (been there, done that). It's clear this would be a great place for a piss up with friends. It absolutely reeks of dive-bar charm, and the comfy benches with traditional Nepali rugs and blankets practically swallow me whole as I settle into the back corner. Over a shockingly expensive local brew, I'm drawn in by the last 20 minutes of La Liga soccer action between Real Madrid and Athletic Bilbao via satellite, on a large flat-screen mounted on a huge rock taking up the near corner. Technically it's more mountain than rock, as the building was assembled with this idio-syncratic detail in mind. The room all but wraps around the hard, sloping intrusion, embracing it as if it were per-fectly natural to build three walls and leave the fourth to nature. Like I said, dive-bar charm, Nepali style.

Another small group of Brits arrives, drawn by the promise of more soccer on the big screen. In the end I'm too tired to wait for the English Premier League games to start, so I pay my bill and go out casually looking for dinner, knowing full well I will end up eating back at my guest house. Real ended up winning the La Liga game 2–1, I think. The power went out during added time.

PART THREE

THE HIMALAYA

13.

LIFE IN METROPOLIS

My body is on pack strike. It flat-out refuses to carry anything. Period. Full stop. My traps are sore, my knee is stiff and my back aches, to say nothing about my motivation. I can't even imagine going through the process of stuffing everything into the backpack, let alone hoisting it onto my shoulders. Nope. Not going to do it. Can't do it. Won't.

This is not that big a deal. I was planning on taking some time off in Namche anyway. A day off a day early here in Phakding isn't going to disrupt the greater workings of the universe. After a handful of very nice days settled into my new rhythm, I hope to see the local sights, absorb a bit of the local culture and then figure out a plan for the high country. There are four major valleys and countless combinations of pathways from which to explore the region above Namche, and I am intrigued by the possibilities. I'm also genuinely curious about my abilities and whether or not I'll be able to reach any of the walk-up peaks or cross any of the really high passes. I've managed to come this far, but further success is by no means guaranteed.

Out my window, the subtle sounds of the pathway below have begun for the day. The Nepali voices, the bells on the yaks as they plod along and the tourists speaking English or German or Japanese, which somehow sounds more harsh and obtrusive than the native language, will all be a fixture until sundown. I can also hear the river off in the distance, rushing by in its relentless fashion; and, far enough away as to not be totally annoying, a couple of dogs are yapping back and forth about something. A handful of crows and the occasional rooster round out the auditory extravaganza, and it's pretty clear I'm not going to be sleeping in this morning.

The Shangri-La Guest House has a dining room inside the main building and a separate sunroom-style café attached to the small outdoor patio next to the trail. I much prefer the café, where I secure the same table by the door that I had last night. As is common practice during trekking season, the same waiter is on shift again this morning. Ngawang is about 20 years old. He's studying graphic design in Kathmandu but is home for a month in order to help out his mom at the lodge. He's hard-working and good on the cappuccino machine and always has a smile on his face.

There's a small group from France at a nearby table and a handful of Americans at another, and they all get to talking with Ngawang about the lodge. I don't quite catch the family history of the place, but when renovations come up, Ngawang becomes excited and animated, and that gets my attention. He is the next generation of lodge owner, and like most people his age, he's got big plans. The cappuccino machine was his idea, and he's got a list of upgrades for this building and the overall operations. He cites what Westerners want and expect when they travel as strong motivation for the changes, but I just hope he doesn't mess around too much with the Nepali-style seating arrangement in this common room. Benches and tables around the outside and a woodstove in the centre – that's the set-up I've come to know and love on these treks.

Ngawang's enthusiasm reflects a certain inevitability. Things are changing. Fast. Memory is an unreliable record, and returning to the places we hold dear can be dangerous. We want to keep our more cherished and idealized memories alive. Returning can burst the bubble. The first time I came here, in 2007, I was remarkably self-absorbed. It was more than a vacation, because of the nature of trekking, but I was not prepared for the cultural shock that comes with being thrust into a completely new environment. A little time off the beaten track in Mexico was not adequate preparation for the widespread poverty and other harsh realities of the developing world. A couple of months in Japan can help you acclimatize to the idea of spending time in a place where you don't speak the language, but the culture of progress is as developed there as in any other Westernized country.

Despite the early challenges, I fell in love with Nepal. I enjoyed the perceived simplicity of life for the average Nepali and was genuinely curious about the plight and the character of the less advantaged. I was eager to understand why they often seemed happier than Westerners in their everyday lives and was compelled to explore their circumstances in greater detail. I didn't want anybody to be poor or to struggle unnecessarily but was intrigued by the idea that people could live a fulfilling life without a car or a big house full of things. But I didn't want to know too much about the painful challenges facing these individuals – that knowledge would ruin the elaborately constructed scene in my head. I wanted them to be different. I needed them to be different. I hoped they could mirror my ideal of a hard-working, egalitarian and compassionate society, if only because I had grown so disillusioned with my own culture.

Real hope for the future, I thought, existed most readily outside the quagmire of modern politics and economics, and so I came to Nepal with unrealistic expectations at first. I didn't want to be disappointed by local aspirations. I wanted the simple (if at times difficult) lifestyle to be enough for these hill people, as an example for us all. I didn't want them to covet TVs and ATMs and cellphones. I mythologized their lifestyle of farming and animal husbandry and taking care of the occasional tourist. I wanted their lives to be free of the burden of endless craving and stress and debt because I yearned for the same for myself.

John Hunt, the leader of the British expedition in 1953, described his experience of the Sherpa way of life: "To travel in the remote areas of Nepal today offers much more than superb mountain scenery. It provides an opportunity to step back in time and meet people who, like our ancestors centuries ago, lived free of complications, social, economic and political, which beset the developed countries. To the Nepal peasant, his life revolves around his homestead, his fields and, above all, his family and neighbours in the little village perched high on a Himalayan mountainside."

The sentiment is extraordinarily idealistic nowadays but appealing nonetheless. The longing for simple community is probably deeply embedded in our collective psyche, from the time when we were all hunter-gatherers and no tribe consisted of more than a couple of dozen individuals. That's how our early ancestors lived for centuries, perhaps even hundreds of centuries, through all the difficult changes that led to the development of modern humans and the spread of more complex social groups. We used to have community; now we have civilization. It is curious to me that Western explorers often found something different in their travels than what the modern world offered, but instead of changing themselves in any significant way, they brought change to the cultures they explored. Modern tourists still do very much the same thing.

Tom Hornbein, a member of the first American Everest expedition, wondered about the consequences of that kind of interaction in 1963, a decade after Hunt passed through here. In his book *Everest: The West Ridge*, he remarked on the symbiotic relationship the hill people had with their environment. He wrote that there was no real wilderness in these hills, at least as a Westerner would define it, but there was a balance between man and nature in the region that even one large expedition could affect. "Although we touched each place for only a day and then moved on, I wondered how many such passings could be made before the imprint would become indelible."

Here, as everywhere, there is desire for progress, for things, for status, for security – but it comes at a cost to traditional ways of living. For example, guest houses are going up all the time because that's where the money is. The Khumbu has one of the highest standards of living anywhere in Nepal, and the amenities offered are increasingly Western in their nature.

Serious climbing, especially on Everest, provides wages for porters and camp cooks and high-altitude guides, and trekking brings hard currency into the region for guides, porters, lodge owners and staff. Not to mention shop owners and vendors supplying building material, consumer goods and food. There is no natural resource extraction, big industry or manufacturing in this part of the country. Farming and animal husbandry remain at a small scale because of the extreme landscape. The soil quality is generally mediocre, and the growing seasons are comparatively short because of the altitude and climate, but the tourists do come in droves. People are the cash crop around here, and that creates obvious challenges.

At the Sagarmatha National Park entrance in the village of Jorsale, a tally of trekkers is kept on a chart pinned to the wall behind the information counter. In 1998, 20,014 trekkers entered the park, 5,987 of them in October, traditionally the peak month. The main climbing season is in the spring, but expeditions are not counted in that total anyway, and neither are guides and porters, so the actual number of people using the trails and lodges is much higher than indicated.

Visitation slumped during the worst of the Maoist uprising, to a low of 13,786 in 2002, but numbers have soared since, breaking the 30,000-trekker barrier in 2008 and hitting a peak of 37,124 in 2014. There was another understandable dip in the earthquake year, but where it goes from here is anybody's guess. The pressures this kind of tourism brings, not only to the culture but also to the very environment where the culture developed in the first place, are difficult to measure.

Dr. David Shlim, a pioneer in travel medicine research, once wrote, "I guess Khumbu cannot remain an anthropologic reserve for the benefit of future generations of Westerners. However, it feels as if it is making the transition to an Alpine-style mountain environment, with more creature comforts. I believe it can be enjoyed for a long time to come as this style progresses."

A new reality has arrived, no question about it. One can only pray it doesn't get completely out of hand.

• • •

"Namche, you magnificent beauty, you."

With the one-day pack strike comfortably behind me, I discover that the notorious Namche hill seems to have mellowed with age. The 600 abrupt vertical metres up to the village after entering Sagarmatha National Park are a slap in the face to the first-time visitor, but with a little experience you eventually get used to giant hills that never seem to end, and simply take them in stride. This hill hasn't gotten any easier over the years; I've just accepted it for what it is, and at the end of the slog is one of the little jewels of the world.

Namche Bazaar (Nauche to Sherpas, Nabouche to Tibetans) is built into a natural amphitheatre 3450 metres above sea level, and it is impossible to avoid marvelling at her improbable presence every time you stand on the slopes of the bowl and peer in. Having a quick look around to see if anyone has heard me talking out loud to a village, I find a quiet spot with a clear view. Panorama Lodge is somewhere on this side of town, near the police post and the school, but I've never come in on this particular trail midway up the bowl, so I have to get my bearings before continuing on.

The most striking physical feature here is the huge northeast face of Kongde. Even four kilometres away and across the Bhote Kosi Valley from town, it is still a presence. Kwonde to the Sherpa, the mountain itself is a collection of high points as opposed to a single distinct peak, and the face looks like a wall of rock and trees, capped at the top with snow and ice. It is a sight to behold, even in a land filled with breathtaking sights, but I have always been more intrigued by the Namche bowl itself.

Chosen as the key trading post and central administration centre of the Khumbu largely because of the spring that provides a reliable water supply, it has transformed over time from an obscure little village in a mysterious and distant land to a bustling town of a couple of thousand people. Photos from as late as 1968 indicate a handful of small homes, no lodges and a succession of terraced fields reminiscent of the smaller villages below Lukla. All that has changed dramatically, but the locale is still compelling.

Today is warm and sunny, and the town is pretty from this vantage point, but a unique added dimension is augmenting the scene: sound. Music from the shops, indistinct human voices and tinkling yak bells drift up from below, carried on a breeze that modulates in intensity as if on a whim. Playing on that breeze, the local crows are incredible acrobatic flyers, using the thermals as adeptly as any bird of prey. I can vividly recall being captivated by a similar scene while standing on the opposite side of the bowl years ago and thinking, *If there was ever an earthquake the entire town could slip into the valley below.*

Mercifully, this did not happen. Namche suffered some damage in 2015, but a short distance away, Khunde and Khumjung were both much harder hit by the Gorkha earthquake.

After taking a wrong turn (surprise, surprise) and ending up in the centre of town, I finally get my bearings with the help of a handy billboard map at a main trail junction. Panorama is not amid the central cluster of lodges. At the end of a long climb, the last thing you want to do is more ascending, but there you have it. It is the way in this country. Everything is up. Mohan Rai, my newest jack-of-all-trades front desk clerk, waiter and local information specialist, checks me in when I finally get to Panorama, and after unpacking and getting my boots off, I settle into the dining room for milk tea.

Sherap Jangbu Sherpa introduces himself. With his

wife, Lhakpa Dolma, he has operated Panorama since the early nineties. The lodge has grown from its humble beginnings and developed a reputation among climbers and serious-minded trekking groups. It would not be unusual to find a noteworthy alpinist, on the way to or from a climb, lounging in the dining room on a lazy afternoon, but today it's just Sherap and me.

"Did you have trouble finding the place?" he asks, after making sure I've got everything I need.

"Sort of. I knew it was on this side of Namche, but I don't know the paths well and ended up down in the main part of the village. There's a big sign and a map with all the guest houses there."

"And you look at it and think, *Panorama Lodge is up. Shit.*"

"That about sums it up, yes."

I know immediately I'm going to like this guy. Sherap is warm and friendly, with a keen sense of humour and a genuine interest in the experience his guests are having. He was born and raised in Namche and has spent much of his life welcoming foreigners to his rugged corner of the world as a guide and lodge owner.

"How was your walk?" he asks, in reference to the trip up from Phakding.

"It was good. Not too hard. I have a sore knee, but it wasn't much trouble today."

"The walking sticks help," Sherap points out astutely.

"Yes, especially on the downs. They give you a sense of security on the big steps."

"Little men, such big steps."

Okay, he's not funny, he's hilarious – and it's true. The mountain people from this region are many things: strong, resilient, determined. One thing they are not is especially tall, and one of the realities of rural life in this challenging landscape is that's the size of the rock, so that's the size of the step; deal with it. Many a time I have stood in awe in front of a particularly robust step, trying to catch my breath, and wondered how anyone ever moved the stone into place to begin with.

After chatting for a few more minutes, Sherap excuses himself to take care of lodge business, and I am left to my tea, my note taking and the realization that I am finally here. I landed in Kathmandu on September 18, and it's already October 30. The approach has been a trip in itself, and there's still a whole adventure ahead. Two hundred and seventy-five kilometres of accumulated biking and walking has been one heck of a warm-up. I'm tired, but I feel good. I'm content. I'm happy to have put in the effort, even though there have been some difficult moments. Now I have the entire month of November to wander around and explore. It's exciting, and as I take another sip of tea, it occurs to me that I am incredibly grateful for all of this.

• • •

True to Dr. Shlim's observations, Namche has grown into a compelling and alluring destination in itself. Even the seven years since my last visit have made a big difference. There are more lodges and more amenities, and I don't even know where to start my reintroduction. Sagarmatha National Park Headquarters is just up the hill behind Panorama, and a Sherpa museum is nearby; both offer valuable insight into the rich culture of the region. On the opposite side of town, the local gompa (as opposed to a monastery, where a collection of monks is present, not just a single custodian) is a great place to begin exploring the finer details of Buddhist practice. I have visited these points of interest in the past, and I look forward to doing it all over again, but a more practical consideration is at hand. I need cash.

"Downtown" is eerily quiet. Everyone is on an acclimatization hike or has headed out on the trails to villages farther up or is making their way down to Lukla. The ATMs here are new and notoriously fussy. The first one I come to is out of order, and the second has a line five people deep, with various friends and acquaintances hanging around looking perplexed. It's difficult to determine where the line starts, so I ask someone near the back.

"What's going on?"

"The bank machine is not working for everyone. Some cards work and some cards don't, but you're welcome to give it a try."

This makes me nervous. If I can't get any money out, I'm screwed. It used to be you had to carry all the rupees for your entire trip as you left Kathmandu. At a time when the only acceptable currency was in coin form, the British expedition that summited Everest in 1953 needed three porters just to carry the wages. Paper notes have made moving money easier, but in rural areas it's still important to have a stash. Credit card advances have been available for about a decade at banks in Lukla and Namche, but at exorbitant fees. I've budgeted well on the journey from the capital, but beyond this point, there is zero opportunity to get more money. Fingers crossed.

The cubbyhole containing the ATM is about as big as a phone booth, and the door doesn't close properly, but the machine does give me money. Naturally, I can only get 10,000 rupees (three or four days' worth of expenses) at a time for a 500-rupee fee, and I have to run the transaction repeatedly. There are three certainties in this life – death, taxes and banks extorting customers – but at least I was able to get some cash. As I walk away, a number of the people gathered around the ATM are still pondering their options. As far as I know, the next-nearest bank machine is in Lukla, a hard day's walk away.

I'm not yet motivated for an acclimatization hike, but the local cafés provide an easy and remarkably comfortable alternative to doing something productive. Sherpa Barista would not be out of place in downtown Manhattan, or even Seattle, for that matter. It's a tastefully decorated modern coffee shop and restaurant, and a caramel latte paired with the blueberry cheesecake is a decadent indulgence. The framed landscape posters by famed photographer and local activist Lhakpa Sonam Sherpa inspire you to climb high and gaze out over some breathtaking scenery. After peeling yourself away from the cheesecake, of course. There's pizza, a variety of sipping whiskeys and even wine by the glass, but alcohol is known to hinder acclimatization, so I refrain, choosing instead to search out another fabulous café for a second latte.

• • •

The next day, I have no hint of a headache, which is a relief. This is where people often begin to feel the effects of altitude, which is why Namche is a scheduled rest day on most itineraries. The walk in from Jiri has served me well, but I don't intend on pushing my luck.

A short, steep walk up from Panorama leads me to an important trail junction, where a large prayer wheel and gigantic Mani stone have attracted a lot of trekkers. The options are to go left and circle the Namche bowl to the helicopter pad at the other side of town, go right along the

main trail toward Tengboche or follow the popular acclimatization hike up and over the hill to the Hotel Everest
View. The hike starts off at a sharp angle, and every tourist in town has decided to do the roughly hour-long walk
right at this very moment. The steep slope allows a good
view upward at what looks like a wheezing, slow-motion
conga line struggling toward the first crest. No thanks.
Tengboche trail it is.

It's an easy 15-minute walk on the main trail to a corner
skirting the hill everyone is climbing, and from there one
of the world's most dramatic valleys presents itself. Ama
Dablam is the most striking mountain from this viewpoint. At 6812 metres, it is tall but doesn't quite reach
the extreme height of some of its near neighbours farther up-valley, notably Lhotse, at 8516 metres, and Mount
Everest, at 8848 metres. What it may lack in stature it
more than makes up for in aesthetic appeal.

From this angle, it peeks out over a lower shoulder on
Kangtega and so is not as prominent as if I had followed
everyone else up over the hill. From a perch a few metres
above the trail, the bottom half of the mountain is hidden from view, but the dramatic main spire is dazzling as it
stabs at the impossibly blue sky. A prominent icy shoulder
also hints at a large symmetrical bowl that can't quite be
seen from here. Ama Dablam means "mother's necklace,"
and part of the hanging glacier that helped give the mountain its name came down in an avalanche in 2006, but it is
still beautiful.

By comparison, Everest is not nearly as dramatic. Both
Ama Dablam and 6367-metre Tabuche Peak, on the opposite side of the view on the far left, appear to be higher,
and the Nuptse–Lhotse ridge dominates in the foreground. The ridge is impressive, filling the view ahead

with near-vertical stone and snow and ice. Everest peers out from behind, barely hinting at its massive bulk.

• • •

Mountaineers call the area near the tops of the bigger mountains the Death Zone, and for good reason. The amount of oxygen available at altitudes above 8000 metres is approximately one-third of what it is at sea level. We can adapt to altitudes above 3000 metres, but the human body is not designed to acclimatize much beyond the 6000-metre mark, at least not enough to spend any significant amount of time. I, of course, have absolutely no intention of going anywhere near that high, but I am interested in experiencing all that can be found a little lower down, and there is a price to pay for that. Travel here is not, and never will be, easy.

This is a dry climate after the monsoon retreats, but the very fine dust left on the trail is a mystery to me. I would expect it to be washed away during the rainy season, leaving the hard, compacted dirt underneath, yet here it is, year after year, at a uniform depth and consistency. The stubborn powder blows around on the wind, or is kicked up by trekkers' boots and passing yaks, and has the added bonus of being mixed with minute dung particles from said beasts of burden that have been trampled into the trail. The "Khumbu cough" is a common and charming upper respiratory illness caused by wind and dust and animal poop.

And while we're on the subject, this is rural Asia, with the inevitable personal intestinal difficulties that go along with it, but I will leave the details to your imagination.

A third inconvenience is that it gets chilly at night no matter how warm it was during the day. All other conditions being equal, air temperature decreases at a rate of 6.5 degrees Celsius for every kilometre of elevation gained, to a height of about 11 kilometres. A sunny day skews that measure, and if the wind isn't blowing it can be very pleasant even if you're wearing just a T-shirt, but the average nightly low in Namche in November is minus three degrees Celsius. Of all the improvements to creature comforts available with the introduction of modern gadgetry (Cappuccino machine? No problem. Flat screen TV? Sure. Full-sized chest freezer? All the big lodges have one.) what you can't seem to get hauled up here is proper insulation.

When I was a kid, my parents renovated the basement of our house and installed polystyrene insulation. Lightweight and moisture-resistant, it seems an amazing product. I can't help but feel there's an opportunity here for someone, because unless you're near a fire, most Himalayan guest houses are freezing at night. If I had any business acumen, I would capitalize on it myself, but there's a reason I'm a writer. I have no idea where to start with an idea like that.

The biggest challenges here come from altitude. Technically, Acute Mountain Sickness can occur at elevations as low as 2400 metres, but the effects are generally minor – symptoms resemble the flu or a hangover. As you go higher, however, the situation can become much more serious. In a curious quirk of biology, the combination of high altitude and lower air pressure can cause fluid to leak from the capillaries to surrounding tissue, most notably in the lungs and brain. High-Altitude Pulmonary Edema (HAPE) and High-Altitude Cerebral Edema (HACE) have serious and potentially fatal consequences. Avoiding them requires a sensible approach to acclimatization.

As the human body ascends into the atmosphere, the amount of oxygen available to feed the muscles and organs decreases. Optimal conditions for humans occur at sea level, where the air is a positively thick 21 per cent oxygen, with an average barometric pressure of 760 millimetres of mercury (mmHg). At 3658 metres, close to the height I am sitting at now, oxygen remains at 21 per cent, but the barometric pressure is only about 480 mmHg, which translates into 40 per cent fewer oxygen molecules available for consumption. The result is an increased breathing rate, even at rest, and it takes 24 to 72 hours for the body to get used to this oxygen deprivation.

While you're busy breathing hard, your body is also making subtle changes to how the internal equipment works. Pressure in pulmonary arteries is increased to force blood into portions of the lungs not used in normal breathing, and the body starts creating more red blood cells to carry oxygen. Production of a particular type of enzyme that helps the release of oxygen from hemoglobin to the body tissues is also increased. This is why I've just been hanging around for the last couple of days. My body is preparing itself to go higher, and from cruel experience, I understand the consequences of rushing that process. If the rarified air above 8000 metres is the Death Zone, I am perfectly happy calling the upper reaches of the trekking circuit above Namche Bazaar the Uncomfortable Zone, and the plan is to spend a month roaming around in all this beautiful discomfort, once I develop the appropriate number of red blood cells for the task.

That's what I keep telling myself, anyway. The lattes, pizza and cheesecake do make it easier to live with the decision to spend a couple of extra days here. Come to think of it, it probably wouldn't be any effort at all getting too comfortable in all this comfort.

14.

RAKSI AND *DAL BHAT*

It might be time to accept a cold, hard fact. I should never be allowed out of the house, let alone out of the country, unsupervised. Chances are I'm going to get lost – in the backstreets of Kathmandu, on the road to a temple or a shrine or along the trail to a relatively easy-to-locate village. When I do manage to keep from going astray, it's entirely possible I'll settle in at the wrong location and not even realize it. What I mean by this will become abundantly clear soon enough.

The Bhote Kosi Valley is an afterthought for most tourists. The Khumbu Valley is the main draw in this region. Kala Patthar, the Khumbu Glacier and Everest Base Camp attract people from all over the world. Roughly parallel to that, the Gokyo Valley has famous alpine lakes, tremendous views of Cho Oyu standing at the head of the valley, and Gokyo Ri, a challenging 5350-metre walk up to arguably the best view of Mount Everest available to the casual trekker. Even the Imja Khola Valley is acclaimed. Imjatse, also know as Island Peak, is one of a handful of trekking peaks where an expensive climbing permit is not required. It sits just up past the village of Chukhung.

The Bhote Kosi is obscure by comparison. Off the main trekking route that passes through Kyangjuma before continuing on to the aforementioned valleys, it receives little traffic other than visitors using the village of Thame as an acclimatizing day hike, or those attempting the Three Pass Trek. Historically, however, it is key to the development and spread of Sherpa culture in Nepal. *Sherpa* means "eastern people" in Tibetan, and, approximately 500 years ago, the first settlers to these valleys came from the Kham region over what is now the northern border of Nepal. They originally crossed the Himalaya slightly farther west but soon began using the Nangpa La, at the head of the Bhote Kosi Valley, as the preferred route. A vital path for migration, and then trade, in recent decades it has also served as an escape route for political refugees fleeing Chinese occupation. I would like to experience it.

Leaving Panorama, I've got to cross the village and head out past the helicopter pad that can be seen from the dining room windows at the lodge. I do want to avoid going down through the centre of town, because that would require going up again needlessly on the other side. It's a lovely walk, first around the Namche bowl, above most of the other lodges, and then along a nice contouring trail through a mixed pine and rhododendron forest. There are no horrendous uphill sections and no horrendous downs either. Stone steps are confined to a few brief sections.

A couple of traditional Sherpa villages dot the route, notable for not simply being a string of guest houses, and on the far side of the river, a small five-to-ten home settlement is becoming, with yaks grazing in small stone-walled pastures. Passing an elderly Nepali man in traditional dress on a deserted part of the trail is like stepping back in time, and it isn't long before I come around a corner to see Thame perched on the hillside. Almost close enough to touch, but still 10 or 15 minutes away.

It has been a couple of hours of pleasant walking, but

this still feels too quick. Normally, I underestimate the distance and challenge involved in any given morning walk, although cycling from Kathmandu to Dhulikhel was less demanding than I had anticipated. It appears today is similarly blessed. I'm not going to complain.

Heading into the village, the trail begins to climb, and it doesn't take long to pass right through. This is the most vertical part of the day, and there are plenty of stone steps now. Although Sherap recommended a guest house, I have missed it in my sweating and cursing against the slope. Having reached the monastery at the top, I have no choice but to turn around or continue on to the next village. On the way back down, I still can't find the guest house and settle for Mount Everest Camp 2 Restaurant and Bar because I don't want to go farther only to come up again, and because it has a charming little stone patio with three tables situated in the sunshine.

Sitting a table over from a couple who are just finishing up their lunch, I can't help but notice that the proprietress looks every bit the Sherpani chic part. Female Sherpas are sometimes referred to as Sherpani, and they have a distinctive style of traditional attire that continues in this contemporary era, but there is a modern twist. She's decked out in a customary thick woolen dress called a *thongkok*, a colourful striped apron and light wool vest over a low-profile, Western-style puffy jacket. This I like. It's a functional blend of cultures incorporating the practical and the traditional. Many of the new-to-the-job porters, the young guys trying to make a name for themselves on the walk in from Jiri, wear jeans and modern trainers. They look like they might be going to the mall, except for the enormous loads they're carrying, of course. It doesn't seem right.

On the other hand, Buddhist monks in traditional robes and modern trainers seem perfectly normal to me. Kinda cool, even, so what do I know.

After my tea arrives, the sun slowly drifts past its apex and becomes increasingly harsh. Perched on the northeast slope, the village is now a direct target as the sun heads west-southwest. The reflection off the white pages of my notebook is blinding, and Kongde positively towers above across the narrow valley. The foliage on that opposite slope has an interesting silvery sheen to it. A progression of clouds form and are subsequently blow apart across the peaks.

Here in the small courtyard, Camp 2 appears to be a one-woman show. The proprietress takes the orders before disappearing into the gloomy interior of the building to do the cooking, and then it's her again, delivering the food and beverages a few minutes later. Fully sated by my veggie fried noodles with egg and cheese, and happy to be idle in the sunshine, I begin to get the odd sensation something isn't quite right. An inquiry about a room draws an odd, mildly surprised reaction, and I am led around the side of the building to a padlocked door leading to a dark hallway under the dining room. The hall leads to a pair of guest rooms to the left and basement storage at the end. The whole area is a bit like a dungeon, with no windows and a musty unused air about it, but the room is clean and the electric lighting is good, so I shrug it off and assume I must have just chosen an unpopular lodge.

Back out on the patio, the first couple has gone down the trail toward Namche, and a new couple, in their mid-60s, at a guess, join me. Clearly, they are heading up; they quickly order lunch and show no indication of stopping over. This is also odd. Carrying on seems ambitious to me. The Bhote Kosi Valley becomes increasingly dry and desolate beyond Thame. The villages get fewer and farther apart, so it's best to explore the area fully rested, but this is not my problem. I'm content and comfortable. It's been my kind of trekking day, out at the crack of 9:30 and done just after noon, with a lazy afternoon of idle observation and casual relaxation ahead. As I open my map and guidebook in order to figure out tomorrow's itinerary, it all seems too easy, and that's when it finally dawns on me: this is Thamo, not Thame.

There are a number of explanations for this latest confusion. The first, and most obvious, is that I should never be let out of the house without adult supervision. But I am not entirely to blame. In my guidebook, Thame is also known as Thami, and on my map, Thamo is marked on the opposite bank of the river. Having not consulted the map all morning, I was easily lured into a premature sense of accomplishment, especially after reaching the monastery at the top of the village. The monastery is new and unlikely to be included in any guide or map. And now that I've finally pieced it all together, I'm already unpacked, my boots are off and lunch is tucked away in my belly. The only reasonable course of action is to go out and see what Thamo has to offer. At least I'll get to see what a sleepy little Sherpa village off the main tourist trail is like.

As I walk back up toward the monastery, the sound of the river below is a persistent companion, and traffic consists of the very occasional trekker passing by. I go up and down the trail a couple of times, taking short breaks for pictures and notes, and settle on the best spot for both near a large Mani stone plunked right in the middle of the trail, almost in the dead centre of the village. The valley is relatively tight here, and as a result my spot is cast in shade by 3:30 in the afternoon. The temperature begins to drop immediately, but the sun will still be shining on the mountaintops down-valley for about two hours.

Waiting for the light to change, for want of anything better to do, is an exercise in tiny tasks and attention to detail. Living in the now consists of short little walkabouts up or down the trail in order to get a fresh angle on a particular peak, and watching the growing cloud cover play peekaboo with the mountains in a constantly changing tableau. Sometimes I get a good shot and sometimes not, but it's cool, I've got time until dinner. As my attention and camera are drawn up by a particularly interesting formation over a nearby summit, the sound of a small group coming down the trail enters my universe. There's no reason to be distracted by this. There are no bells and so no yaks or horses to be wary of. It isn't until one of the group asks a question that I'm even consciously aware of their presence.

Whoops.

"Hey, are you from Canmore?"

I'm 11,000 kilometres from home, so this does manage to get my full attention. I'm not even in the biggest obscure village around here. I'm in an obscure obscure village. It's absurd. Spinning around, I recognize one of the three young faces immediately. He's a kid I know from when I helped coach the high school soccer team back home, but it's been a few years. I don't recognize the other two, but it turns out they're all classmates.

"Yeah, I am. Spencer, right?"

"Yeah. Jamey?"

"That's right. What are you guys doing here?"

This is a dumb question; clearly they're trekking. What I meant to ask is where are they coming from: it's late in the day to be passing through Thamo on the way down.

"We were in Gokyo this morning. We got over the pass and made it to Thame and figured we'd push on to Namche."

This is an impressive feat. The Renjo La sits at 5417 metres, and, together with the Cho La and Kongma La, is part of the increasingly popular Three Pass Trek. Wisely, the boys have chosen to do the circuit counterclockwise, so they were well acclimatized before attempting the Kongma La and are now incredibly fit. It's 28 kilometres from Gokyo to Namche via this route, and my guidebook suggests at least six days for the unacclimatized going from Namche to Gokyo. The western slope of the Renjo La is particularly daunting, 1135 metres from the village of Marlung to the top. They've come down it, but still.

"Wow, that's hardcore," is about all I can manage. I'm blown away by their effort, considering how pokey I've been in comparison.

"Yeah, we're pretty tired, but we're psyched for showers and beer. Any idea how much farther it is?"

"At the pace you're going? An hour, maybe an hour and a half."

"Great. Thanks."

And with that the three of them disappear down the trail at a pace I wouldn't be able to match first thing in the morning. But impressive and surprising are not at all unusual around here. On my second night at Panorama, Sherap sat me next to a Canadian couple at dinner, figuring we might have plenty to talk about. Bryce and Sunny are climbers, here to make an attempt on Cholatse. It's Bryce's ninth visit to Nepal and Sunny's sixth. Our mutual obsession is indeed a fertile talking point, as is the fact we share the same adopted hometown of Canmore. For over five years we've lived in close proximity and have only managed to cross paths here in the Khumbu.

Later the next afternoon, a rising star in the climbing world checked in at Panorama and had tea with friends a little farther down the table from where I was sitting. Pasang Lhamu Sherpa Akita was voted *National Geographic*'s People's Choice Adventurer of the Year in early 2016, and her list of accomplishments is impressive. The first female mountaineering instructor in Nepal, she was born in Khumjung, grew up in Lukla and has been a tireless advocate for her people. She raised money and delivered supplies in the aftermath of the 2015 earthquakes, and this led to an ongoing commitment to the less advantaged across the country, which has all but overshadowed her notable ascents on Everest, Ama Dablam and K2.

I only mention any of this because about an hour ago I saw her once again. She walked past with her small group on the way to Thame, and my only thought was, "I bet she knows exactly where she is."

• • •

I live with an impossible dream constantly bouncing around in my head. For my whole life, I've had an overwhelming urge to find the place where I feel at home. The trouble is, I have a wandering spirit, so that place is constantly shifting in my imagination. Despite my general cynicism, I believe the planet is a beautiful place, and where we have slipped off course is where we have tried too hard to make the world. We try to build it and shaped it to the latest whim of convenience and comfort, and often lose our way. In his book *The Lost Continent*, Bill Bryson went searching for Amalgam, a town described on the dust jacket of the book as "the kind of trim and sunny place where the films of his youth were set."

It was an impossible objective but well worth pursuing, and so I persist in my own comparable quest. While I may be searching for a perfect I'll never find, I'll gladly take interesting and engaging in the interim. But it is remarkable how often I get close to my goal.

After the sun descends deeper behind the mountains, the foot traffic peters out completely and Thamo presents as peaceful and near perfect. The only visible activity in the growing gloom is a stooped and aged Sherpa woman watching over a toddler in the yard of a nearby house, and a yak out on his own on a late-afternoon stroll through the village. As the temperature continues to drop, smoke from a few chimneys begins to appear, but otherwise the fifty-odd small buildings that make up Thamo show no sign of activity. The sunset light show I was hoping for on Thamserku has not materialized. As is common at this time of year, clouds have slowly moved up the valleys as late afternoon progressed. Just as the colours begin to get interesting on all the rock and snow and ice higher up, the views disappear completely. So I make my way back to the lodge for dinner without getting the shot I was hoping for.

It appears I will be the only overnight guest at Camp 2, and possibly even in the whole village, and as a consequence I receive tremendous service. Without a paying guest, the dining room stove would probably not be lit this evening, and I could easily do without, but my Sherpani hostess goes the extra mile and starts a fire. At first the room fills with smoke, but after a few minutes, with the windows and door propped open, the fire establishes itself and the smoke dissipates. After a slow start, the small stove becomes remarkably effective at beating back the evening chill, and my hostess insists I sit close for warmth. She plies me with tea and makes sure I have enough water, and eventually serves a very good *dal bhat*, with the customary generous second helping.

After a time, a neighbour drops by to share the local gossip and watch a bit of TV. Televisions are comparatively new and increasingly common in the Khumbu region. I can only recall seeing a single TV on my first two visits, a small tube-type version in a guest house in Namche, but now that flat screen and satellite technologies have advanced, screens are popping up, usually in dining room corners. Viewership is not yet as dedicated as in the West, but the contraption is catching on.

Tonight it's a Nepali version of CNN, followed by coverage of a weird political reception in Kathmandu for the president of India. Broadcast live, CSPAN-style. It's about as exciting as watching paint dry, and for some reason the proceedings are being translated to English. In true bureaucratic form, the monotone droning sounds like nothing more than glad-handing, with a little arse-kissing mixed in, as opposed to a serious attempt at creating effective policy between nations. It occurs to me in passing that I should try and get a job in politics. It doesn't appear that you ever have to *do* anything except prattle on nonsensically. As long as the occasional platitude is mixed into the talking points, everyone pretends to be happy with the outcome. It's quite easy to lose interest in this broadcast and get back to my notes and my maps and my daydreaming, which is probably a good thing.

In his book *The Age of Missing Information*, written pre-Internet, Bill McKibben examines the effect of television on our daily lives. He tries to figure out why the flood of information coming right to us in the comfort of our own homes might actually be making us less aware of (or at least unconcerned about) the outside world that exists just beyond everyone's front door. It is a thought-provoking exploration of the tube and our strange love affair with it.

McKibben references a study by Robert Kubey and Mihaly Cziksentmihalyi that tried to identify the reasons we watch TV in the first place, and the results are interesting for anyone who feels that maybe their life lacks a little in the get-up-and-go department. The idea that TV has an addictive quality has been around for almost as long as the first commercial broadcasts, but Kubey and Cziksentmihalyi found that this addiction is no rush. Quite the contrary: they found TV has a sedating quality, and that we seek it out in order to wallow in that sedation. The study even suggests, "watching it actually makes us feel more passive, bored, irritable, sad, and lonely." Instead of being a portal to learning or an important cultural record, as it is sometimes championed, television is a tranquilizer that we use "to even things out, to blot out unpleasantness, to dilute confusion, distress, unhappiness, loneliness."

Stephen King, in his memoir of the craft called *On Writing*, has some ideas about the value of television and the effect it can have on aspiring writers. King notes that he was among the last of the American novelists who learned to read and write before "they learned to eat a daily helping of video bullshit." King doesn't flat-out say television is bad, but he insinuates that if you have higher aspirations than just sitting around watching it, you might do well to "strip your television's electric plug-wire, wrap a spike around it, then stick it back into the wall. See what blows, and how far." The advice isn't just for writers, obviously. We could all do with less video stimulation in our lives. Unfortunately, I love television documentaries, but at least the good ones are informative, insightful and inspiring. The problem is, I'm also addicted to television dramas.

I find the writing, the acting and the overall slick production irresistible. A well-executed program is an exciting and thoughtful story played out in less than an hour, and the beauty of it is that I don't have to risk anything to take part, except my time, of course. I'm not going to get shot or stabbed or put in jail. I don't have to worry or risk injury or deal with any of the messy consequences of all that conflict. I just have to sit there. And therein lies the problem. I just sit there, for hours, until my body starts to melt into my easy chair and I begin to feel lobotomized.

And now that I think about it, my other big vice, booze, is a lot like that too. It's a shortcut to an altered state. Why not skip the effort and risk of dealing with the challenges of life and get right to the insight and pleasure and inspiration. Or just dull the pain. Why not have a couple of beers and get to your destination in 45 minutes, instead of the days or months or years of patient and determined effort that real insight sometimes takes? And if a couple of beers are good, then a half dozen must be great. Most of us have done it at least once, and some of us are prone to repeated attempts at proving the multi-drink theory, but even that is not as bad as the "a couple here and a couple there" that turns into a few all the time, because then it's a habit. Then you might as well be home watching TV.

A few more locals drop by to chat and watch the idiot box. I think it might be the cops from the police post across the "street." I noticed them earlier as I set out on my walk. A crime wave is surely not under way in this valley, because they looked awfully bored. Surfing the channels on offer now, they spend a lot of time on bad Indian music videos and WWE's *Monday Night Raw*. I've been over-stimulated and desensitized by the medium for going on 40 years, but it is interesting to be in a place where the technology is only now getting widespread attention. I've been daydreaming about *raksi* and *dal bhat* in a tiny village at the edge of the known world. Tonight the *dal bhat* is some of the best I've ever had, but instead of *raksi* by the fire and stories of derring-do in the mountains, I get professional wrestling on TV.

Modern Nepal is nothing if not interesting.

15.

THE OTHER BASE CAMP

Above Thame, a difficult landscape grows increasingly harsh. As the altitude inches ever upward, the wind becomes a more noticeable and persistent force, and vegetation grows increasingly hardy and sparse.

I got to Thame yesterday, which was easy enough after covering the equivalent of more than half that distance, from Namche to Thamo, the day before, and the walk up the hillside spur to the monastery in the afternoon was an excellent acclimatization hike. The monastery was founded over 300 years ago. Nestled high above the village, it is a collection of stone buildings cut and pasted and balanced into the surrounding rock. Each May, the springtime Mani Rimdu festival is held at Thame gompa and, along with the fall Mani Rimdu in Tengboche, is among the most important festivals for the Sherpa people.

This morning I've scaled the hillside spur once again, but instead of following the ridge up to the monastery, I've descended the other side to Thame Teng, a sister village to Thame proper. Almost immediately the surroundings appear drier and windier. A few kilometres along the left bank of the river, even the occasional small juniper tree has trouble maintaining purchase, and before long a sketchy part of the trail forces all travellers across a slide path with huge boulders dangling precariously overhead. The lower part of the valley, nearer to Namche, was steep and deep, with the mountains towering above, but gradually, as the landscape begins to dry out to stone and dirt and scrub, it opens up slightly. The right side of the valley continues to provide a formidable barrier, but it is becoming increasingly clear with every step I take that the Nangpa La and Tibetan Plateau just beyond are growing ever closer. The pass is still much too distant to see – two to three more days' walk, at a guess – but I can feel its pull.

Nine years ago, I stood on the far side of the historic pass at the head of this valley, not entirely sure what I was looking at. Over the border in Tibet, approximately 50 kilometres directly north of here, is the town of Tingri. The Friendship Highway between Lhasa and Kathmandu passes through the town, which is also one of the overnight stops on the week-long jeep tour between cities. Gazing wistfully in the direction of the Nangpa La from the top of a small hill at the edge of town, I imagined walking the pass one day, and then abruptly forgot about the plan for nearly a decade.

It is interesting that, even in the politically charged climate that surrounds a sensitive border, Sherpas from as far down as Lukla can cross the Nangpa La to Tingri with nothing more than local documentation, and Tibetans can descend as far as Namche. But cross-border transactions between historical trading partners is a far cry from freedom to travel, and merchants and everyday citizens alike understand the consequences of violating the rules. In 2006, 75 political refugees from Tibet were shot at by Chinese soldiers while trying to make an illegal crossing of the border in deep snow. Seventeen-year-old Buddhist nun Kelsang Namtso was killed, and a number of others were injured. Forty-two members of the group did escape to Nepal and eventually made it to Dharamsala, India, where the Dalai Lama's Tibetan Government in Exile continues to lobby for Tibetan rights and freedoms. Seventeen people from the party remain unaccounted for, absorbed into the Chinese penal system and not heard from since.

Needless to say, it is illegal, not to mention dangerous, for Westerners to make the trip without passports, proper paperwork and a Chinese government-appointed minder. Political considerations have no place in inspiration and curiosity, however, and I found the allure of the journey nearly overwhelming, despite the tragic events that had occurred only a year before. I was being pulled toward Nepal not by the road that eventually descends the Sun Kosi drainage to the west of Tingri but by the centuries-old footpath that links the Khumbu with its ancestral roots. In retrospect, it seems odd that my imagination was drawn so strongly not to the mountains on display from the viewpoint but to the passes that lead off of the plateau.

Everest, roughly 40 kilometres to the southeast of Tingri, was just a large nub poking out above an extensive ridge in the foreground. Cho Oyu, while undoubtedly more robust due to its relative proximity, was also comparatively subdued. The Tibetan Plateau is both high and vast. One thousand kilometres wide by 2500 kilometres long, it contains most of the Tibetan Autonomous Region, and its average height is more than 4500 metres. Subsequently, the snow-capped peaks that make up the border are not nearly as imposing as they appear from similar distances in Nepal. They are pretty, yes, but they almost ease up from the high, dry landscape brushing their flanks. The deep valleys and tight canyons that accompany the very same mountains on the opposite side are not a common feature in Tibet.

Picking my way along sections of trail cut by countless yaks over untold decades, I've strongly renewed my interest in this valley, but in the end I only venture as far up as the village of Marlung, near where the trail splits on the way to the Renjo La. From what I have read, there are not many facilities for trekkers beyond Marlung in the direction of the Nangpa La, and I don't have the proper gear for camping. I'm also not yet acclimatized for such an ambitious adventure; the pass does sit at just above 5800 metres, after all. So, instead, I have lunch and return to Thame in the afternoon, passing a handful of yak trains heading toward the pass.

It's a surprisingly bittersweet return to Thame. I hadn't thought much about this valley before heading up it. I only knew I wanted to have a look. The 14-kilometre round trip has given me a feel for the conditions and rekindled an interest in exploring the Bhote Kosi Valley in more detail, and maybe even walking up to the border. I don't yet recognize it as such, but a seed has been replanted. A new idea has been embedded in my subconscious, from which it will be very difficult to shake loose.

• • •

Returning to what I'm beginning to think of as my alternate base camp at Panorama Lodge, my home base in the Khumbu, I relax with a pot of milk tea in the sunshine on a terrace overlooking Namche and endeavour to do nothing more than enjoy the music and voices and bells wafting up from the village below. Sherap is on laundry duty but stops by briefly for a chat. It isn't until later in the afternoon that I sit down with him and Lhakpa in the dining room and get a privileged peek into the history of the Khumbu, as well as a brief look into its possible future.

Sherap was born in 1954 and, as a child, would have witnessed climbers becoming an increasingly common sight in a land not accustomed to white-skinned foreigners. When he was a teenager and young adult, trekking was the new novelty, before it exploded into big business and eventually brought about such improbable adaptations as ATMs and cappuccino machines. Out of context, the shift from a self-sustained agrarian society to one driven largely by tourism seems tremendous, but at ground level none of it happened overnight. All of us (or at least all of us of a certain age) have witnessed massive cultural and technological transformation, regardless of our background. The differences are in the details.

"The changes here were not that fast," Sherap points out. Over a 60-year stretch, the biggest transformations in the Khumbu have come in the last couple of decades. But he takes me back in time to his very humble beginnings. "I remember when I was 5 or 6, we didn't have proper shoes. We had only Tibetan shoes. Up above it was cloth, and down below it was leather."

Sherap is describing a common early indigenous approach to footwear, one that uses the materials at hand – in this case, cloth or felt attached to a buffalo or yak hide sole. What makes the description so vivid is that I'm not talking to the curator at a museum about an ancient culture that has disappeared. Seeing a pair in a display would have far less impact than hearing them described from personal experience. The Sherpa people have moved along with the times, and Sherap happens to be old enough to remember the beginning of that transformation. The amazing part is that he's only 14 years older than I am. I have a brother farther away in age.

"Inside the shoes, the cushion was hay," Sherap continues as my mind reels, and then, as if to accentuate the point, adds, "everything else was made of yak wool."

This reshaping of circumstance is difficult to grasp. I grew up lower middle class, and the closest comparable personal reference from childhood is that my first bicycle only had a single gear. Now Sherap and I have similar cellphones and laptops. I may have lived through the 1980s and the continuing evolution of pop culture as a dominant influence on ways and norms in the West, but Sherap has witnessed his whole world change on a much broader scale.

Sherap's father was a high-altitude Sherpa with the Hillary expedition in 1953 and went against type early on in his career. It was the one and only expedition he participated in. As Sherap describes it, his father didn't like the job, vowed not to make a living in tourism and became a trader instead, crossing the Nangpa La to Tingri and Lhasa many, many times over the course of his life. He couldn't, however, keep his children from getting involved in what would become the biggest growth industry for Sherpas over the following decades.

"We were not smart enough to be like him," Sherap says with an infectious laugh.

"So he was a good barter man, then?"

"He made very good deals in Tibet, yes. We couldn't be that way, so..."

One of 14 children, Sherap worked as a climbing guide for one expedition, just like his father, and then restricted his adventures in the mountains to guiding trekkers. In 1991, Sherap and Lhakpa began running the lodge. A number of expansions and upgrades have been undertaken, and, as is common practice in Sherpa families in similar situations, Lhakpa has been in charge of operations, while Sherap continued guiding until 2012. The lodge and guiding have been successful ventures. To hear Bryce and Sunny tell it, Sherap is the unofficial mayor of Namche, and the couple are well-respected pillars of the community. Overall, the standard of living has improved markedly for all the people in this region. That doesn't mean there haven't been growing pains or challenges.

In most cultures, prosperity breeds an expectation of more prosperity, and education, somewhat ironically, has begun to create a brain drain in the Khumbu. As more rural children receive basic education, higher education becomes a viable and desirable option, but that means going to the city. Not everyone comes back. Coupled with a low birth rate, this creates a vacuum. The Sherpa are not alone in facing this problem. What young people plan on doing is a key component in the long-term viability of a society. As the fates of the 15-to-25-year-olds go, the established traditions are sure to follow.

"It's a little bit hard," Sherap says. "Once they get a good education, then it is hard to come back, because there is not much opportunity here except running the lodges or climbing. So I think those guys who have a good education either want to be a doctor, or a pilot..." Sherap trails off for a moment to collect his thoughts. The options for young people are far greater than they were even a decade or two ago, and the ambitions have grown proportionally, but the Khumbu is still a small place, supporting a population of about 3,500 permanent residents in roughly 13 main villages. Kathmandu is compelling; so are the United States and other overseas destinations.

"Everybody wants to look for better," Sherap says. "A bigger place, better money, better opportunity."

To my mind, it doesn't get much better than this: a small, tight, comparatively affluent community surrounded by magnificent scenery is pretty damn close to my version of Bryson's Amalgam. Although this has been personally gratifying to search out and discover, it brings up the question of perception. This is my vision but not necessarily theirs. I admit, I want to blindly embrace this place as the harsh idyll it appears to be to an outsider who doesn't have to make a living here. I also don't have to endure the cold, quiet winters, when around 1,000 trekkers a month visit. Or the wet, quiet summers, for that matter, when it's fewer than 500 visitors on average in the months of June, July and August.

After I romanticized the spectacular landscape while stuck on my couch, recovering from major surgery, walking up here has helped me get over that particular mental distortion. Grinding up and down these huge hills has a way of keeping illusory thoughts in check. Boots on the ground makes for a sobering exercise, because it's beautiful here at every turn, almost to the point of being mundane, but it's also hard travelling. This is an important and irreplaceable characteristic of this place. You must respect the real effort in getting around, or the opportunity for a full experience could pass you by. It might even kill you if you're not careful. That's why, in my opinion, it would be disappointing if a road ever extended to, or even above, Lukla. Convenience and efficiency would be gained, but something more profound and less easily measured would be irrevocably lost.

But it is not my place to pass judgment on the possible spinoff consequences of a road, even one that only reaches Lukla. Much like the airport 50 years ago, a road to the village is envisioned not necessarily as a way to move tourists but as a way to move goods and provide an alternative to walking when the airport is closed by bad weather. Sherap expects regional tourism would increase as an ancillary benefit, with other Nepalis and Indians taking advantage, for the most part, but the cost of moving a kilo of freight from Kathmandu to Lukla is approximately 100 rupees. It's an additional 50 rupees a kilo from Lukla to Namche, a distance roughly 14 times shorter.

A ropeway has been floated as an alternative to porters and pack animals for the final stretch, but the idea is still just that, an idea. It isn't hard to imagine a continuation of the road in the event the opportunity presented itself. Progress is progress, after all.

Veering away from that potentially contentious subject, we instead focus on how well the Sherpa people have adapted to massive change in a relatively short period of time. After a challenging adjustment to the early surge in tourism, Khumbu is becoming self-sufficient once again. Nearly all the fruits and vegetables consumed by locals and foreigners alike are now grown in the Dudh Kosi drainage. Cooking fuel regulations are helping alleviate pressure on local forests, and community projects like small hydroelectric stations, schools and accessible health care have been a tremendous success. Namche's population is stable, and, for the time being, visitation remains at a sustainable level, but only just. It wouldn't take much to tip the balance.

Native sons and daughters have not abandoned their roots, despite the lure of the big city. Seasonal migration has always been part of life here. Whereas once that meant moving to summer farming or grazing high up the valleys as the seasons permitted, now it also presents as people returning home periodically to help in the lodges or work on other community initiatives. After making their way in the world, some are returning for good.

"We're always trying to convince our young Sherpas to stay, or to come back," Sherap says. "After 35, 40, then they realize this is home, this is their place, and they are coming back."

This development bodes well for the future of Sherpa culture and traditions. Which, in turn, bodes well for the Sherpa people.

• • •

There's a lot to stew on, and for a couple of days after returning from the Bhote Kosi Valley, I don't get much done apart from puttering around Namche. I eat delicious thin-crust pizzas and drink an untold number of lattes in cafés. There are photos to edit and blog posts to write, and the lattes are an easy excuse as I search for a convenient plug-in for a laptop charge paired with reliable Wi-Fi. The combination proves elusive. The average adapter that allows a Western plug to fit a Nepali wall socket is not a tight fit and falls out easily under the weight of a cumbersome MacBook plug. The Wi-Fi? Well, the Wi-Fi is advertised everywhere but is rarely of the high-speed variety. I think it's a running inside joke: put up a Wi-Fi sign and watch the tourists go crazy when their pages won't load.

In between cafés, I cruise the shops for books, supplies, gear and knock-off clothing.

Wandering aimlessly in this fashion has a surprising amount of purpose, as it turns out. Insight takes time. Ideas need to percolate between "flash of inspiration" and "cogent finished thought." As the hours pass, I can't help but reflect once again on the gentrification of Namche.

Clearly, the Khumbu is one of those places I hold dear to my heart, but I worry about it, and for good reason. I have seen runaway growth change the complexion of my hometown of Canmore first-hand; I have watched as some of the charm was bludgeoned out of the place by tourism and "progress." It's not a big stretch to imagine that happening here; the seeds have been sown. More guest houses, restaurants and shops open up every year. Understandably, everybody wants a piece of the action, but as Paul Theroux once wrote, "It is almost axiomatic that as soon as a place gets a reputation for being paradise it goes to hell."

What if things do keep getting busier around here? What if visitation doubles, or triples, or any other multiple you care to imagine? What if the two distinct trekking and climbing seasons expand into a year-round situation? What if the improbable does become real and a road finally does reach this place?

My friend Frances Klatzel is a fellow Canadian currently living in Kathmandu, and her experience in this part of Nepal is extensive. In the early 1980s, when there were only three trekker lodges in Namche, she began exploring these valleys and making friends with the people who call Khumbu home. She has subsequently led upwards of 40 commercial treks to the region. From 1983 to 1989, Frances worked closely with Tengboche Rinpoche, the Abbot of Tengboche monastery, on the Sherpa Cultural Centre, a museum dedicated to preserving and promoting Sherpa culture. There are few Westerners who know the Khumbu better, and her book *Gaiety of Spirit* is a thorough exploration of the history, religion and customs of the Sherpa people.

We have been talking about Nepal for almost a decade, casually over dinner in Kathmandu, or back in Canmore, where she still spends a small part of the year. Once she realized that my growing fixation with the Khumbu included a desire to write about it, she reminded me of the pitfalls of romanticizing the Sherpas and their way of life. I suppose it would be equally unfair to judge too harshly the changes that have been going on. As I grapple with the details of my own experience here, I often turn to her for insight.

Over coffee one afternoon in Canmore, Frances said to me, "When I was reflecting on the big 'so what' – when I asked myself, *What difference has eight years living in Khumbu made on my life?* – I realized a part of it was experiencing a different way of seeing the world. A lot of us, as we look at other cultures, see them as different, and then we're afraid of that, rather than seeing them as other human beings with the same basic needs as we have. Their way of explaining the world is different because of a different cultural situation, a different geographical situation, a different historical situation and a different survival situation. But if we could look at the commonalities between cultures, instead of the differences..." When seen through a common lens, other people's core challenges, desires and hopes look remarkably similar to our own. It's the details in process that are unfamiliar. It makes it easier to identify with, and eventually understand, other people's actions and motivations.

There are unmistakable similarities between Sagarmatha National Park and the Rocky Mountain National Parks system where I live, so it is easy to draw parallels. The physical landscape and many of the activities people engage in are much the same here as they are back home. The obvious difference is that bigger mountains and more extreme hiking and mountaineering can be found in Nepal than in Western Canada. The parks have comparable mandates for protection and restoration of species and habitat, and both are now UNESCO World Heritage Sites. But the circumstances that brought about the creation of these parks are distinct.

Banff, the first national park in Canada, began as a small protected reserve in 1885, largely as a resolution to a land dispute. Sagarmatha didn't gain protected status until 91 years later, in 1976, after it became clear the alpine landscape needed a measure of safeguarding as interest in the area grew. The local histories are also clearly different. Early isolationism and a difficult landscape have been both a curse and a blessing in this part of Nepal. On the one hand, formal education and accessible health care were slow to find these valleys, but the Sherpas in this area have managed to hold onto their land. Back home, the First Nations of Stoney-Nakoda and Blackfoot, who used the Bow Valley as part of their territory, have been pushed to the margins, replaced by largely white interests.

The challenges each region must now manage in the face of popular appeal and increased visitation is where common ground is found once again. With ongoing urbanization and the continued loss of wild lands across the globe, protected landscapes will inevitably struggle to maintain the current level of safekeeping. In an urbanizing world, people want jobs and opportunity and financial freedom, and then they want to get away from it all for awhile. According to the World Tourism Organization, international tourist arrivals across the globe have gone from 25 million in 1950 to 1.133 billion in 2014. These numbers do not reflect regional or even national travel, where a vacationer never crosses an international border. People are exploring unfamiliar landscapes in record numbers.

Different only in detail from Canmore and Banff, Phakding and Namche are now tourist towns. A service industry economy drives growth. It could help explain why I am unconsciously drawn here, and why I feel so comfortable. The mountain views and long walks through wooded hills are the obvious, almost clichéd commonalities between regions. The struggle to balance economic growth, quality of experience and sense of place are also shared obstacles. It has just taken me awhile to figure this out, which is strange, because the particulars have been hiding in plain sight.

Combing through my notes from this trip, I find what you would expect from a travel journal. Highs and lows scattered across the page in barely legible script, surrounded by heaps of observations that seemed prescient at the time but in hindsight are just common details, sometimes interesting, oftentimes not. But two themes recur. The first is that I'm clearly trying to figure something out – what I think, what I feel and where I might fit in this world. No surprise there. This is a pilgrimage, after all.

What is a surprise is the second major topic of interest: the details of service, and, more importantly, my unspoken camaraderie with those who provide it. How they do it here, what could be better and what I already think is done better here than back home. Sometimes I'm annoyed and sometimes I'm appalled, but mostly I'm delighted, and I am almost always paying attention to the particulars in restaurants and bars, guest houses and hotels, and tea shacks and small takeaway shops.

It turns out there are a number of weighty reasons to have come back to Nepal: to escape a tired situation, to be challenged anew, to strive toward something. Without question, there's a captivating desire to search out the exotic and to find insight into another way of being. But part of the reason I'm comfortable travelling in this fashion – i.e., alone, for months, in a sometimes complex and baffling collection of foreign cultures packed into a very small country – is that I've worked for over 20 years in the service industry. Even when I don't speak the language or recognize the food or know exactly where I am on the map, I inevitably encounter a group of strangers performing a set of tasks I recognize intrinsically. It makes me feel at home anywhere.

The realization is stunning, and obvious, and has escaped me until just now.

A couple of days after chatting with Lhakpa and Sherap, I end up tucked off in the corner of the dining room because the lodge is busy tonight. Mohan has his hands full. I feel for him. During the high season, he puts in long hours and needs to be constantly available to serve breakfast, lunch and dinner. He is also responsible for the dining room being clean and tidy at all times. He checks in trekkers and climbers, and he checks them out again after collecting payment, on top of the thousand other small details that go into an enjoyable guest experience. Sherap and Lhakpa are still active in the everyday running of the lodge and shoulder more than their share of the load, but Mohan has a ton of responsibility, and handles himself well. He doesn't let the irritating details of the job show, at least to the uninitiated – under the professional veneer is a hint of longing I recognize all too well. We never do completely escape our experiences. We may move past them to other things, but the most innocent of situations can bring the memories flooding back. Watching Mohan subtly hustle through his duties has triggered a strong memory in me.

After the initial challenges of recovery, my hip

271

improved quickly as the summer of 2015 began. Within two and a half months, I was back at work with no issues, nearly a month sooner than anyone expected. I was happy about being ahead of schedule, and I could walk! Without pain! I was even optimistic my Forrest Gump attitude could be carried over after the medical sabbatical ended, but it didn't take long for the same old workaday bullshit to overwhelm. It's in the nature of the job, no matter how much I would wish it otherwise. After a month back to work, I might as well have been stuck on the treadmill the whole time.

"Hey, Jeremy, how are you?" I asked, passing the bar during a long, busy Sunday afternoon after my return to the business. I had two plates of fish and chips in hand, and Sundays are my Friday, so I had already had a long week and probably shouldn't have been interacting with anyone more than was absolutely necessary, but I like Jeremy. He pours me beer down at the Canmore Hotel and is part of the fraternity of misfits, degenerates and fools who are such a big part of the service industry. He's also one of those guys you don't need to explain things to. One of those guys who *doesn't* ask, "Oh yeah, well, what's the matter?" He lives it. He gets it.

"I'm okay, you?"

"I'm a miserable prick, actually, now that I think about it."

The comment didn't so much slip out as it desperately needed to get out before the top of my head blew off. To be honest, the little outburst surprised even me. I didn't realize my emotions were *that* close to the surface, but Jeremy took the exchange in perfect stride.

"Yeah, I'm actually not great either. I was just trying to

be polite. But at least I've got today off," he said before taking a long swig of beer.

"You're a lucky bastard," I said, and pulled myself together enough to carry on with my duties in a largely mechanical and detached fashion, so as not to frighten the customers.

In Canmore, Sundays in the business are referred to as either Sunday Funday, if you happen to find yourself with the day off (by some miracle of scheduling, or if it's raining hard enough to close the various patios in town), or Suicide Sunday, if the juggernaut that is the tourism trade in the Bow Valley looks to keep on rolling right on through the end of the weekend, dying off only after the sun has finally dropped behind the impressive bulk of the Mount Rundle massif to the west, something that doesn't happen until after nine p.m. in the summer.

I don't know the details of what's got Jeremy down, but I understand the gist of it: he's a senior bartender down at the Canmore Hotel, and, as such, gets busier shifts and makes more money than a newbie would, but with that come the inevitable headaches. Have a look on the Internet for a video titled "Shit People Say to Bartenders." It's hilarious, and we have all dealt with those exact scenarios. Not all in five minutes and 34 seconds, of course, but often enough to make you roll your eyes and wonder what the fuck is wrong with people. Jeremy is probably just coming down from a particularly interesting combination of drunk and stupid.

But we who bring you all this food and drink are not exactly innocent victims. After taking up a position in management, I must admit that we the employees don't do ourselves many favours. With new information born from suddenly being responsible for more than just my own behaviour on the front lines, it has become easier to see the opposing point of view. It's probably no secret that many of us in the business are alcoholics, and some of us are drug addicts as well. This *might* affect our overall performance. At the very least, there are times when the level of professionalism in food and beverage leaves something to be desired, that's for sure. I could tell stories. Oh boy, could I tell stories.

The fly-by-nighters and occasional petty larcenists aside, most people in the business are decent and hard working. They are also my friends. We are, as a group, professionals, in the loosest sense of the word, getting the job done despite our frailties and addictions. It's a hard job to do well, and in the end it's just a job, not a life ambition. Sometimes it doesn't go very well on our end, and that's when you, the customer, have a bad experience in a bar or restaurant. I'm genuinely sorry about that. We are human and doing a job that is not necessarily enjoyable to us, and this is the unmistakable and far less obvious downside to growing success, in an individual business, or even in a region that has seen an increase in popularity: the strain of keeping up.

Sitting in my little corner of the dining room at Panorama, thousands of miles away from any responsibility to service, I have to admit I don't miss it at all. I like being on the other side of the table, especially when things are going so well. It's a joy for me to watch. A couple of small groups checked in today, and the lodge is almost full, but the kitchen team is getting meals out in an orderly and efficient manner. Sherap and Lhakpa are handling their hosting duties with charm and grace, seamlessly pitching in wherever an extra hand is needed in the kitchen, out at the front desk or behind the counter, where the bar and snack cabinet are located.

Meanwhile, Mohan is killing it. I know he would rather be out guiding trekkers instead of serving them milk tea and Sherpa stew, but he's still getting the job done. He's on top of the 13-table, 52-seat section like a true professional.

I'd hire him in a second.

16.

DEATH VALLEY

Winter is not far away here in the Khumbu. Every night
when the sun goes down, it gets a little bit colder, and
if a cloud cover persists during the day, the temperature
won't make it to double digits on the Centigrade scale.
Any breeze invariably carries at least the hint of a chill.
Anticipating this, I have worn pants instead of shorts and
have chosen a dark-coloured top to help absorb the sun's
precious rays should they present themselves.

This has been a mistake. A big mistake.

Right now the sun is blazing down and there isn't a
breath of wind and the heat is making me cranky. My sinuses are acting up, I'm sweating like a madman and my
Khumbu cough is exhibiting a notable determination after
having subsided for a few days. I feel so shitty that the idea
of altitude sickness does cross my mind, but the self-di-
agnosis doesn't make any sense. The village of Marlung,
where I had lunch four days ago, is at 4210 metres, and
navigation aside, I didn't have any problems at all during
the entire foray up the Bhote Kosi Valley. I'm roughly 600
metres lower; why would altitude be a factor now?

Near the village of Sanasa, the main trail intersects
with a trail leading up to the Gokyo Valley. To access the
valley, it is necessary to climb a substantial ridge in order
to bypass a canyon where the Dudh Kosi rushes past before joining the Imja Kola. Almost straight away, the trail

veers upward along a set of stone steps cut directly into a rocky outcropping, and a mid-morning orientation only accentuates the powers of the sun. It is among the more extreme sections on the standard trekking routes, and it's not difficult to imagine the entire face giving way at any moment. That is how the cliff came to be in the first place, after all.

Once I've cleared the impediment of the stone steps, the trail continues at a persistent angle to an open hillside that looks like a typical high mountain meadow, only tilted badly to one side. The trail cuts across it, and the views are tremendous. Ama Dablam is appropriately regal, and the village of Phortse, perched on a comparatively flat piece of ground on the lower slopes of Tabuche just ahead, seems almost close enough to touch. Tengboche, on its wooded ridge across the valley to the right, also appears much closer than it is.

Despite the glorious weather and Ama Dablam acting coquettish off to my right, I can't get over the fact that I feel horrible. I'm not dying (I don't think), but my incessant and aggressive coughing does catch the attention of another solo trekker making his way up to the small village of Mong. I just want to be alone and get through the current torment in quiet martyrdom, so as he gains ground up the slope, I stop next to a conveniently positioned rock, drop my pack and sit and pretend to enjoy the view. His concern is genuine, but somehow I convince him I don't have altitude sickness, and he carries on. But I'm not so sure myself anymore. My experience is with the cerebral symptoms of the condition. I've never even given the possibility of pulmonary issues a second thought.

So lunch in Mong is an exercise in worry as I wait for my Rara noodle soup. Should I go back and regroup or continue into an uncertain situation only to end up suffering unpleasant circumstances? In this landscape, that is a persistent, and valid, question. The goal for today is Phortse Tenga, a small collection of guest houses near the river, 300 metres below Mong. Phortse is upslope on the other side of the river, 150 metres above Phortse Tenga. Dole is up-valley toward the village of Gokyo, 365 metres above where I plan to overnight tonight. If the situation were to deteriorate, I would have to climb to get out of Phortse Tenga in any direction. Decisions, decisions.

The valley I'm trying to get into has at times been overlooked. It is not a trade link with Tibet, nor an access route to the most sought-after climbing in the region. What are now lodge villages were originally *karkas*, or yak-grazing stations. Later, potatoes were found to grow well there, and more small, stone-walled fields were erected. Some were to keep the yaks in, and some were to keep the yaks out and give the potatoes a chance, but there weren't any permanent settlements, just primitive shelters. Adventure tourism, specifically trekking, precipitated a transformation. Once rumours of the beauty of the Gokyo Valley leaked out, lodges and staff became necessary.

There is a part of me that wonders if I will get to see that beauty again.

After lunch and some Coconut Crunchees, I have decided to take the chance. A core mountaineering principal is "climb high, sleep low." The concept applies to trekking as well. Descending to Phortse Tenga should help, but it is a relentless descent, and after the first few hundred metres it proves as difficult as the ascent to Mong. Struggling down, I must look geriatric. My joints feel stiff and my muscles seem uninterested in engaging forcefully enough to halt gravity. As a result, I'm taking even smaller steps than usual and stopping far too often to cough my brains out. I would love to report the challenges of the trail as extreme in order to have an excuse for my poor form, but there is nothing unusual about it. I'm just off my game.

Near the bottom, I come across a designated rest station and take the opportunity to unburden myself from my pack and take in some fluids. Three porters are resting there before continuing up, but none of them speak English, so beyond *namaste*, not much is said. They do seem to exchange information among themselves about what they are up against, and it isn't long before they hoist their loads and slog slowly upward.

Strategically placed, these porter stops are handy. There are rest stops all over the trail – stone seats built into retaining walls or on the sides of lodges, mostly – but the difference here is that stone-and-mortar garbage bins have been added. The rest stations are often at the top or bottom of a particularly challenging section of any given route, and the bins have done wonders for what was once a growing litter problem. The Khumbu appears much tidier to me than in the past, but trail maintenance and garbage collection must be two of the most difficult municipal jobs on Earth. Replacement stones can weigh hundreds of pounds and are difficult to move into place, and collection points on any given trail can be 300 vertical metres apart.

While musing on the practical workings of a growing community, I still can't escape my uncomfortable situation. I'm sitting on a hard stone bench, and I don't want anything to do with carrying my pack and camera bag even a foot farther. I'm suddenly feeling so, so, so disappointed in my body as another bout of coughing takes hold. To add insult to injury, I look positively ridiculous.

My trekking pants turn to shorts by unzipping them at the knees, and, because it's so hot, I did just that two hours ago. Problem is, I couldn't get the bottom half off over my boots, and I wasn't about to take off my boots only to put them right back on again. As a result, the lower portion of my pants are bunched around my ankles like baggy leggings. I look like the member of the Village People that didn't quite make the cut: Hiking Aerobics Guy.

Stepping to the edge of the trail and looking down into the valley, I try to rally my emotions. Part of the reason I feel beaten down at the moment is that the Bhote Kosi Valley was so encouraging. An inspiring and interesting landscape, coupled with some solid walking up to Marlung. Even the Namche hill about a week before that was gratifying. It was physically challenging, no doubt about it, but never felt overwhelming as long as I kept putting one foot in front of the other. The accumulated mileage was finally paying off. When I did start to lag, near the end of the 14-kilometre round trip to Marlung, a small guided group stopped nearby while I was having a water break. They had come over the Renjo La and were on their way to Thame. What set this group apart from the others I had encountered over the previous month is that one of the members only had one leg. The other had been amputated above the knee

Talk about a kick-start to the old "suck it up and get on with it" argument.

Granted, he didn't look particularly comfortable at that moment, placing each of his walking crutches carefully on the rough trail before swinging his good leg forward, and then repeating the process over and over again. But he was there! Fulfilling an ambition many of us have:

to trek in the Himalaya. Clearly, he wasn't going to let a disability keep him from it. I don't know if I have ever been quite so impressed in my entire life.

Properly inspired, I resolved to crush this next part of my adventure. Stomp up and down the Gokyo Valley with confidence and vigour. Bask in the beauty and wonder of a spectacular landscape taken on at ground level. I was going to walk confidently and with purpose during the day, and revel in the afterglow of honest effort over tea and *dal bhat* in the evenings.

So much for that idea. Right now I'm contemplating never picking up my pack again. I've been taking things slowly and sensibly, working my way up to bigger distances and full fitness, and all of a sudden this short section has proven very difficult. It's not fair. Feeling sorry for myself, I pick up my pack and strap on my camera bag and continue down the final bit of trail to Phortse Tenga, and admit to being disproportionately relieved when the first of the lodges does finally come into view. It has only been seven kilometres, and I'm shattered.

Strategically located where the trail splits to go down to the main part of the village by the river or to contour the hillside briefly before the steep climb to Dole begins, the lodge is understandably busy – nobody wants to travel farther down than necessary, only to come back up in the morning. So I end up getting the last room. I've worried that as a solo trekker in the busy season I would have trouble securing a room, but today is the first day it has even been close. There are so many new lodges in the region that this has yet to be an issue, and, in a pinch, space would undoubtedly be made for me on the dining room benches, where the porters sleep after all the Western trekkers have gone to bed.

After I've checked in and changed, there's nothing more to do than have a pot of milk tea, read my guidebook and take some notes on the day. Before dinner, there's an opportunity to take a short stroll, over level ground, with no pack, and it's a beautiful start to the evening.

The walk here was accompanied by spectacular views at every turn, but plunging into the canyon after Mong has restricted the dramatic effect. This is a shame, because for the first time in a few days, the clouds have not rolled up-valley by late afternoon. The sky remains crisp and clear, and the moon that has just risen is somewhere past half full, which means there should be some spectacular combination moonrise-sunsets a couple of days from now farther up-valley, if my wholly unscientific calculations prove correct.

At this comparatively low elevation, tree cover is quite thick, and animals could very well be lurking. Musk deer and Himalayan tahr are the most likely occupants of this area of forest, but Himalayan black bears and red pandas are also possible. It has been reported that Himalayan wolves and the highly reclusive snow leopard still roam in remote areas of the Sagarmatha National Park, but I'm not expecting much within 50 metres of the lodge. If a yeti does happen to amble by, I'll ask if he wants to share a room. I've got an extra bed.

As the sky begins to grow dark and the temperature drops, I make my way back inside to the busy dining room and find a spot in the corner. It's a shame I couldn't enjoy the day as much as I should have, but now I just want to eat, give my emergency antibiotics a try and get some sleep. Life often looks grim when you don't feel well. Hopefully, things do get better tomorrow, because a rescue helicopter would have a difficult time landing in this narrow canyon.

•••

I'm beginning to get the clear and distinct impression this valley doesn't like me very much. The first time I ventured up here, nine years ago, I was rebuffed before reaching Gokyo. Altitude sickness drove Jocey and I down from Machhermo, and now I'm struggling once again. The cough-filled day out of Namche was followed by a cautious climb up to Dole, where a fresh headache has laid me low. The antibiotics have kicked in and my sinuses and chest issues are no longer a concern, but if I jostle my head even a little bit, a pain jumps from the shadows into my frontal lobe to remind me that all is not clear sailing yet. I don't feel nearly as bad as I did nine years ago. Overall I feel quite a bit better than I did yesterday, but I don't want to push it.

Altitude sickness sneaks up on you. There's often a time lag between the moment you take a step too high too soon and the onset of the worst of the symptoms. It's an ambush illness, and it doesn't make any sense to risk it, even though I'm far from debilitated. Guidebooks call this Death Valley for a reason. Trekkers have been known to perish here because the trail from Phortse Tenga to Dole is steep but short, and the subsequent two days to the village of Gokyo are arduous but not terribly long either. From Namche, Gokyo is only 22 kilometres away, but the recommended travel time is four days for the unacclimatized. The urge to push on is strong when you reach the day's destination before lunch, and some people can't help themselves. I don't want to be that guy again. The icing on the cake in all of this is that I just found out that Donald Trump has won the U.S. election.

Talk about kicking a guy when he's down.

The owner of this lodge has been on the summit of Mount Everest three times and fully endorses the decision to stay put. It has been a pleasant enough afternoon, drinking tea and shaking my head from side to side to gauge the returning pain signals. It's a decidedly odd sensation to be able to feel your grey matter. Sometimes my headache seems better and sometimes it's status quo, but it never gets worse, which is a good thing. On the advice of the owner, I took a short acclimatizing hike up the ridge behind the village about an hour ago. Near the makeshift cairns and attendant prayer flags high above the village, I met an older British couple, and they have turned up here in the dining room.

They are nice, easygoing people, and the common-between-trekkers "where are you from, how long have you been here and how many times have you visited Nepal" conversation is a welcome distraction from my cranial troubles. In international news, the American election has been on everybody's mind due to the improbable run of controversial real estate magnate turned TV personality turned bizarre caricature of himself Donald Trump. Hillary Clinton was ahead in the polls and still projected to win when I left Namche a couple of days ago. I left all devices capable of connecting to the outside world in storage at Panorama, and this is the first conversation with Westerners I've had since. As the exchange winds down, I can't help but ask, almost in passing: "So, who won the election anyway?"

"Trump did."

There's a big, pregnant pause while I wait for the punchline, but it never comes.

"No, seriously."

"It's true. No one is as surprised as we are, and we lived through Brexit."

Wow. And let me say it one more time just to be clear. wow!

I have only recently woken up politically. I've always had an opinion, to be sure, but it was largely uninformed and anchored in emotion. In my mind, politicians are liars and thieves, but as long as the least egregious of the offenders steered the most influential countries on a path that resembled fair dealings and equality, I was happy. I could get righteously indignant at the appropriate times, complain about the hypocrisy and shady behaviour for an hour or two, and still sleep at night. I'm Canadian, so the adage "not my country, not my president" offers a level of insulation in this new development, but it still hits a little too close to home.

"How is that even possible? The guy's a moron."

The Brits are too polite to go that far in their assessment – they're too properly British – but a spirited conversation on the subject ensues. If you are prone to bouts of rational thinking, no matter how sporadic, the recent global shift toward right-wing nationalism is a topic that can leave one simultaneously speechless and apoplectic, but we couldn't help but make the effort.

The political situation in Nepal is troubling – it is jarring to witness neglect and incompetence and corruption first-hand – but there is hope in the equation too. Hope that the next generation of leaders will be better, that the country will grow stronger, that the populace will finally prosper. You hope against hope that an emerging country will catch up.

I never envisioned the gap closing because the supposed superpowers would choose to take giant steps backwards, moving toward corruption, oppression, racism and division. Short-sighted policies aside, the new leader of the free world speaks and thinks and acts at an upper-grade-school level, surviving and even thriving on bravado, bullying and bullshit. How is this a good thing for anyone? How is this setting an example for a nation? Or the world?

The next morning, I'm still reeling from the bombshell the Brits dropped, but my headache is gone and the trail beckons. Travelling up-valley is slow going but thoroughly enjoyable and, despite the dangers to the unprepared or inattentive, stunningly beautiful. It is one of my favourite parts of any trek, anywhere in the world. The trail is high up the western slope of the Dudh Kosi, and the valley is impossibly deep. Quite often the swirling torrent isn't even visible below, obscured by the lumps and bumps of the hillside between trail and river. The views across valley are spectacular as well, and the much more challenging local's route between the villages of Na and Phortse is clear to see, a pencil-thin line swirling along the steep lower slopes of Cholatse and Tabuche.

The landscape has a humbling bigness to it, one that makes you feel inconsequential in comparison. Yet that feeling is oddly comforting. It says, "I am here, and here is all that matters."

I see the Brits often at rest stops along the way, but we don't talk about politics anymore, preferring to exchange lighthearted observations about the challenges right under our feet. The route is straightforward but relentless. In the high meadows, ribbons of worn trail meander through the low scrub, cut 6 to 12 inches into the earth by the footfalls of countless trekkers and yaks. Where the trail navigates mountain spurs, it narrows to a single wide and dusty track punctuated by the occasional giant stone.

There are a couple of groups out today, but there's never a traffic jam. Everyone takes their water breaks a respectful distance from everyone else, as if inspired to quiet introspection by the grand and sweeping landscape around them.

Reaching the top of the final hillside spur before Machhermo is an effort in breathless exertion. When I walk straight into the wind, whatever diminished oxygen is available at 4465 metres seems to be ripped away before ever reaching my lungs, and every infinitesimal rise on the rounded slope is always "just a little bit farther." But at the top a small Mani wall has been fashioned in the shape of a stupa, and at the head of the valley the gigantic, snow-covered bulk of Cho Oyu stands in stark contrast to the brown hills that frame it. It is impossible not to linger. I have made it back to Machhermo, and I don't have a headache!

Dropping into the small valley that cradles the village, I again take my time, not because it requires any significant effort but because I want to soak it all in. The handful of lodges, the well-maintained stone-wall-enclosed pastures and the burbling stream cutting through the middle are hopelessly picturesque in the sunshine. It isn't hard to locate Namgyal Lodge on the opposite side of the creek, and after checking into the same room where I stayed during my ill-advised adventure of 2007, I'm enjoying tea in the dining room by noon. Perfect.

• • •

High on this western side of the valley, direct rays from the sun disappear by three p.m., so I go back to the room, read for awhile, and then just lie in my sleeping bag, hands in pockets, to contemplate the small joys of this hard place.

A small pot of tea, a simple lunch, a warm sleeping bag and an uncomplicated afternoon with a clear head are precious things indeed.

At around 4:30, I begin to get restless, but instead of going to the dining room for more tea, I head out to explore the village and take some pictures. The light is flat and there's not much going on in the village, so I meander up-valley in hopes of finding something interesting, to no avail. Mercifully, the wind has died down, so it's not uncomfortably cold, and for awhile I'm content to sit on a rock and see if anything happens. A pair of sturdy ponies graze in a small pasture just below, and a trio of yaks is walled up in another, so at least there's something to look at.

But, in the quiet, I can't stop thinking about Trump, which is as disturbing a sentence as has ever been uttered.

Hard as I try, I can't seem to wrap my head around the whole thing. Can't shake the ominous overtones. Call me a cockeyed optimist, but I have always thought the forces of good would prevail in an often tumultuous world. I could afford to be an obnoxious youth in that scenario. The world was a mess, but it would get better, and I would eventually come around to being somewhat engaged and be able to say, "See, that's better." Along the way, we would have continued to grow and mature as a species. I assumed logic and thoughtfulness would win out in the end. But lately, it appears, the world is dead set on consuming itself, and too many of those aspiring to power are poised to accelerate the process for personal gain.

In the jockeying for position, a schism has developed in modern politics. A division. A fundamental split in thinking and ideology that now overlooks the fundamental principle of addressing the issues. Partisan bickering that serves no one has won the day; it's all just yelling back and forth across a divide, born of a need to be right at all costs. We are being forced further apart. It has the effect of making you feel like you should give up, like you should give in. Go along to get along, succumb to the never-ending distraction or conveniently ignore everything that is happening. Is this the best we can do?

In 1989, Lawrence Kilham wrote, "One of the most difficult of all things to endure for a crow, a raven, a wolf or a human is to feel alone and separated from one's own kind. A sense of belonging is one of the most universal of all feelings."

My question is: What happens when the system you grew up in, the system you're supposed to believe in and follow, is nothing more than a series of half-truths and flat-out lies, perpetrated by governments and corporations with an overwhelming vested interest? What happens when a startling percentage of the population buys in, with nary a second thought? It would be difficult for me to feel any belonging in that, any kinship. There's no great overarching conspiracy in it, it's just human weakness masquerading as strength. Our system is too big, the superstructure too weak, the key participants too greedy. The rot has reached a tipping point where fiction is as good as truth and critical thinking is dead. Common sense is no longer common. Transparency is nonexistent, and even the good guys are full of shit.

The thing is, I do believe there is still a great deal in this world to be inspired by, an abundance of people to adore and cherish and champion. There is much to go and do and see, plenty to be in love with. There are still things worth fighting for. I'm just not sure our modernized version of society is one of them. Not with the current roster of leaders, anyway. First World, developing world, it doesn't seem to make a difference. Collapse is inevitable unless we change course.

Strangely enough, admitting that dark belief makes me feel better. Accepting the very real possibility of what looks to be unavoidable – that we are poised to destroy ourselves and don't much seem to care – is strangely liberating. It makes me feel better to admit this truth.

About once a month, I have beers back in Canmore with Bob Sandford. He's a friend and a fellow writer and also happens to be the EPCOR Chair for Water and Climate Security at the United Nations University Institute for Water, Environment and Health. In his capacity as Robert W. Sandford, dedicated professional and water and climate expert, he's a good guy to know. He's a wealth of information and stats and projections on our current environmental trajectory. The one made ever more challenging by this new political development. Over beers, however, he's just Bob, someone who's fun to blow off steam with. Someone with whom I can reaffirm, in this age of fake news, misinformation and misdirection, that those with a curious inclination and a modicum of concern are not making this shit up. We're not jumping on a bandwagon of mass liberal hysteria. We're not simply taking an alarmist position over growing neo-conservative and corporate greed.

In a moment of solemn clarity during one of our big-picture conversations, I once said to Bob, "We're going to get what we deserve."

"We are going to get what we invested in," he replied matter-of-factly.

This *is* real, this *is* now and this *has* consequences. We are creating a problem for ourselves that may soon be irreversible, and in November 2016 the accelerator has been pushed a tiny bit harder.

As the light in the valley turns gloomy and the smoke from the guest house chimneys thickens, I begin to make my way back to the village. The narrow trail is well worn and smooth, and as I reach the first of the guest houses, the last of the sunshine brushing the peaks directly across the valley burns off. Almost immediately, the sky slips from a pale, almost anemic blue to a richer, warmer shade. In behind the large rounded ridge in the foreground, two harder, sharper rock outcroppings split the scene in two, and through the gap between them, a main peak remains in the dimming sunlight. The orange and red hues grow ever more dramatic in their contrast. The scene is more than worthy of a photo.

After I switch to the telephoto lens and find a convenient rock wall on which to steady myself against the heavier set-up, the framing works out perfectly. At a 310-millimetre focal length, the rounded foreground ridge appears dark, and the slightly brighter rock faces to the sides, dusted with light snow, offer a ghostly contrast. Through the gap, the main ridge with its heavier snow crown practically glows in comparison. It's a beautiful sight, and I quickly snap off a dozen or so shots in order to assure a stable focus, before letting the camera fall to the side to enjoy the scene with my naked eye. A part of me wants to shout to the surrounding guest houses and alert the other visitors to the wondrous natural process unfolding right before me, but in the end I get it all to myself.

Just as I'm about to put away my camera and go for dinner, a strange white glow appears along the very edge of the left-hand rock face. It's far too harsh to be a part of the warm glow of the fading light, and it takes me a few seconds to figure out where this new illumination could be coming from. Sunlight reflecting off snow does not look like this. Impossibly faint at first, it grows quickly and mysteriously until a tiny sliver moves out from behind the rock. Now I get it.

"Well, hello, moon."

The moon is two nights from full, but the side coming into view is a perfect sphere. It takes about two minutes for the moon to move a full width in the sky, but I hang around for 20, watching it climb as the sunlight drains off the last mountaintop. After this impressive show, I resolve to stop thinking about the ugly big picture, preferring instead focus on the big beautiful picture that is this collection of remote valleys. It will be nearly a week before I return to Namche, plug back into the Internet and waste an entire day surfing for evidence that the latest political development is just some kind of sick joke.

The only time it comes up in the interim is when I have to explain to American trekkers I am not in a position to grant their asylum requests.

17.

A SUPER MOON

Gokyo Ri is there out the window, waiting for me. A huge mound of earth and stone tilted at what looks to be an impossible angle, and I admit I'm a little nervous. What if I can't do this?

I can do it, of course. The bike ride from hell near Mude and the Lamjura La were comparable, if not more difficult, individual challenges. They were much longer climbs, but at significantly lower elevations, so it is ultimately impossible to assess which should be rated as "hardest." The psych-out comes from being able to see almost the entire route from the comparative warmth of the guest house dining room, and I will probably spend half the day staring at it and wondering, *What if?*

What if I run out of energy and can't make the top? What if I go through the effort and do make the top, only to have the clouds roll in so there's nothing to see? What if I turn an ankle or break a leg and am left out in the cold and dark? What if I fall down some obscure gully?

Ultimately, I'm sitting here fretting about these possibilities instead of joining the half-dozen, ant-sized people picking their way up the trail in the distance, because sunrises are overrated, in my opinion. They happen very early in the day for one thing, and the angle of these valleys and the trajectory of the sun is not quite right for better-than-average photos. The very best early light hits the most desirable mountain faces at an unflattering inclination, so why bother? But there are also practical considerations. Each morning, before a fire gets going in the dining room, I can see my breath, and my water bottle froze to a slushy soup last night, *inside* my room. Go outside? Ha, ha, ha. I don't think so.

Besides, the whole morning-light-show thing is usually over too quickly. Sunsets this high up, on the other hand, do tend to linger, and so I will wait until this afternoon before heading up the Ri. In the interim, I will think about it too much. A welcome distraction while I wait is the Brits. Not the couple I met in Dole, mind you, but the Midlands Gang of Six, who are a diversion because collectively they've got a keen and slightly acerbic British sense of humour, which I appreciate, and because there's now only three of them. Hilton and David are back in Kathmandu already, searching out the best pub after dutifully checking in with Tony, who remains in hospital for tests. The missing half of the group has recently taken an unscheduled helicopter ride.

Machhermo strikes again.

"It was quite lucky, really," Amanda says, after ordering a pot of tea for us all. "The guys weren't faring well with the altitude, and we weren't sure what we were going to do. The health post in Machhermo was only a couple of days from being shut for the season, but fortunately there was still someone there."

As it happened, Hilton began feeling ill when they reached the village, so he went to see the doctor, complaining of severe fatigue. After some tests, it was revealed he only had 52 per cent of the normal oxygen saturation in his blood, and he was immediately given supplemental oxygen. After Rob came back with the news, Tony went over to see Hilton and had a massive angina attack en route. When Tony didn't return, David went to find him. Turns out David himself had the beginnings of cerebral edema.

"The doctor decided all three had to be evacuated on the first available helicopter," Amanda says, as I try and insert all the players on the board. Once I've confirmed that everyone is okay, it's hard not to imagine the scenario as a distressed-trekker Keystone Cops episode, the participants travelling back and forth to the health post, missing each other along the way and coming back with a different ailment after each visit. I need a scorecard to keep up, but at least I'm not thinking about the Ri anymore.

My new friends Amanda, Paul and Rob are from the Midlands region in England, and the group came to Nepal for the usual variety of reasons. Amanda, Paul and Hilton had been to the Khumbu before but had yet to see the Gokyo Valley. Tony had been to altitude before but not in the Himalaya. David's children are autistic, and he was on a fundraiser for their school. Rob got caught up in the excitement of the pre-trip discussions and was ultimately dragged along for the ride, the silly sod. The evacuation has not deterred their spirits or their focus on the overall goal, but it didn't exactly go smoothly.

"Our lodge owner was a piece of work," Paul says.

"She was nasty," Amanda adds. "Wouldn't let the guys get on the helicopter."

"Even though they were sick?"

Amanda, Paul and Rob nod a contemptuous affirmation.

A helicopter in a tiny village on the side of a mountain in the middle of nowhere would be an exciting story all by itself. It is a juxtaposition. These remote mountain villages with no road access, no expensive infrastructure and no high-rise buildings are often buzzing with multi-million-dollar machinery. It is one of the quirks of this place. I figure I've seen three or four helicopters a day on average since reaching Namche, and a disagreement over landing rights simply upped the ante this time.

"The pilot was meant to land in a field adjacent to the lodge," Paul says. "But there were too many people milling about, so he ended up in her garden by mistake. She was not pleased."

After extorting an illegal landing fee from the pilot, the lodge owner refused to let the evacuees on the helicopter. So the pilot took off and landed again at the upper end of the village, near the health post.

"The guys had to walk over, bless them," Amanda says.

"The best part of it though," Paul says with a gleam in his eye, "is after getting everyone on board, the pilot buzzed the lodge on the way out of town. Could've flown down the creek and out into the main valley, but purposely went over the lodge. Real low."

I take a second and look over to Rob, who has a big grin on his face.

"No."

He nods.

"Sent the washing all over the place," Amanda says, describing in detail sheets and blankets, laid out over stone walls to dry in the sun, suddenly leaping into the dust. "She was furious."

"I think he even flipped her the bird on the way by," Paul adds.

As I've mentioned, aggressive and obnoxious behaviour is usually a specialty of entitled Western tourists, but Nepalis are catching on, and this is a scenario that could not have taken place anywhere else on Earth. I only wish I had been there to see it.

Finally, at about 1:30 in the afternoon, I can't contain myself any longer. The heli story has been properly memorialized, and I'm not in the mood to take any more travel notes for the moment. The thing is, I can't pretend to read my book in the room when the words just slide by without penetrating my distraction with the task ahead, and I'm not interested in strolling around the village to kill time when I can see the Ri from everywhere in town. So I head out with my camera bag, some water, a few snacks and a flask of tea for the top, determined to get myself there.

The scramble up the Ri is about what you would expect. It is a relief to not have my full backpack, but after I cross the meagre flats where a small creek feeds into the turquoise lake in front of the village, the recurring word that comes to mind over the next two hours is *steeeeeep*. It's amazingly steep. Deceptively steep. The whole slope verges on what appears to be impossibly steep – a few more small degrees and it would surely be unable to support itself, collapsing into a series of landslips and cliff faces that would not bear the weight of a proper trail. Then it would be rock climbing.

The other notable feature early on is the wind. A powerful force that was battering the side of the guest house all morning, it is a juggernaut out in the open. Fortunately, the wind is hitting the area around the trail at such an angle that the bulk of the hill deflects some of the gusts. Other times, the wind, being so pliant, massages the hillside in a new way and just slams right into me.

At these high elevations, the trusty yak is the only animal you're likely to see, apart from the occasional bird or very tough pony, but *yak* isn't always a completely accurate name for the assortment of hairy beasts working the local trails. First of all, a female yak is referred to as a *nak*, but it's doubtful I'll ever venture close enough to one of the notoriously temperamental animals to figure out the difference. Muddying the waters further, many of the pack animals working the moderate elevations are hybrids. Domestic cattle and yak/naks crossbred, to mellow them out. A male is a *dzo*. A female is a *zhom*.

The big, scruffy guy who has appeared out of nowhere around the edge of the slope while grazing the short brown grasses, and has come up short, clearly surprised to see me – well, he is almost definitely a yak. He's enormous, for one thing. Even domesticated yaks can stand close to six feet at the shoulder and weigh a thousand pounds. Wild yaks are generally black or brown, but this guy's long, shaggy fur is streaked with cream-coloured accents, so he's probably tame, to a degree. I'm having the same combination of reactions I always have when I come upon a large animal in an uncontrolled setting. There is an inevitable "Oh, hey, cool." Followed by an immediate step back: "What if my new friend here is in a bad mood?" After initially being startled, however, he doesn't much care about me and carries on grazing the steep hillside, eventually disappearing back around the corner from where he came.

As the air thins, my upward progress slows and breaks become more frequent. It's an odd sensation. I don't feel tired, exactly, but I can't keep the gears engaged. I'm sucking at air that just isn't there. Most notably, the will for the effort fades as I get higher, and the whole thing becomes a mental exercise. *I'll make it to that odd-shaped rock just up the trail,* I keep thinking. *Then it'll be the small cairn after that.* But the body would just as soon stay put as carry on. The urge to simply stop must be nearly overwhelming at more extreme altitudes. Taking a moment to gaze over my shoulder at Mount Everest in the distance, the top of which is still roughly 3600 metres above this already lofty position, I can't even imagine it.

I haven't spoken about mountaineering much to this point, mainly because it's neither the focus of this book nor the reason I'm here, but I would be remiss if I didn't cover the topic a little bit. I am, after all, in one of the meccas of the sport. Those who dream about climbing really high mountains dream about this place. For mountaineers, this is Yankee Stadium, Wembley and the old Montreal Forum all wrapped up in one. It is the big time.

At 11:30 a.m., on May 29, 1953, Edmund Hillary and Tenzing Norgay reached the summit of Mount Everest. They were part of the 1953 British Mount Everest expedition, and their success was a worldwide sensation. Everest was often referred to as the third pole, and many wondered if it even could be climbed. Adventurers had been trying for decades, and although a few had come relatively close, the cost in human lives prompted some outside observers to question whether mountain climbing was worth the risk. Thirteen people died in the attempts prior to 1953, and countless more had been beaten back by the difficult conditions. The extreme height of the mountain only supported the argument that the summit would remain unreachable.

So when Hillary and Norgay achieved the improbable (only one of the world's 14 8000-metre peaks had been climbed previously – Annapurna, in 1950), it changed mountaineering forever. High-altitude climbing found a prominent place in the growing sport, and, within 11 years, all of the 8000-metre peaks had been climbed. Gokyo Ri is a mere 5357 metres and is pretty much the upper edge of my high mountain abilities, but having reached the top, I can see a handful of those loftier peaks clearly.

Mount Everest is directly ahead and looks appropriately massive, even from a distance. The upper portion of the standard southeast ridge route is visible in profile on the right side of the mountain, but Mount Nuptse obscures the south col. The west ridge plunges at a diagonal down the middle view of the mountain, and the north ridge, one of the routes on the Tibetan side, stands in dramatic profile on the left. Two things catch your attention from this vantage point: the lack of snow up high, due to fierce winds that batter the mountain much of the year, stripping it down to its hard stone base; and the sheer magnitude of Everest. Those who would disparage it say the mountain lacks the aesthetic appeal of an Ama Dablam, or even Pumori. I admit it is a touch stout, but some have called it nothing more than a rubble pile, which is dismissive at the very least. From here, it's an imposing-looking rubble pile. After spending two hours grinding my way up to 17,575 feet, I can only speculate what ascending to 29,028 feet would be like, although the word *relentless* does spring to mind.

Off to the right of Everest, and also partially obscured by Mount Nuptse, is number four on the list of mighty mountains, Mount Lhotse. The name means "south peak" in Tibetan, and the mountain is part of the Everest massif. At 8516 metres, it is without question a giant, but only the top and the southeast flank are visible. From Gokyo Ri, it is remarkable only in being so nondescript. Number five on the list of highest mountains in the world is Makalu, about 20 kilometres to the east. That distance allows it to blend into a horizon littered with peaks, and a number of those lesser summits in the foreground appear taller, most notably Cholatse and Tabuche, which are roughly 2000 metres shorter.

Off to my left, however, Cho Oyu is, by virtue of its proximity, everything you would expect a Himalayan giant to be and more. Number six on the big list, it fills the head of the valley, and although it is considered the easiest of the big boys to climb, I would hardly character-ize it as inviting. It's draped in snow and littered with gla-ciers; a captivating feature is the minor ridge tucked in the bowl created by the larger sweeping ridgeline in the back-ground. In any other setting, this peak would be a domi-nant mountain unto itself. Here it is simply a small, craggy outcrop tucked in the bosom of a much larger eminence. As the sun's long descent in the afternoon sky softens the light cast on the mountain, I begin to struggle to find the right superlative to help define the overall view. It's mag-ical, magnificent and marvellous, and that's just the *m*'s. It takes an aggressive gust of wind to shake me from my musings.

The top of Gokyo Ri is a jumble of giant boulders spread along a ridge running roughly north and south. Although awkward to navigate, it does allow for multiple viewpoints tucked away in relative isolation. Perched out on a rock, his tripod impossibly balanced at the edge of the void below, the famed photographer Sonam Sherpa is already prepared for what the evening might bring, and I have managed to find my own little slab of rock tilted at a clumsy angle and have set up shop as well. After a brief reprieve, the wind is picking up again, and my hands get cold every time I take off my gloves to change a lens, but I'm ready.

As the afternoon wears on, most of the dozen or so peo-ple I saw on the way up have now descended, but a trickle of newcomers has been slowly arriving. Most of them have camera bags at hand. It's no secret that tonight is the full moon, and it also happens to be a "super moon," the infrequent event when a full moon is closest to Earth during its orbit. I only figured out the timing while taking the moonrise shots in Machhermo a couple of days ago, and now I don't want to miss the opportunity to witness it. The sweep of the Himalayan range, Mount Everest and a super moon sometime after sunset – you can't make this stuff up.

I've already spent 45 minutes moving to a different location every few minutes, but other people have taken up the best viewpoints, so it's always a few quick shots before scurrying back to my perch, lest someone muscle in on my turf. Before long, I spot Marlene and Pega, who have just made the top and are searching for somewhere to wait out the sunset. I bumped into them yesterday at about this time on the ridge in behind the guest houses. Marlene is a fellow Canadian, a photographer from Vancouver, and she's hired Pega Sherpa as her guide.

The ridge we were on is the lateral moraine of the Ngozumpa Glacier, which is reputed to be the longest in the Himalaya. I had been sitting there appreciating the views, and perhaps more notably the sounds of so many small rockslides triggered by the gigantic ice sheet grinding past, when they made the short climb up the moraine. I was enjoying the solitude, but we ended up shooting pictures, talking about travel and contemplating when and where the moon was going to rise. In the trekking world, this is how you make friends.

After inviting them over to my perch here on the Ri, I learn Pega's home village is Phortse, which is becoming an epicentre for local climbers. In 2003, the Khumbu

Climbing Centre opened in the village, and over 700 Nepalis have since taken advantage of the opportunity to develop better technical skills. As it turns out, Pega is a natural, and at the age of 22 has already been on the top of Cho Oyu and Everest, which you would never guess after just meeting him. He's a nice, unassuming, young man with a well of skill and determination he keeps largely to himself.

Later, after returning to Kathmandu, I will talk to him about his accomplishments over lunch. Pega explains his modesty in simple terms: "In the Sherpa community, climbing Everest is not a big deal," he says, with a laugh to underscore the slight exaggeration. Climbing the mountain will always be difficult and hazardous, but in the six decades since the first successful summit, Sherpas have gained a worldwide reputation for being exceedingly competent at high altitude. According to the Himalayan Database, 4,469 different people have reached the top of the world a total of 7,646 times as of December 2016. Sherpas and Western guides account for nearly half the total number of summits.

"From my village, there are 67 Everest summiteers," Pega continues.

"Sixty-seven!"

"Yes, only from my village of Phortse."

"It doesn't look like there are 67 homes there."

"There are almost 90 houses. Some of those 67 people have been on the top of Everest many times. A few have been up six or seven times."

High-altitude climbing is part of Pega's history and heritage, and just as young, ambitious athletes in Canada would aspire to play in the National Hockey League, young, ambitious Sherpas aspire to Everest, for many of the same reasons. Prestige, respect and money all enhance an already innate drive to achieve. While only 1,134 players had won the Stanley Cup, the pinnacle in hockey, as of 2015, it is also far less likely a player will get killed in the attempt, so for argument's sake I'm going to give the nod to Everest as the tougher challenge. Both are a pretty big deal.

After an interminable wait, it's finally showtime. The light lingering on the mountains to the east continues to soften and develops a subtle red-orange tint as the shadows cast by the western side of the valley wall creep slowly upslope. The tallest peaks hold the light longest, for the most part, but a couple of smaller mountains happen to be aligned in gaps that keep them in the late-day sun, where they peek out in sharp contrast to their larger neighbours. When the light can finally touch only the very tallest summits, the sky behind them takes on a purple hue that gradually spreads up the entire eastern sky. The otherworldly purple is eventually followed from below by a darkening blue that fades imperceptibly to black as night takes hold. It is then that Everest comes into its own. As if the dark, bare rock has absorbed the sun's rays all day, only to slowly release the energy again as night falls. I know it's impossible, but I swear it glows from within.

On the way down from the Ri, a desire to reach the warmth and safety of the lodges before full nightfall battles with the surreal picture being painted and repainted with each passing moment, but walking and admiring the view simultaneously is a dangerous act in Nepal. So I concentrate on my footfalls in the beam of my headlamp and stop every few hundred metres to take in the view, when suddenly there's another, different sort of glow across the valley. I've seen this before, and quite recently.

"Here comes the moon."

I have not said it so much as shout it, before realizing I'm not at all prepared for this development. Last night, Marlene, Pega and I stood out in the cold after the best of the alpenglow had faded, just to see where the moon would rise, hoping for the best. In disappointing fashion, it came up directly over a nondescript hillock that from our angle of view was backed by nothing but sky. Not much exciting in that, and we certainly didn't expect much better tonight, anticipating a much later rise, much closer to the head of the valley. It turns out our calculations are wrong. They are very, very wrong.

"And it's coming up right behind Everest!"

I don't know if anyone has heard me over the wind, and after hastily pulling out my camera, I've dropped the bag, and it almost rolls down the steep slope, but I don't care. I've got bigger problems. It's gotten way too dark to shoot hand-held, and I don't have a tripod. I didn't bother bringing it up, based on last night's calculations. A few metres farther downslope, a trail cairn looks to be my only option, so I shuffle down, lie in the dirt and find a flat spot on the low cairn to balance the camera. It seems to work when I peer up the viewfinder, and a few small stones tucked under the lens create the perfect angle to the top of Everest, now strongly backlit by a moon that has not quite risen.

The next 15 minutes are a blur as the moon sweeps through the aforementioned two minutes for every full width. I want to get a good picture, but I also just want to stand and stare at the spectacle. While only backlit, the mountain retains enough dim light to create an unusual and stunning contrast, but when the moon breaks over the ridge, it overwhelms the sensor and appears as a fiery orb. I did notice one of the other photographers at the top of the Ri had two cameras strapped to each other, and now I get it. Each was likely set at a different exposure to capture the moon and mountain separately, to be rejoined later in Photoshop. Smart move, says the guy with no tripod.

As the moon climbs higher, the last of the colours in the scene fade and a black-and-white world emerges. Most of us pack our gear quickly and continue down by headlamp. The adrenalin is pumping and the wind is howling, and it almost turns into a race to the lodges. It's easy to get sucked up in the excitement of the moment. Stopping a little farther down the trail requires an effort of will. Turning off my headlamp, the lake is cast in the ghostly moonlight below. I feel like I'm on top of the world, which is not entirely accurate, but I can see the top of the world off in the distance, a silhouette on the skyline with the moon almost directly above. As the half-dozen or so other hikers in the vicinity get farther away, I experience a moment of profound peacefulness; I just want to stand here forever and let the sensation continuously wash over me.

The spell is broken only when the wind, in its infinite ability to conform to the surroundings, finds a new route around the shoulder of the slope and slams us all with renewed vigour. Suddenly, I'm freaking out because I don't want to be left alone on the mountainside, just in case. A couple of stragglers come down the trail, and I can't help but get sucked back into the rapid group descent. Before long, my thighs are burning and my knees are aching as I scuttle along in the beam of my headlamp, but the light coming from the lodges below draws me ever forward. Somewhere along the way, I lose Marlene and Pega, and quite suddenly, it seems, find myself standing in what feels like a completely foreign environment: the warm, bright, somewhat loud dining room of the lodge. It's a rapid shift in circumstance, and it takes a moment to get my bearings, but the recently downgraded Gang of Six is off in a corner with a space to spare.

"So how was it?" Paul asks before I can even sit down.

I'm so pumped up with excitement and leftover adrenalin I can barely speak. It takes me a moment to find the proper context. It's too easy to simply say "best day ever," but it was pretty awesome.

"In the top five experiences of my life. No question."

"Really? How so?" Amanda asks.

"Hard to say, kind of a perfect balance of everything," I finally manage as I try to think and speak at the same time. "The effort getting up there, coupled with the unknown element of coming down in the dark did make it exciting. And then there's the ridiculous sunset. The alpenglow here is off the charts, and the sky moves through these crazy shades of blue and purple. Then, as we were coming down, the moon rose over Everest."

"No," Paul says.

"Yup, right over the base of the north ridge. Fucking unbelievable."

I'm practically vibrating, but I'm also starving and want to get a dinner order in, seeing as it's getting close to eight p.m. For awhile, I babble nonsensically about the details while trying to read the menu and drink a celebratory beer. When Marlene and Pega roll in after a few minutes, they share their own versions of events, and we cram all the details together, filling in each other's gaps. We're like a bunch of kids who have just come back from an outing at the zoo. We're exhausted but don't yet want to let the day be over. It's not often life lives up to our expectations, but every once in a great while an experience steps up and exceeds them.

I wonder, as I dig into my pizza and spoil myself with a second beer, is it worth it to travel halfway around the world for a single extraordinary sunset? With a super-moonrise tacked on as a bonus? Yes. Yes, I think it is, because one thing is certain: I'm never going to forget this day for the rest of my life.

18.

TENGBOCHE

Sometimes I wish I was a more religious person. Millions upon millions of people around the globe find strength, solace, peace and purpose in their chosen faith, so there has to be something to it. I have just never been able to connect with the concept, let alone the application, of organized religion in any meaningful way. I realize faith does not necessarily equal religion, and adhering to a religion does not necessarily mean someone is a good person – or has any true faith, for that matter – but that is an argument far removed from the scope of this journey. The point is, many people can and do look to organized religion in its various forms for guidance and comfort. But it has never worked for me. Not that I haven't, on occasion, tried.

In New York for a soccer tournament as a teenager, I went to an old-school Catholic service with my host family. Removing the wafer from my mouth during communion (I was genuinely curious about what it was made of) did NOT go over well. Over the years since that unfortunate faux pas, I have also participated in Christian services of various denominations in a number of cities and towns out west, where I now live, usually with friends who are more dedicated to their spiritual commitments than yours truly. God bless them. I'm even baptized Serbian Orthodox but have never felt the calling to pursue what it means to be devoted. In a way, that's too bad, because if I had a stronger religious background, the spiritual intricacies of this place might make more sense to me. But I have stopped over here in Tengboche to try once again.

After a few days of rest back at my Namche base camp, I am finally on my way to the real Base Camp at the foot of Everest. Along the way is the village of Tengboche and its famous monastery. I have passed by here three times before, once on the way up-valley, and twice on the way down, but it has always been around lunchtime. Consequently, the visit has been a quick stopover before moving on along the trail. I have never even had a good look around. I have stood at the ornate main gate to the grounds and peered up the stone steps at the main building but have been inexplicably nervous about ever stepping inside. With no religious history and no familiarity with the monastery's customs and practices, I am simultaneously standoffish and overly reverent as I lurk at the edges and try to figure out what's going on. I want to be respectful, and I am curious, but I also don't want to get in the way.

Interestingly, during my most recent stay in Namche, I spent time in the book section of one of the general stores. I needed something new to read during the long evenings but couldn't decide from the wide variety of adventure offerings available, most of them to do with Everest, Nepal or the Himalaya. Granted I've read many of them before, including Jon Krakauer's *Into Thin Air*, Peter Matthiessen's *The Snow Leopard* and Michael Palin's *Himalaya*, but adventure travel just wasn't on my mind. My eye was drawn to the bottom shelf and the gentle, friendly face of the Dalai Lama staring out from the cover of *The Art of Happiness*.

The 14th Dalai Lama, Tenzin Gyatso, is a remarkable human being. Born in 1935 and identified at the age of two as the *tulku*, a reincarnate custodian of the teachings, he took over the responsibilities of the position of Dalai Lama at the age of 15 after years of intensive study in Lhasa. In 1959, the Tibetan Uprising forced him to flee Tibet ahead of invading Chinese troops, and to this day he leads a government-in-exile and promotes Tibetan interests from Dharamsala, India. He is among the most recognizable and respected people on the planet. *The Art of Happiness* is not an autobiography or a précis of the Buddhist philosophy but a thought-provoking conversation about the human experience between a Western psychiatrist, Howard C. Cutler, and His Holiness.

In a way, it all fits together nicely. After a long and pleasant walk from Namche, I'm lying in bed with my weary feet up on the wall in my guest room and an interesting book in hand. Mount Everest and the Nuptse–Lhotse ridge are an inspiring sight out my window, and a visit to one of the most famous Buddhist monasteries in the region is scheduled for later this afternoon. I feel calm and content, as if there's nothing else in the world I should be doing at the moment. If I'm not careful, I might start to get a handle on all this spiritual business after all.

• • •

Buddhism, according to Wikipedia, is "a religion and dharma that encompasses a variety of traditions, beliefs and spiritual practices largely based on teachings attributed to the Buddha." Where it gets complicated is that the term *religion* is fairly broad in its definition, and Buddhism is often viewed as being on the spiritual-practice end of the spectrum – a technicality, perhaps, but not necessarily the easiest place to start from. What is clear is the origins of Buddhism are in India, and versions of the practice have spread throughout much of Asia. Most Sherpas adhere to Tibetan Buddhism, which has its roots in Mahayana Buddhism, one of the two major tenets, and the Tibetan version is further broken down into four schools that overlap in philosophy to a large degree. The Dalai Lama is the spiritual head of the Gelug, or Yellow Hat, school.

There is little chance I'll get a handle on all the intricate details right off the bat, but I have to admit, I genuinely appreciate the painted Mani stones and laboriously constructed Mani walls that appear along the trails. Stings of colourful prayer flags are easy to spot in the village, and can be seen in some unlikely and amazing places throughout the countryside. They appear on mountaintops and high up on crags that look impossible or impractical to get to. In the small communities, the stupas, gompas and monasteries are a big part of everyday life and a continuing influence in the expression of the larger cultural narrative. There is a demonstration and celebration of belief here that is publicly visible but not at all imposing or oppressive. Buddhism is simply a part of the fabric of this place.

I am reverent as often as I can be, to the point of occasionally getting the stinging nettles treatment or walking a couple of dozen yards out of my way, often uphill, in order to pass on the left of a Mani wall or stupa – when you're hot and tired, this is a bigger effort than it sounds, believe me. But I enjoy it. I look forward to the opportunity to pay homage in this small way. It's a very personal and private way to worship, even though it is often done in public. I'm not nearly as comfortable with the more formal situations, like being inside the monasteries, for example, where I feel like I'm intruding.

Inside the large main chamber of the monastery there are huge supporting beams, and intricate detail accentuates any painted surface. Prayers today are soothing and hypnotic but do not appear to be a strict recitation from sacred texts, as I have seen elsewhere; portions are performed largely from memory. Bells, horns, cymbals and drums accompany the chanting, but it is impossible to decipher when and where the musical backing will kick in. That part seems kind of random. Colourful tapestries and murals – and, of course, incense – complete the scene.

About 20 Westerners are with me, taking in evening prayers, and at the entrance to the monastery is a list of rules, roughly translated into a number of languages that goes like this:

YOU ARE ENTERING A HOLY PLACE
PLEASE RESPECT WORSHIP + MEDITATION

WE REQUEST YOU KINDLY TO:

1. NO MOVIES WITHOUT THE PERMISSION.
2. DRESS RESPECTABLY – PLEASE NOT IN SHORTS.
3. NOT TO SIT OR WALK OVER ANY OF THE CUSHIONS.
4. NOT TO PICK UP ANY RITUAL INSTRUMENTS.
5. PLEASE DO NOT MAKE NOISE OR WALK AROUND.
6. PHOTO IS STRICTLY PROHIBITED INSIDE THE MONASTERY.
7. WAIT UNTIL ALL MONKS ENTERED AT CEREMONIES.

8. PLEASE LOOK AFTER YOUR BELONGINGS –
BE MINDFUL.

9. NOT TO KISS PLEASE.

THANK YOU

While grammatically imprecise, the spelling is spot on, which was better than I managed in transcribing it. More importantly, it is only now I realize I've still got my toque on. While hats aren't forbidden per se, it does feel like poor form. Maybe not as bad as urinating in front of a group of monks on a trail somewhere, but still poor form. This is why I don't spend a lot of time in places of worship. I'm a bumbling buffoon more often than not.

Tea service for the monks begins. Fifteen of them are present, sitting in rows facing the centre of the room, and their raised benches prop them up about two feet off the floor. There are men of various ages who have worked their way up the ranks, but two younger monks are in charge of serving tea, and the chanting is not interrupted en masse. Each monk takes a break at an individually convenient time, and then slips right back into concentrated worship without missing a beat.

By now, most of the Westerners have lost interest and wandered off, but the senior monk in my line of sight is mesmerizing, so I stay to watch him for awhile longer. His concentration and devotion to the task at hand is impressive; he's as immersed in the moment as anyone I have ever seen. I can feel he *believes* in the words he is reciting, even as I don't understand a single one. Then, just as I'm about to leave a donation and sneak out for the sunset, everything stops abruptly: the chanting, the bells, the drums, everything. It's snack time.

In the sudden quiet, the chamber takes on a cavernous

quality. I'm standing now but don't want to move because it would be too obvious. The awkward moment only lasts a second or two but feels much longer. I'm like a cartoon thief caught in the police spotlight, scanning the room with my eyes without moving a muscle. Only a few murmured voices punctuate what would be a total silence, and nobody cares what I'm doing, but I am paralyzed in place. Rule number 5.

The snacks are trekker-style, like Crunchees and candy bars, along with a few homemade items I don't recognize, and they are delivered around the room on trays and in bowls by the same young monks who served tea. As one of them is doing the rounds, he offers me a prawn chip. It's sort of like a pork rind but not as heavy, and I admit I don't know what to do. Accept. Demur. Eat it. Don't eat it. It's communion in New York all over again. In the end, I decide to accept, and once the chanting and music start again, I slink out for the sunset, relieved I have managed to avoid another unfortunate faux pas.

Outside, the air is crisp, and the light has already left the valley, but the Nuptse–Lhotse ridge and the tip of Everest are a fiery pink. The customary, high-altitude cloud plume is anchored over Lhotse for a change, leaving the top of Everest clear, and watching for awhile eases my spiritual anxiety. *Om mani padme hum* – the mantra that is recited in prayer, carved on Mani stones and printed on prayer flags – floods my mind. Strict translation and interpretation of the mantra is thought to be secondary to the mere existence of the six syllables as a symbol of the essence of the entire teaching. I like that. I don't have to take it in all at once but can still be strongly connected to the underlying principals, because the mantra is everywhere.

I am drawn to a further understanding of Buddhism

and its practice, no question, and suspect I'll be creeping around the edges of every learning opportunity that presents itself from here on. Samma-Sati, or complete awareness, is part of the Eightfold Path to Enlightenment. It is mindfulness of all things, internal and external. For the rest of the evening, however, the natural world is going to be my church, my synagogue, my mosque and my gompa. As I work on unravelling a few more of the intricacies of faith, religion and right practice, I will continue to have a much clearer understanding of what's going on out here. For the time being, anyway. But I am trying. If I understand correctly, the path is a process.

19.

THE END OF THE ROAD

From Tengboche, it was a pleasant and challenging walk to the village of Dingboche, and after visiting the upper Gokyo Valley, I expected to be acclimatized for the Khumbu proper, but a headache laid me low once again. It exposes 4000 metres as my altitude threshold, and I'd better schedule a rest day no matter how much clomping around I've been doing. In accepting this, I have finally grown more relaxed about the process. I'm connected to the trail, more attuned to the challenges and distances and more appreciative of the effort it takes to get around. It wasn't until after Dingboche that I finally found the strong yet comfortable rhythm I had been working toward for two months.

The hill straight out the door of the lodge in Dingboche is an unpleasant way to start any day, 15 minutes of lung-searing climb right off the bat, but the long, high traverse toward the two lodges that make up the village of Dughla is ample reward. It is one of the premier sections of trail in all the Khumbu, a wide, slowly ascending bench, with Tabuche and Cholatse soaring across the valley on the left. The mountains offer different yet no less compelling faces than they do when viewed from Gokyo. I have the walk largely to myself, with only the occasional trekker, a few *dzos* and *zhoms*, and a couple of unoccupied *karkas* to complete the charming mountain scene.

At the top end, near where a swift river cuts a gully with meltwater from the Khumbu Glacier, Pumori emerges on the right to stab at the impossibly blue sky and hint at what's to come.

From Dughla, it's necessary to ascend the edge of the Khumbu Glacier moraine, and, to my surprise, clambering up to the memorials for fallen climbers proves simple enough. A few short breaks along the way to catch my breath, and I am at the top. While I have a snack and explore the monuments, a big black dog makes his way up the trail and, just short of the top, promptly lies down without warning. He looks healthy enough and doesn't seem to be travelling with anyone, and after a couple of minutes he simply pops up and continues on.

After a surprisingly comfortable sleep at a new lodge in the village of Lobuche, a hard slog into a fierce wind between Lobuche and the final lodge village of Gorak Shep requires a perfection of the zombie walk. Head down and tucked under the brim of a hooded jacket to keep the dust out of the eyes, and just enough forward lean to keep from being blown over. Mind turned off. Although, it is interesting that my friend Dog shows up again to saunter along by my side for ten minutes before striking out ahead. A day and a half after leaving Dingboche, I find myself near the top of Kala Patthar, 11 kilometres and 1200 vertical metres later.

Found my rhythm indeed.

The first Westerners to climb Kala Patthar were Bill Tilman and Charles Houston, in 1950. Nepal had only recently been opened to foreign scientists, and the pair were among the first to explore the Khumbu Valley in search of a viable route to, and eventually up, Everest. Kala Patthar is actually part of Pumori, a minor ridge on the much bigger mountain, and although it is roughly 150 metres taller, I've found it easier to get up than Gokyo Ri was. After a similarly steep beginning, a lengthy traverse on Kala Patthar moderates the effort for a time, but nearer the top, it is just as challenging as the Ri. A steep trail along a rocky hillside, with very little oxygen to help in the effort, is mitigated only slightly by the inspirational view of Pumori lurking above.

Kala Patthar is a much more distinct peak than Gokyo Ri, which is essentially a ridgeline, with plenty of nooks and crannies among the boulders where you can find your own space. The top of Patthar is a sloping dagger with a comparatively narrow point. With more than a few trekkers, it can get crowded fast, and this afternoon it's crowded. I'm nearing the end of my journey and want to be alone up here with the mountains and the wind, so I am irritated, but I probably wouldn't go to the very top anyway; I never do anymore.

The first time I consciously stopped a few feet short on a mountain was not far away, over on a lower hillock on Chhukung Ri, back in 2009. The thing is, there was no real forethought about the decision. No earth-shattering philosophical revelation. It just kind of happened. At the time there was a collection of man-made junk on the ridge above town, possibly a mini–cellphone tower or assemblage of weather instruments, but, whatever it was, it felt decidedly out of place. I didn't want to add myself to the mess. It didn't make any difference if I took those last few steps anyway. The work was done, I was there and I suddenly had an overwhelming sense I shouldn't take those last steps.

I have since read the book *Touching My Father's Soul*, in which Jamling Tenzing Norgay, son of Tenzing Norgay, writes, "Some climbers are driven by personal achievement and the desire for a trophy. Others are drawn to the mountains by something more mysterious, something more deeply personal. Perhaps they are motivated by a need for understanding, by a desire to gain freedom from the Wheel of Life, the cycle of birth, death and rebirth."

Talk about a passage to stop you dead in your tracks.

My meagre grasp of the intricacies of Buddhist philosophy prohibits me taking on the implications of the Wheel of Life in my current quest, but there is something mysterious and deeply personal about being in these mountains again right here, right now. I feel this place in my bones. More than anywhere else on Earth, on these trails I feel like I'm living in the now. Norgay goes on to suggest climbers searching for understanding are sharing his pilgrimage. I would not recognize the man if he walked past, but I would like to think we are all on the same pilgrimage when we go out in search of what we feel but don't yet fully comprehend.

I've been thinking of my new friends Bryce and Sunny these last few days, and their attempt on Cholatse. At about the time I was skittering around on Gokyo Ri, they were bivouacking under a tarp in a small crevasse. Experienced mountaineers at high altitude, they were denied the top by less than 100 vertical metres due to high winds and cold temperatures and couldn't make it back to their high camp before dark. What stuck me as important in their telling of the story over dinner at Panorama was not the peak missed but the experience gained. The lessons learned.

You come here because it's beautiful and foreign, you return because the people are welcoming and the culture is intriguing, but make no mistake, you are inevitably testing yourself against a challenging environment every step of the way, regardless of whether you're a climber or a trekker. Everyone has a different definition of challenge and a different threshold for engaging it. To my mind, Bryce and Sunny's story wasn't about the climb, or coming up short of the top, or the sketchy night spent under a tarp at 6100 metres. It was about the deeply personal element in experience we are all searching for. It was about taking another step toward understanding. I believe anyone who comes to the Khumbu is bound to experience something different and something interesting in an environment that by its very nature pushes us up against our limits – and what we really want to find out is something about ourselves.

As the sun descends and Everest begins to take on a softer tinge, more trekkers have come upslope. I've taken up a spot a dozen metres below the summit in a jumble of boulders but have been having a difficult time getting comfortable. The winds are persistent and my hands are cold and it's awkward to move around in search of new angles for pictures of the surrounding mountains. Wedged in the cracks between the rocks are a couple of discarded water bottles, and I can't help but wonder, *What is wrong with people?* Who comes to this incredible place, grunts their way all the way up here and decides this is the appropriate spot to leave a plastic bottle that weighs less than an ounce?

Stepping down from the growing congestion, I'm not at all bothered about not touching the peak. I've just got to get away from everyone. We might be sharing a pilgrimage, but there's nothing that says we have to do it in lockstep.

Descending to the area around a small col a short distance from the top, I find temporary relief from the wind.

323

Ama Dablam is tremendous in the distance, a stunning pyramid thrust against the sky on the southern horizon. Away from the small crowd, I have space to further reflect on my time in the mountains. I have succeeded a handful of times on a few simple trekking peaks at home in the Rockies, and now here in the Himalaya as well, but the specific destinations are not really important. This is not a mountaineer's résumé but a keen amateur's scrapbook of adventures, punctuated by the fact that I have failed, not just stopped short, on more than a few attempts.

The reasons for the failed attempts are varied: bad weather, hiking partners unwilling or unable to go on or, more often than not, a lack of will myself. Turns out I am drawn across the landscape as much as up it. A high pass or a sufficiently elevated view of the valley below is often enough. Once I was just way too hungover to reach the top of Mount Nestor, in Kananaskis Country, and quit tantalizingly close to the summit after getting drawn off the easier path up the ridge and struggling on the scree slope.

The odd thing is, almost every time I didn't make the top, I felt like a failure and ended up missing the point of the whole experience, which was to be out in the mountains. To be exploring a piece of the landscape I had never been to before, or simply to get some fresh air and exercise. Mountains are compelling, challenging and beautiful, and most of the time it is enough just to be in among them. I have not always been so relaxed in my thinking, but I'm getting there. Maybe this is also a form of payback for previous misdeeds.

In early 1988, I was a 19-year-old kid intent on seeing a bit of the world, and curiosity about what was out there led me to the centre of the Australian continent and a visit to one of the most recognizable rock formations in the world: Uluru. The sandstone inselberg is important in Aboriginal creation mythology, and although it is not forbidden to climb it, the local Anangu people would prefer if no one made the attempt.

It is a steep but not overly difficult walk up that takes about an hour. The formation rises to 863 metres above sea level and 348 metres above the surrounding desert, but the easiest path up also happens to cross a sacred dreamtime track. I could understand the situation in theory, but at the time I was young and selfish and still driven by adolescent desires. I grew up in a culture that encouraged the strong to take what they wanted, one that rarely stops to think about the consequences of actions when those actions serve our own self-interest. So, of course, my concern for the wishes and feelings of the people who had been living with Uluru for hundreds of generations was quickly pushed to the background. I had come from the other side of the world to witness this geological anomaly first-hand. Crossed prairies and mountains and oceans and deserts by bus and airplane, and spent thousands of dollars for the experience. Tens of thousands of years of culture, tradition and responsible stewardship of the land – well, that was not my concern, I was climbing it.

Increasingly, I'm not sure what's right or what's wrong in this day and age; I just know how I feel. You wouldn't catch me dead anywhere on the slopes of Machapuchare in the Annapurna Region, or Mount Kailash in Tibet; they are sacred mountains that remain off limits, and stopping a little short here on a popular knob in a corner of the Himalaya in order to pay homage feels right after a lifetime of doing whatever I want. Instead of pushing my way onto the busy summit to bask in the glow of minor accomplishment, I'll pick up another water bottle to bring down with me as I wait to enjoy the coming sunset. It's a little thing, inconsequential in the grand scheme of things, but this is the deal I have made with the mountains. This is the deal I have made with myself.

• • •

For a second morning in a row, the temperature in my room is a pleasant surprise. The sun is not yet up, but the sky in the east is growing brighter by the minute, and it's not absolutely freezing in here. This is a lucky break as much as anything else: my window looks out on the enclosed outdoor courtyard of the guest house and is largely shielded from the worst of the weather. I can see prayer flags being blown sideways, and I hear that same wind battering the outside edge of the building. I bet the rooms across the hall are not quite so agreeable.

That said, I'm not exactly rushing to get out of my sleeping bag. I have slept well, considering the altitude, but walking up from Lobuche in the morning yesterday and then climbing Kala Patthar in the evening proved a big day. I'm not sore, exactly, but am experiencing a deep muscle fatigue that comes from insufficient recovery after exercise. I also feel groggy and sluggish in general. Pulling the bag to my chin, I decide breakfast can wait; it is only 6:30 in the morning, after all.

Staring at the ceiling, I realize this is not how the last big day of my trip was supposed to play out. Imagination is a powerful thing, and you tend to create an idealized image of what the key moments are going to look like, in order to get through the more difficult days. Overcoming doubt and discomfort and boredom is a mind game. Creating lofty goals and imagining optimum scenarios helps tip the scales in your favour. In a perfect world, you hit peak performance in ideal weather on the last day so you can tie the experience up in a nice bow and go home. Life doesn't work like that.

Instead of a dream scenario, the wind is blowing relentlessly, Base Camp is two hours away, it's cold outside and I'm tired.

After breakfast, the outlook doesn't get much better. Out in the open, the wind is indeed ferocious and blowing down-valley directly into my face. Dog looks up at me from the sheltered spot he's curled up in as if to say, "You're on your own this time pal." I don't blame him. At a guess, it's minus ten degrees Celsius with the wind chill. The lake beside the guest houses has always been more like a large pond, but in recent times water usage has increased in Gorak Shep, and an oversized frozen puddle at the far end of the flats is all that's left. Walking across the dried-out lakebed is like walking across the desert in a sandstorm. The only sane way to approach it is the zombie walk. Head down, brain off.

At the end of the flats, the trail scrambles onto the lower slopes of Kala Patthar and weaves up and down and around various boulders and outcrops. In the lee of the hillside spurs, it is pleasant enough walking, but at any exposed corner the wind is strong enough to knock over a man who isn't paying attention. Off to the right and across the glacier, Nuptse is a gigantic, imposing wall of snow and ice that blocks any direct morning light. I have inadvertently walked into that shadow since starting out from the lodges.

Nuptse is a dramatic presence viewed from Gorak Shep, and it towers above the walk to Base Camp, but it is not an independent peak. It has a topographic prominence of only 319 metres. As a result, it is not ranked on the list of highest mountains in the world; it doesn't meet the 500-metre threshold. The ridge between Nuptse and Lhotse does not dip low enough. This seems a bit unfair, because it is arguably the most striking mountain to be viewed from the bottom of this valley. A wall of rock and ice and snow that presents as nothing less than modern sculpture on a massive scale but is really just a 7864-metre-tall sub-peak of Lhotse.

On the other hand, that's part of what makes this area so interesting: the little quirks. I like the little quirks. They impart character on a place.

After about 40 minutes, just as the sun is about to come over the shoulder of Nuptse, I begin to get the sensation I'm being followed. I have not seen a single soul up ahead all morning, and this is a strange place to feel the unknown presence of others. Scanning the trail behind, I see nothing but rock and earth and dust. For the next ten minutes, I stop and look back every few minutes as the feeling grows. The trail is still rough going and wildly undulating. By chance, my company is revealed as we pass along separate trail spurs simultaneously: a pair of hikers, catching up fast.

This throws me off. I suddenly feel an irrational need to stay ahead. I have left my backpack at the lodge to be picked up later today, but my camera bag is still heavy enough, and my legs and mind remain sluggish. In the thin air I don't stand a chance, and by the time the trail crosses onto the glacier's lateral moraine, Patrice and Christophe, two gendarmes from France, have caught me. This turns out to be a relief, because my only crime is being slow, and I don't think I could have kept up the pace for long. We chat for a moment, and I let them pass so as not to feel dragged along.

Near the end of the lateral moraine, at the point where it mashes into the lower slopes of Pumori, the trail drops down steeply onto the Khumbu Glacier. From that vantage point, my final destination, Everest Base Camp, is just below but blends imperceptibly into the surroundings. There are no expeditions on the mountain and so no tents on the glacier. At first I'm confused: maybe I'm in the wrong spot. It wouldn't be the first time I've gotten lost on this trip.

Scanning the entire valley for a sign of the temporary settlement, I see only broken rock covering ancient ice on this near side. On the far half of the valley bottom, sun-battered seracs have come tumbling out of the icefall, turned left around the end of Nuptse and merged with the main body of the glacier. It takes a keen eye to eventually spot a couple of small, colourful rubble piles dead centre on the ice sheet. From a distance they are almost imperceptible, but they are the only indication there was ever a camp here at all.

At the start of every climbing season, a number of pujas are performed. The ceremonies are meant to bring good fortune to the climbing team and show respect for the mountain before stepping onto it. A lama officiates, juniper branches are burned, food and drink are left as offerings and prayers are recited. The location of the ceremony is an altar made of stones gathered from the glacier, and each team attaches prayer flags to the altar for luck. These rubble piles heaped with prayer flags are all that's left from the most recent pujas. The slow motion of the underlying ice has rattled the stone structures back toward their original form.

Down on the glacier, the sun is now all the way up and in full force, and the wind is less of a factor. Up close, EBC is not necessarily what you would expect. This part of the glacier has come down from the head of the valley and has been bombarded with scree and stones coming off the surrounding mountains. The underlying ice is hard and white and smooth, but it is largely buried. I wouldn't in a million years think, *Cool, let's put our tents here*. It's rocky and uneven but out of range of most avalanches. I chat again with Patrice and Christophe, and we share the wonder of the locale and take a few pictures before a small group makes their way down from the moraine. They also want the trekker's version of summit photos, and I drift off toward the second mound of rocks and prayer flags.

Beyond the second mound, the glacier drops off slightly. Running parallel to the main body of the glacier, the pinnacles and old seracs look like hoodoos of snow that slowly dissipate the farther down-valley you look, until they are absorbed and buried in stone. Just beyond the degrading seracs, steep, towering ramparts rise 2000, 2500 and even 3700 metres above a valley floor that already sits at over 5100 metres. It boggles the mind. This is the world on an epic scale, which is why it so easily draws the imagination and stirs the emotions.

This place dwarfs the troubles of a single human being. The sheer mass of the earth pressed up to the sky is humbling. This place is nothing if not a lesson in perspective. It's also somewhat amazing to think there is almost 50 per cent less oxygen available here (based on an average barometric pressure of 54 kilopascals) than if I were sitting at the beach, looking out at the ocean. To me the air looks pretty much the same. As I'm contemplating the enormity and power of this place, a middle-aged woman from the group comes by to take a few photos from the high point I happen to be standing on, and without provocation states, "I never expected it to be so beautiful."

It is. It really is, as long as the weather cooperates and you're not stuck here for close to two months as you try to claw your way up a dangerously temperamental mountain. There's a rough and wild element that for the moment has been pushed to the background. The wind has dissipated somewhat, and the temperature has soared to the upper single digits. There is not a single cloud in the sky in any direction. The dark stones covering much of this part of the glacier collect the sun's rays and don't exactly radiate the heat absorbed but do manage to provide a strangely comfortable base at odds with the inherent harshness of the surroundings. There is nothing but snow and ice and rock everywhere, but I have stumbled on a small window where EBC is pleasant and welcoming. Although I suspect spending significant time in a tent at this spot would be somewhat less agreeable.

A second group shows up at Base Camp, a larger group operating at a much higher volume. When one of them shouts, "We got to get a group picture, but we can't just stand there. Everyone's got to do something fun and crazy," I wander off around a hillock of ice to find some privacy. Finding an appropriately sized boulder, I sit down to have a snack and some tea. Out of the wind, it's quite cozy, and part of me is again overtaken by the urge to never move. I want to capture this moment in time and stay with it because it feels so perfect. I'm wind-burnt and exhausted, which is how every long, hard journey should end. Funny; there was no indication this morning that the day would turn out so great.

I will be home again soon, back to my humble mountains in the west of North America, and I will appreciate the comforts associated with that transition for awhile, I'm sure. I will probably wallow in them. Jocey's company, my own bed, a duvet instead of a sleeping bag, the breathtaking view from my balcony, TV with more channels than I could ever watch, central heating. What I'm not going to miss is washing my hands in the morning with water that comes in two temperatures, cold and ice cold. Treating my water with chemicals or fluorescent light every. single. time. I'm. thirsty? Over it. Repacking my backpack every morning – over that too. My knees and my back are certainly not going to miss the inevitable long, hard descents after all this altitude gain.

But I am going to miss this place, the rawness of the landscape, the hard beauty and the experience that is by necessity a million miles from my everyday routine back home. I'm going to miss the simplicity of purpose that comes with a regimen hinged on eating, sleeping, walking and taking in yet another spectacular view. After awhile, everything else proves superfluous. My responsibilities and expectations. Trump and the narrow-minded, self-absorbed GOP world view. The equally asinine Canadian Conservative Party's policies and ideals. The petty quarrels, the politics of division and the despair and worry that go along with a growing capitalistic exhaustion. So many of us running around, fighting for power and chasing a buck while a big beautiful world passes us by. Sad!

In a quiet moment, when the wind dies out completely, the only sound to be heard is pebbles tumbling down the uneven surfaces on the glacier, shaken loose by the imperceptible motion of billions of tons of ice succumbing to gravity. I am reminded that, despite EBC's reputation as a destination (in the climbing season, it is a tent city housing upwards of a thousand souls), this is a location in concept as much as in geography. I'm sitting on a huge glacier slowly creeping down-valley. As a result, this place is never in exactly the same place every year. Perhaps that is part of the mystique of Base Camp. It doesn't really exist, yet here it is.

It is interesting to note Everest does not lord over would-be climbers as they prepare for the attempt on her. You can barely see the upper half. Depending on where you stand, it's not much more than a thin sliver of the southeast ridge poking out over the massive base of the west ridge. It's little wonder there are four advanced camps on the route to the top, and I can't even imagine the effort of moving on from here. It's been 69 days since I landed in Kathmandu. To climb the mountain would require another six weeks and a force of will that is beyond me. I am again amazed by the scale of this place, and the determination of those who do climb on from here, but am not beckoned upward. This is plenty. This is enough.

Since the only place left to go is up, I guess this is the end of the road. The trouble is, I've still got to get out of here, and it's not like I can simply call a cab. The Khumbu versions fly, and cost about $5,000 one-way. So, I take one last look at the stunning scenery bathed in bright mid-morning light, sling my camera bag over my shoulder and start making my way back to Gorak Shep.

PART FOUR

EPILOGUE

20.

THE CANADIAN ROCKY MOUNTAINS

From as far as you can go in the upper Khumbu without
a climbing permit, it took me four and a half days to walk
out of the high mountains to Lukla, including a day off
in Namche to gather my things and say goodbye to the
new friends I had met there. By 10:30 in the morning on
the fifth day, I was sitting on a bed at Karma Travellers
Home in Kathmandu, marvelling at the change in circumstance. I didn't have to walk anymore. Didn't have to push
against gravity or a growing natural tendency toward idleness. Essentially, the trip was over. Tired and beaten up by
the rigours of the trekking lifestyle, I was happy about that,
but the realization carried a depressing subtext as well. I
didn't have to walk anymore. As I sat there I wondered,
What am I going to do now?

In the planning stages of the journey, I'd thought of
trekking all the way back to Jiri and then bicycling back to
Kathmandu as well. The early Everest expeditions, which
entailed walking in from the capital, climbing the mountain and then walking all the way out again, are more impressive to me than more recent ascents. Thrilling as they
may be to read about, they lack an element that helped define Everest for decades. Not only was it thought impossible to climb; for a time, it was nearly impossible to get
there. That's what originally inspired me: the "warm-up"
to the more celebrated event. The sheer magnitude of

the complete act, not just the part that gets in the papers, helped shape my itinerary and route even as I knew I would never do the climbing part.

In the cold light of day, however, I realized before I even got to Base Camp that it was time to invite my ambition to join me in reality. Five hundred kilometres of bicycling and walking, first around Kathmandu, and then through country that can charitably be described as undulating, was enough physical effort. Continuing would have been overkill. Just as the concept of climbing Everest existed in a realm I wasn't motivated to visit, retracing those early kilometres in reverse no longer sounded like a great idea. My prolonged approach had helped me experience Nepal, not just the Khumbu, and an abbreviated exit would still be long enough to engender reflection.

Writing a travel book requires a certain amount of foresight. To imagine, plan and execute a trip to the other side of the globe and then bring back a compelling story about the experience requires an ability to see a sweeping arc of time that reaches into the future. You envision a path ahead and then engage it in order to find out what happens. Some of it turns out pretty much as you expected, most of it does not, and inevitably there is a disaster or two along the way that you could never reasonably have seen coming. The setbacks are the circumstances that test your intestinal fortitude, your desire to follow through with the blood-and-guts part of a flash of inspiration.

My big disaster did not happen on the ride along a narrow mountain road used by impatient drivers and a dizzying array of vehicles, many of which would never pass anything resembling a safety inspection. It didn't happen during the couple of hundred kilometres of walking on dirt trails through earthquake- and landslide-prone countryside. It wasn't illness, or altitude sickness (this time), or any of the other challenges travel throws in your path. I didn't get robbed; I didn't collapse in a weeping heap at the prospect of another long climb that required picking my way on awkward rocky steps or through a minefield of ankle-turning stones. My big gut check came before I even left: in the familiar confines of my condo, 11,000 kilometres from the Himalaya, after emergency knee surgery put an abrupt and painful halt to everything that was going on in my life.

It came from out of nowhere, as disasters often do. My hip was doing fine; this manuscript was beginning to take shape, with background research and anecdotes spread across the page in the scattergun fashion of my process. But I was struggling with work/life balance; part of me that wanted it all – the job, the money, the travel, the stories to tell – and I had failed to prioritize my efforts. Like so many misguided modern souls, I thought I could have it all if I just tried hard enough.

Instead, I found my life was too busy, too messy and too complicated. My desires and core values didn't match my efforts and actions. Something had to give. Eventually, the universe got tired of my wishy-washy attempts to make it all work and jumped up and bit me on the ass – or, in this case, in the knee. I went for a simple cortisone injection to ease my arthritis and came away with a nasty infection that penetrated deep into the joint, by all accounts a 1-in-10,000-injections turn of events.

Those first three weeks after surgery, I was in more pain than I had experienced in my entire life combined. I couldn't get out of bed or even change positions without someone supporting my heel in order to keep pressure off the joint. This tiresome production was required every six or seven minutes, or so it seemed. I got distressingly comfortable peeing into a bottle kept by the bedside and was up every two hours, night and day, for my pain medication. If I happened to oversleep because it was three a.m., my knee would begin to howl at me through my dreams, "Hey, asshole, where are my drugs? We're 15 minutes overdue here! WHERE ARE MY DRUGS?"

Saying this will make me appear tougher than I am, but a full hip replacement was a breeze compared to one small microbe getting into a joint and partying with his friends for a weekend. Eventually, a surgeon had to come in, turn on all the lights and throw everybody out. That was March.

In June, three months after surgery, I still couldn't walk properly, navigate a flight of stairs without clutching the handrails for dear life or ride a bike. That's when I began to wonder if my active travel days were behind me for good. There are always challenges and setbacks. As I have written about before, money and time and age and responsibilities all take their toll on the adventurous spirit, but for the first time I worried that my situation wasn't just an obstacle to overcome or an alteration in the original plan. This was different; this was serious. In 2015 I got better after hip surgery and just went back to the same old workaday bullshit because I was terrified of giving up the paycheque. In 2016 I didn't get better, and I was scared.

The months that followed became an exercise in patience and attention. The world went on spinning around me and I spent the time quietly watching it pass as I tried to figure out how I was supposed to fit in. "It takes the time it takes" is a concept not well understood in our culture anymore, confused as it sometimes is with idleness or sloth. There were days where I struggled mightily. I had four months of unemployment insurance benefits from the day of my surgery, and six months of salary saved on top of that, so I was in no rush to get back to work, but it was surprisingly difficult to unplug and just be. The tired old harangue was always there in the background, barking for attention. "You should be [insert responsible, good-citizen-type actions here]. And what are you going to do for money, anyway? You know it's not acceptable to just loaf around, don't you? *Don't you?*"

When I got bored or began to feel like the hippy-dippy "take what the universe gives" mentality was a waste of time, I would meet up with my old colleagues for a cocktail, things would inevitably get out of hand and I would wake up the next morning with a thumping head and a fresh patina of guilt. Sooner or later I would need to find gainful employment again. I understood that; I just couldn't face it.

But I *was* doing work; it just wasn't a job in the traditional sense of the word. Reading and writing and planning – that was my job, and I loved it. It *felt* like the right thing to do, but I remained vaguely embarrassed as well. I felt ashamed of my simple desires in a society that has grown impossibly complex. All I wanted out of life was to travel around, meet new people, experience a bit of the world first-hand and write books. That's not respectable or responsible, unless you happen to be penning an endless string of bestsellers. For the rest of us, this is a perfect example of what you can't do as a grownup. To the system, I was simply unemployed. I was just another artsy-fartsy type avoiding "reality." The effort contained noble elements to be sure, and with luck would generate enough income to help fund the next adventure, but it wasn't going to pay the mortgage.

It's funny how often we think of a job as a means to an end, and then somewhere along the way the job becomes the whole point to everything. Given the chance to do whatever we wanted, most of us wouldn't know what to do with ourselves. That's probably when we begin to wonder where our dreams went. I had pulled one of those dreams out of storage and remained committed to it, even when it didn't "make sense." Staying the course wasn't easy.

Finally getting back out to the local mountains helped. By mid-July, I had gone up and down the stairwell at my gym hundreds of times and done my assigned rehab exercises thousands of times, and my knee was finally stable enough and strong enough to attempt some moderate outdoor activities. Visiting family in Quebec, I took the first tentative steps off smooth surfaces and through the woods. It was slow going; I had to be attentive to the terrain for fear of falling down, and, in turn, that forced me to be present in both my actions and the moment. It became a form of quiet meditation, and when I walked with someone else, I found it distracting.

Upon my return to the Rockies, I was able to get on my bike again and manage complete rotations on the pedals without pain, so I rode. I also walked. It was a challenge to stay motivated, and there were plenty of days I just wanted to skip the effort, but it was always kind of fun once I got going. I was learning to move around in my environment while constantly expanding my frame of reference, just as a child would. I was getting reacquainted with my mountain home all over again, in a slow and deliberate fashion. It peeled me away from the TV for a few hours every couple of days. On alternate days, I went to the gym to continue with the rehab exercises and throw the weights around. For the first time in five years, I began to feel good. I lost a bit of weight and built up some muscle tone. I began to feel like myself again.

Staying committed to this new process wasn't just a physical challenge, however. It was still awkward interacting with, well, just about everyone. After a serious wake-up call, I was taking the time and making the effort to have a different experience, and that proved a strain on my social life. Injury and illness can be isolating and lonely and unsettling. Throwing yourself into the healing process gives you something to fill the void previously occupied by your habits and routines, as well as all the people who inhabit that part of your universe. I missed my friends and coworkers, but our schedules and priorities were out of sync. Staying true to the new path I had chosen, at the expense of hanging out and having a laugh, was one of the most difficult parts of my recovery. I wasn't lonely; I just felt like a bad friend. Fortunately, most of the people who know me are used to my eccentric and sometimes erratic behaviour, but I remained guilt-ridden.

The hardest part of finding an authentic path is not the effort involved in following through but missing the friends you leave behind. You constantly want to shout over your shoulder, "Come on, gang, we should all go." But finding yourself is not a group effort. In mid-September, a year and a half after getting my hip replaced and six months after having my knee cleaned up, I got on a plane to Kathmandu with no idea how the surgically repaired parts were going to hold up to more rigorous activity. But I was determined to find out. It was what I was inspired to do. I knew I had to try.

This unusual conclusion to my rehab program turned

out far better than I ever could have expected. I stood on the summit of Gokyo Ri exactly eight months to the day after being rushed to the hospital for emergency knee surgery; this pleasing coincidence of timing and endeavour is a memory I will never forget.

As I write this, my friend Pega Sherpa has just summited Everest for a second time, and I am happy for him also. We all have our mountains to climb, figuratively and literally. I hope our paths cross again soon.

Now my Himalayan adventure is over, now that I'm home, I'm not sure what it is I'm supposed to be doing. This place is the same, but I am different. I still don't fit in and am certainly not inspired. Canmore is a perfectly lovely and typically modern version of a North American mountain town, but does it represent my values or my desires? Does it support my hopes and dreams? Is this even my home anymore? I admit, I don't know.

Fortunately, the surrounding landscape has not changed at all. It has always been there in the background, looking pretty and anticipating the day I might get my act together. For years I was lost to the perils of 21st-century life in a growing tourist trap. A medical emergency forced me to take a big step back and have a good look at what was going on. The resulting adventure sent me halfway around the globe. Through it all, these local mountains have patiently waited for me to come out and play. It would be a shame to disappoint them.

• • •

I step out of my condo building at 6:45 a.m. The air is cool, and Bow Valley Trail, normally a busy road into the town centre, is deserted, save a single jogger and a cyclist in full restaurant apparel pedalling to a breakfast shift. Or maybe home from the after-shift get-together last night. You never know; Canmore is a party town.

Making my way through the Kananaskis Way neighbourhood on foot, I don't realize until I reach the pedestrian underpass for the Trans-Canada Highway that I've forgotten my surgical mask. I weigh the options. Go back and waste the 20 minutes it's going to take round-trip, or just get on with it already. High, thin cloud is brushing over top of Mount Lady MacDonald and Grotto Mountain to the east, but to the west the sky is clear. A little hazy, maybe, but I can't smell smoke. I'm going to risk it.

You see, the Verdant Creek drainage, a couple of valleys and 30 kilometres away, has been on fire for a week. Air quality around here has been hit and miss. Just yesterday, we had a bluebird day until three o'clock; then the wind shifted, and within half an hour the skies were an Armageddon shade of orange. Flakes of ash drifted down on the town like a subtle warning. So far today, it doesn't look like the world is going to end, but the forecast for later this afternoon is 32 degrees Celsius. If the wind comes up, everything could change in an instant.

Just beyond the underpass, a trail connects to Cougar Creek, and the walk up the left bank leads eventually to the trailhead for Mount Lady MacDonald, my destination for the day. I can see Lady MacDonald from my condo building, and as I approach, her shape constantly changes until I step into the trees at her base.

The plan when I got back from Nepal was to carry on with the walk-a-day routine; I wanted to reinforce the newly rebuilt, adventurous me. But that has proven somewhat impractical in the "real world." Somehow six months have gotten away from me. Time has a way of doing that, of disappearing when you're not paying attention, and it happens in the usual ways. I've been trying to fit in with civilized society again, I swear, but it has not been a smooth transition. Balancing a desire for a more relaxed lifestyle with work, this manuscript and the occasional freelance writing job has been no easy task. It all adds up, and I'm in danger of managing my life again, not living it.

In Jamling Norgay's book, he writes, "In an earlier era it sufficed to sit and simply observe and perpetuate the cycles of life, to pray and to practice, to eat and to sleep. But by the terms of the modern age, to practice such a routine was only to move backward."

I sometimes wonder: Was I born in the wrong age?

As a hike, Lady Mac is relentless, and three hours after stepping out my door, I arrive at the wooden platform that straddles the ridge just above treeline. It is all that's left of an ill-advised tea house plan, and from this lofty position I can clearly see Canmore spread out in the valley below. I can even see my condo building from here. What is amazing, and somewhat disappointing, is that I can also hear truck tires humming on the highway 1000 vertical metres below.

Across the valley, the views are sweeping, from Mount Lougheed to the left, all the way down to Cascade Mountain and beyond to the right. There are only occasional patches of snow hanging on in deep cracks and sheltered gullies, but even without the winter contrast, the chain of peaks and outcrops is amazing. I check for ticks, slather on some sunscreen and pull out my water bottle before sitting down to enjoy it all.

Up-valley and to the right is where the haze is the worst, and beyond Cascade Mountain it is clearly smoke. It's strange. I'm intrigued by the fire more than worried about it. Jocey and I have go-bags packed at home, just in case, but in the end conditions are going to be what determine the outcome of this event more than anything else. Emergency crews are containing the blaze, but if the wind comes up or lightning strikes another valley close by, everything could get out of control in a hurry.

When I passed through Tengboche on the way down from EBC last fall, a pre-dawn earthquake that registered 5.6 on the Richter Scale shook the guest house I was in. I was simultaneously woken up and almost thrown from my bed, and as the room rattled around me, I imagined the whole building coming down. I even contemplated jumping out the second-storey window in my underwear. In moments like this, it is clear the larger world still operates on a massive scale. Earthquakes and forest fires: just two reminders we are not in charge.

Returning to the task at hand, the top of Lady Mac looks tantalizingly close, but this is an illusion. The toughest part of the scramble is still ahead. As I shuffle up a small knob on the ridge, the temperature creeps uncomfortably upward. The trail is filled with pebbles of all shapes and size – it's not quite scree, where each step up has a corresponding slip back, but it is a bit of a slog as the gravel absorbs each footfall. After trudging along with my head down for awhile to ensure solid footing, I stop to scan the trail ahead and catch my breath. You can imagine my surprise to be standing face to face with a solitary bighorn sheep, not six metres away. She's coming down the trail and is equally startled to see me, and for a moment neither of us knows what to do.

Not wanting to spook her, I take two big steps to my right and stand perfectly still. She's a mature female, slightly smaller than your average deer, with narrow, nearly straight horns and a sandy-brown coat. Having come over the crest of the knob, she stands in silhouette against the blue sky and after a moment of indecision calculates I'm probably no threat. She moves three paces off the trail on the opposite side, hesitates and then walks cautiously past, looking back occasionally to see if I'm following, which is a strong prey-species instinct.

Beyond the knob, the final slope to the top of the mountain gets increasingly steep. Continuing on up the ridge toward the lower south summit looks the easier option, but soon the trail deteriorates into tiresome scree. About three-quarters of the way from the platform to the top, it gets a little too steep for comfort, and I pull the chute, proving beyond any lingering doubt I'm no mountaineer. My knee and my hip are simply not up for this kind of foolishness anymore – a convenient out for my waning ambition. But I did enjoy the walk up – the sweating and heavy breathing aside, of course.

In his essay "Out of Your Car, Off Your Horse," Wendell Berry writes: "If you want to see where you are, you will have to get out of your space vehicle, out of your car, off your horse, and walk over the ground. On foot you will find that the earth is still satisfyingly large, and full of beguiling nooks and crannies."

In a world full of distractions and responsibilities, it is these beguiling nooks and crannies that inspire. The discoveries we make there are the truly valuable ones. Pinned to my fridge, in among the magnetic knick-knacks, postcards and family photographs, is a sticker for an outdoor outfitting store stencilled with what is, to me, a prophetic slogan. It's part of a famous John Muir quote: "The Mountains Are Calling."

Yes, they are. And they don't seem to mind that, when I do visit, I often come up a few feet short.

THE END

ACKNOWLEDGEMENTS

First of all, there are people I missed the first time around when I tried to do this thank-you thing. With every book you write, I suspect, the thank-you list gets longer because you realize just what a tremendous debt you owe. Writers can be selfish and self-absorbed at times, maybe even much of the time. It's a shame that, even when a simple "thank you" is the best we can do, we manage to screw that up. I would like to acknowledge these people now and apologize in advance to everyone I'm going to miss this time.

In Calgary, Michelle Brown and Karen Allen (RIP) were supportive of the idea of writing books before that first one began to take a recognizable shape. Karen gave me a copy the *Oxford Paperback Dictionary & Thesaurus*, with an inspiring inscription, that I continue to use to this day. Arlene Penny and Ladislav Zevnik (RIP) put me up in a spare room at their house in Calgary when I first moved out west, and listened to my endless ravings about how cool writing a book one day would be. This was long before I realized the most important part of writing was writing, not talking about what you wanted to write about.

While still living back east, I was blessed with too many friends and influences to name here, but Tracy Fenton and Greg McDonald deserve special mention; Tracy for putting up with my endless ranting about the wonders and magic of the mountain west while still trying to navigate a relationship in the east, and Greg for unwittingly donating his copy of *Walking on Alligators*, by Susan Shaughnessy, to my office library. I became enthralled with the book on a visit to his apartment in Toronto one summer in the early '90s and borrowed it with every intention of giving it back. That never happened. I hope the guitar I left behind was adequate compensation.

Six months after my first book was released, I went to my 30th high school reunion, and it was an enlightening experience. It turns out Dan Mosevich, Glenn Chisholm, Mike Soutter, Kathy Czuba, Ankur Barthakur, Julia Mackey, Kim Shatilla, Sue Bedard, Lu Grundhofer, Tracey Larder and Dave Hayden, among many, many others, were a bigger part of my early growth as a person than I ever stopped to seriously contemplate before. Reconnecting with them, both in person and through the Internet, was more rewarding and enjoyable than I ever could have expected. Social media can be a deep black hole where creative time and energy disappears without a trace, but it is also an instant portal to distant areas of the globe and a different way of sharing experience. That's why I continue to log on. Without all my friends there, both old and new, I wouldn't see the world in quite the same way. The key is recognizing when it's time to log off for awhile.

I would also like to take a moment and thank the universe at large. I am immensely grateful for the opportunity to do this storytelling thing. In a newspaper review of my first book, Rob Alexander called me an "ogre philosopher," which is not far off the mark. Without writing, without the ability to have an opinion and express it in my own peculiar way, I would simply be an ogre. So for this latest book, the usual suspects must be acknowledged; without them, a second miracle never happens. Don Gorman and the Rocky Mountain Books team deserve a lot of credit for somehow making me look better, and sound smarter, than I really am. Design, editing, layout – I provide the words and pictures, and they provide the platform and the all-important finishing touches. Peter Norman has proven especially helpful in this regard. He keeps me on track during edits, and makes sure I don't make a fool of myself, at least in print. Chyla Cardinal makes everything look exactly as I imagined it in my minds eye, only better.

For this book, a big thank you goes out to Frances Klatzel; her help in trying to understand the subtle details of the Nepal experience has been invaluable. I continue to enjoy our conversations about writing and travel and the evolution of place. Sherap Jangbu Sherpa and Lhakpa Dolma at Panorama were gracious hosts and generous with their time on this last visit to the Khumbu, and Mohan Rai always had a smile on his face when I stumbled in off the trail. I am grateful to Pega Sherpa, Marlene Ford, Bryce Brown and Sunny Twelker, not to mention Norman, Darryl, Jo, Amanda, Paul, Rob, Patrice, Christophe, Arjun and Ram never-got-any-of-their-last-names, for sharing small parts of the journey. And I can't forget the gang at Karma Travellers Home in Kathmandu, who surely thought it was strange I spent three weeks walking up and down the stairwell at the hotel as last-minute prep instead of just going out trekking already, but they were quick with a *namaste* and were always helpful when I needed something.

Many of my friends in Canmore who supported my first book are still around and continue to encourage the process, and are available whenever I get stuck on the page and need to blow off steam. My brother Jesse and the rest of the crew at the Rose & Crown will always be close to my heart. We made some money, had some laughs and managed to avoid strangling any tourists. Angels, love you ladies always. I also can't forget the boys from the Drake, you know who you are. And no, I don't want another pint. Okay, maybe a halfer.

My friends Neil and Joyce were fun to travel with on my first trip to Nepal, and it was nice to share the experience of the place with my mom, Dena, and stepfather, Brian, the second time around. My brother Scott and his wife, Haley, took an interest in the early manuscript when they were out in Canmore for a visit, and I'm sure one day I will end up going back to Nepal with them. My partner, Jocey, deserves a lot of credit for this book. She dragged me to Nepal the first time, encouraged and welcomed the in-laws the second time around and never once doubted a solo trip on a bum knee and fake hip was absolutely the right life choice for me to make that third time. I love her. She's so great.

Special mention goes out to Bob Sandford, who has become something of a mentor over the years. We get together every once in awhile to have a beer and talk about, well, everything. He's one of the smartest guys I've ever met, and one of the nicest as well. The 35 books he has authored, co-authored or edited inspire me to continue with this writing thing. Thanks, Bob. And, finally, to my fellow dreamers, seekers and creative types, this kind of path through life probably won't make you rich or famous, but it just might make you happy, or at the very least thoughtfully engaged. The work you do might also inspire others to find their own path as well. Live your life. Share your stories. That's all there is.

RECOMMENDED READING AND SOURCE MATERIAL

Armington, Stan. *Trekking in the Nepal Himalaya*. Lonely Planet Publications, 1997.

Berry, Wendell. *Our Only World: Ten Essays*. Counterpoint Books, 2015.

Bhatt, Damodar Prasad. *Ecotourism in Nepal*. Anju Bhatt – Quality Printers, 2006.

Bryson, Bill. *A Brief History of Nearly Everything*. Anchor Canada, 2003.

Bryson, Bill. *The Lost Continent*. Black Swan, 1999.

Chand, Diwaker. *Nepal's Tourism: Uncensored Facts*. Pilgrims Publishing, 2000.

Curtis, Rick. Outdoor Action *Guide to High Altitude: Acclimatization Guide and Illnesses*. Princeton.edu, 1999.

De Botton, Alain. *The Art of Travel*. Penguin, 2002.

Harris, Michael. *The End of Absence: Reclaiming What We've Lost in a World of Constant Connection*. HarperCollins, 2014.

Harris, Michael. *Solitude: A Singular Life in a Crowded World*. Doubleday Canada, 2016.

HH Dalai Lama and Howard C. Cutler, *The Art of Happiness: A Handbook for Living*. Coronet, 1998.

Hillary, Sir Edmund. *Nothing Venture, Nothing Win*. Coronet, 1975.

King, Stephen. *On Writing: A Memoir of the Craft*. Pocket, 2000.

Klatzel, Frances. *Gaiety of Spirit: The Sherpas of Everest*. Mera Publications, 2009.

Krakauer, Jon. *Into Thin Air*. Villard, 1997.

Kropp, Goran. *Ultimate High: My Everest Odyssey*. Discovery, 1997.

Lineen, Jono. *Walking the Earth's Spine*. Pottersfield Press, 2012.

Matthiessen, Peter. *The Snow Leopard*. Penguin Classics, 1987.

Mayhew, Bradley, Lindsay Brown and Stuart Butler. *Nepal*. Lonely Planet Publications, 2015.

McGuinness, Jamie. *Trekking in the Everest Region, 5th Edition*. Trailblazer, 2009.

McKibben, Bill. *The Age of Missing Information*. Random House, 1992.

Norgay, Jamling Tenzing and Broughton Coburn. *Touching My Father's Soul*. HarperSanFrancisco, 2002.

Palin, Michael. *Himalaya*. Phoenix, 2004.

Potts, Rolf. *Vagabonding: An Uncommon Guide to the Art of Long-Term World Travel*. Villard Books, 2003.

Reynolds, Kev. *Everest: A Trekker's Guide*. Cicerone, 2011.

Rubinstein, Dan. *Born to Walk: The Transformative Power of a Pedestrian Act*. ECW, 2015.

Shaughnessy, Susan. *Walking on Alligators*. HarperSanFrancisco, 1993.

Solnit, Rebecca. *Wanderlust: A History of Walking*. Penguin, 2001.

Theroux, Paul. *The Tao of Travel*. McClelland & Stewart, 2011.

Whelpton, John. *A History of Nepal*. Cambridge University Press, 2005.

ALSO BY JAMEY GLASNOVIC

LOST AND FOUND: ADRIFT IN THE CANADIAN ROCKIES

For many people, moving to a mountain town is the realization of a dream, the final step in a pilgrimage to a relaxed lifestyle in a rugged and beautiful setting. After a long journey that began when he was a teenager in the 1980s with the vague idea there might be a better life somewhere "out west," Jamey Glasnovic eventually fled the chaos and stress of the big city and tried to settle into an uncomplicated Rocky Mountain existence.

Canmore, Alberta, a small community nestled in a picturesque valley situated right at the edge of Banff National Park, should have been the perfect end to his searching. A rapidly growing town emerging on the tourism radar can strain anyone's definition of paradise, however, and Lost and Found is Glasnovic's account of his attempt, in the fall of 2008, to recapture the simple wonders of living on the boundaries of a vast wilderness.

A spirited amble by bicycle and on foot, inspired by the work of Bill Bryson, Lost and Found explores the heart of the Rocky Mountain Parks, a UNESCO World

Heritage Site known for its staggering beauty, and examines the consequences of celebrating that beauty too effectively with mass tourism and over-ambitious development. Eschewing the convenience of motorized transportation, Glasnovic earns every kilometre that passes beneath his feet, and along the way he learns a thing or two about feeling profoundly connected to place. An experience some would describe as being home.

TRAVEL WRITING

9781771600514

$25

JAMEY GLASNOVIC was born in Montreal, Quebec, in 1968, and grew up in the suburb of Beaconsfield. A family trip to Spain when Jamey was seven was the first step in creating an avid traveller, and he was drawn early in life to such faraway destinations as Australia, Japan, Mexico and Ireland. He has visited much of North America, from Florida to Alaska, and repeated trips to the mountain West led to a move to Calgary in 1995. After relocating to Canmore in 2004, Glasnovic began freelancing for newspapers such as the Banff *Crag & Canyon*, the *Canmore Leader* and *Rocky Mountain Outlook*, and he continued to roam. Hong Kong, Singapore, Thailand, Nepal and Tibet have since been checked off his life list of destinations. His first book, *Lost and Found: Adrift in the Canadian Rockies*, was published by RMB in 2014. More stories and photos by the author can be found at jglas.com. Jamey Glasnovic lives in Canmore, AB.